Computer Security

Threats and Countermeasures

K Bhaskar
CIRU

MANCHESTER • OXFORD

British Library Cataloguing in Publication Data

Bhaskar, Krish
Computer Security : threats and countermeasures
I. Title
658.478

ISBN 1-85554-174-2

Published by:

NCC Blackwell Ltd, 108 Cowley Road, Oxford OX4 1JF, England.

Editorial Office: The National Computing Centre Limited, Oxford House, Oxford Road, Manchester M1 7ED, England.

Typeset in 11pt Times Roman by CIRU and printed by Bookcraft (Bath) Ltd.

ISBN 1-85554-174-2

Preface

This book has been prepared by CIRU (The Computer Industry Research Unit Ltd) from information contained both in the official documentation and the background research material of the ESPRIT Project 998 (Measures and Requirements for Security) MARS.

As part of the European Community's European Strategic Programme for Research and Development in Information Technology (ESPRIT) the MARS project was undertaken between 1986-89. The aims of the Project were to perform a thorough state-of-the art study of IT security, and to produce guidelines and specifications in the area of highly secure office information systems. The overall objectives, within the context of the ESPRIT Programme, were to contribute towards Europe's competitive position in the international IT market and to provide input to the production of European standards.

The MARS Project was performed by a consortium of six partners throughout the Community:

The Computer Industry Research Unit (UK); BBN Communications (Denmark); Bertin et Cie (France); COPS (Ireland); Protexarms (France) and the University of Cologne (W. Germany). The partners provided a wide range of backgrounds both in information technology and in workstation security, communications security and auditing. Thus allowing the Project to cover a very broad range of security issues.

CIRU's involvement with the MARS project began when it was a research unit in the School of Computing Studies at the University of East Anglia, and was led by the School's founding Professor of Accountancy and Finance, Krish Bhaskar. Professor Bhaskar led the CIRU team in the MARS project and the team has since continued its security interests in EC research programmes through participation in the MERCHANT project (RACE No. 1057). and is currently also involved in DIVIDEND (RACE No. 1059, Advanced communications, financial services sector), CITED (ESPRIT II No 5469, Electronic Copyright) and DITTTO (RACE II No 2063, Remote video data capture).

This document is a summary of the work performed during the MARS Project. Its purpose is to make the results of the project publicly available. It is aimed at a wide audience and is, as far as possible, written in a style which is understandable to those who have a basic knowledge of computing. It will be of interest mainly to DP professionals, academics and students.

iii

The subject of security has been rising in prominence in the Computing Industry for some time. This is partly a result of the increasing number and variety of attacks on computer systems. A number of recent trends have contributed to this. Firstly, with the increased power and performance and the decreasing cost of workstations, there has been a general shift away from the mainframe environment, where security has traditionally been quite strong, towards the minicomputer and microcomputer (PC) environments.

Secondly, with their relatively low cost and ease of use, microcomputers are being used by an increasing number of non-technical people with minimum support levels, and often in roles where security is required to protect information from unauthorised personnel. Furthermore, these computers are often attached to networks, where sensitive data can potentially be accessed from any terminal if it is insufficiently protected.

Thirdly, there is an increasing interconnection between workstations and between computer systems, both within and between organisations. This is of particular concern as it opens up the system to external threats, especially where public telecommunications systems are in operation. Unauthorised external access either by hackers or more sophisticated criminals is increasing and motives range from the more innocent 'challenge' right through to theft, espionage and malicious damage.

The increase in computer crime is evidenced by the regular reports of hackers breaking into various systems, of banks and companies being defrauded and of widespread damage due to computer viruses. Furthermore, the problem is probably far greater than it appears on the surface, as the victims of such attacks, particularly financial institutions, will try their utmost to avoid publicity.

The subject of security and the need to protect computer installations of all types can no longer be ignored by those responsible for computer systems. The MARS Project addressed the risks, threats and countermeasures in detail and in its later stages was largely concerned with practical approaches to securing computer systems. This document can therefore be read as a comprehensive introduction to the subject, as a reference on specific issues within computer security, or as a guide to effecting practical solutions where a system is not sufficiently secure.

INTRODUCTION

The subject of computer security can be examined from the point of view of a three-axis model of threats, components and countermeasures (see below). Threats are directed towards system components and countermeasures are used to guard the components against those threats. It is this concept which forms the background to our approach.

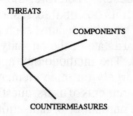

Three axis model of threats, components and countermeasures

The three main parts of this document - *State-of-the-art study, New models and guidelines and Specification and design of a secure treasury management system (MARS)*, correspond to the three Phases of the (MARS)Project. These sections are quite distinct from each other, although each stage of the project drew heavily on the work performed in previous stages. Different readers might, therefore, use the book in different ways.

Part 1 can be used either as a reference text to provide insight into specific areas of computer security or can be read as a detailed general introduction to the subject. Part 2 presents models and guidelines in different areas of computer and data communications security. This work is intended to provide a yardstick for decision-makers and to provide an input to standardisation efforts. In Part 3, the results of the final phase of the project are presented. Here a theoretical specification and design was made for a secure treasury management system. This will be of particular interest to those involved in either financial systems or in communications security.

PART ONE: STATE-OF-THE-ART STUDY

We begin with an analysis of the security *threats* facing computer systems. A threat can be defined as a source of danger or as a potential attack on the system. An examination of threats is an essential prerequisite to a study of the security required to protect the system. A threefold distinction is made in this chapter between accidental and deliberate, physical and logical, and active and passive threats.

Chapter 2 contains an introduction to *risk management* concepts and techniques. The object of risk management is to assess the cost-effectiveness of security policies and countermeasures before they are implemented. There is little point, for example, in investing in a security policy or countermeasure if it costs more than the potential loss involved in a successful security breach. Therefore, the likelihood of a threat materialising, together with its potential loss, should be quantified and compared with the cost of guarding against such a threat.

In Chapter 3, the results of a state-of-the-art study into *user requirements for security* are presented. The methodology applied to identify user requirements was based largely on three elements: existing literature relating to the security requirements of users, questionnaires sent to users, and case studies made at a number of organisations.

Moving on to the subject of countermeasures, Chapter 4 examines one of the most important aspects of computer security, access control. It is a very broad subject and is inherent in most other security topics, whether it be in user identification and authentication, terminal identification and authentication, or in auditing. This chapter gives a brief introduction to access control, distinguishing physical access control from logical access control.

User identification and authentication, the subject of Chapter 5, is a necessary feature of access control procedures. The user must identify himself/herself and that identity must be proven before access to the system and it's resources can be granted or denied. The general principles of identification and authentication are examined, along with methods for performing these steps.

In Chapter 6, *terminal identification and authentication* is studied. It is very desirable for a host machine to be able to verify the identity of a communicating terminal, especially if that terminal is connected through an open network. The purpose is to prevent remote access from an illegal user. User identification and authentication is usually performed as well, thus providing a two level system to control initial access. Terminal identification and authentication is strongly linked to the subject of secure data communications, covered in the next chapter.

Secure data communications is the subject of Chapter 7. In some ways data communications forms a distinct sub-topic within information systems security. Whereas a standalone computer (or a local area network) can be locked securely within the physical confines of an organisation, wide area communications links with data being transferred over them are potentially much more vulnerable to the outside intruder. This is particularly the case where a public network is used, which can potentially be accessed by anybody. Communications security is a subject which has grown in importance tremendously over recent years. With this, the general trend has been towards a rapid increase in the interconnection of equipment, both inside and between organisations.

Auditing is a very important aspect of security, in that good audit techniques should allow the *ex-poste* identification of a security breach. These different approaches which exist for auditing computer systems are examined in Chapter 8. Some make greater use than others of the computer itself and, therefore, differ far more from the traditional techniques of auditing manual systems. Usually a combination of techniques are used in a computer audit.

In Chapter 9, we look at *security modelling*. A very useful tool for assisting the security designer in that it gives a simplified overview of the system as a whole, provides a means of designing and implementing security as an integral part of the system, and is a tried and tested basis for implementing security. Although a great deal of work has been performed in this area, we provide only a summary of what we consider to be the most important examples. Some of this work was drawn upon by the consortium in its work on new models and guidelines, which is discussed later.

PART TWO: NEW MODELS AND GUIDELINES

During the second phase of the MARS project, the MoSel model (MOdel for Security devELopment) was developed. Its purpose being to assist in the design and testing of secure communications systems. The MoSel model, described in Chapter 10, provides a systematic approach to security design and testing and a medium for expressing the results of that activity. A 'process' model provides the essential methodological framework for security design and a 'product' model guides the activity of designing and testing security aspects of communications systems.

At the same time, a model for workstation security was developed by the Computer Industry Research Unit. This then became the basis of the *Guidelines for Workstation Security*, which are presented in Chapter 11. These guidelines are considered to be one of the most important results of the Project and will form the basis for further work in this area in the future, with possible input into the development of European standards. The guidelines themselves draw heavily upon the United States Department of Defence (US DoD) 'Trusted Computer System Evaluation Criteria' [DoD 83], known as the Orange Book. The concepts used by the DoD have been adapted in order to make them applicable to the office environment.

The guidelines are intended to be used by a system designer or security manager as a basis for providing a comprehensive set of security countermeasures at a level appropriate to the system in question. The methodology behind the guidelines is independent of the type of system and countermeasures available and in this sense is completely independent of technology. However, countermeasures and components are defined, which although not product-specific, could change or be added to as a result of technological change over an extended period of time. The structure of the guidelines is such that they can be adapted very simply to take account of any technological changes which may be of importance.

The workstation is defined in terms of a series of components, each of which requires it's own security countermeasures. This ensures that the workstation as a whole is protected and that no 'link in the chain' is left unguarded. An important feature is that different levels of security are defined according to what is required on a specific system. The methodology allows the user of the guidelines to determine the level of security required according to the level of sensitivity of the data on the system and by the 'clearance' level of the system users. The countermeasures required for each component are then determined according to this 'workstation security level'.

The importance of the guidelines lies partly in the fact that there are presently no accepted European standards to compete with the US DoD Criteria referred to above. This means that American products and systems, which can far more easily obtain security certification, have a marketing advantage over European products which might be equally secure. It is intended that the guidelines presented here form part of the initiative for a proposed European Security Evaluation and Testing Centre.

A further outcome of the MARS project was a set of guidelines for auditability (see Chapter 12). Auditability, from the auditor's point of view, can be defined as 'the facility for a competent and qualified auditor to independently convince himself of the proper design and functioning of a system and its internal controls, in order to form an opinion on the propriety of generated information for the user and on the efficiency, of the process by which it is produced, within reasonable time and without undue difficulty. (A. D. Chambers *Computer Auditing* , 1981)

Auditability is a subject which has received insufficient emphasis in view of its importance to computer security and the success of systems auditing. In an attempt to correct this oversight, the MARS project aimed to propose solid guidelines for facilitating the inclusion of auditability considerations during systems design.

PART THREE: SPECIFICATION AND DESIGN OF A SECURE TREASURY MANAGEMENT SYSTEM

In the final phase of the Project, the consortium undertook the theoretical specification and design of a secure treasury management system, the purpose being to apply the results of previous phases of the Project, including those on modelling and guidelines work, to an actual system. The results are described in Chapters 13 - 15. Chapter 13 gives a general introduction to the treasury management system itself, Chapter 14 describes the operations and functionality of the system, and Chapter 15 presents an overview of the security design.

Although the design was theoretical and as such not applied to a real-life system, a case study was performed at a large motor manufacturer using an existing cash management package as a hypothetical subject, in order to determine the security required by the user. The Guidelines presented in this document formed part of this study.

The emphasis of this phase of the project was largely on secure communications, with schemes for encryption and key distribution being considered very important in the context of the system in question. The results will be of interest particularly to those involved in financial systems and in communications security.

Contents

1

Threats

1.1 INTRODUCTION

Before building any defence system, one of the most important considerations is to know your enemy. As a starting point, we consider the threats facing computer systems. A threat can be defined either as a source of danger or as a potential attack on the system. In order to assist the reader in analysing the consequences of an attack, we have put together a classification of threats.

Depending upon the information contained in a computer system, an attack can jeopardise not only the security of the computer but also the whole organisation. By determining the vulnerabilities and susceptibilities of a system, Threat Analysis forms the logical basis for Risk Analysis (see Chapter 2), the assessment of a threat's potential for loss or damage to an organisation's assets and the consideration of possible countermeasures.

1.2 CLASSIFICATION OF THREATS

We have classified threats according to a three dimensional model outlined in Figure 1.1 below. This chapter analyses the threats which face a computer system, under headings corresponding to the subdivisions of this model.

The distinction illustrated on the vertical axis of Figure 1.1 is between accidental and deliberate threats. Accidental threats may or may not involve people. Deliberate threats always involve people who consciously decide to breach security.

On the right-hand, horizontal axis, threats are then further subdivided into Passive and Active threats. Passive threats are those which, if successful, would not alter the data or the computer system. An example of a passive threat would be the unauthorised disclosure of information. Active threats are potential breaches of security which, if successful, would alter data or the computer system. An example of such a threat would be the unauthorised modification of information.

1

The left-hand horizontal axis, shows the distinction between logical threats and physical threats. Logical threats affect the information stored or transmitted by the computer system, and the manner in which this data is processed. Physical threats affect the actual existence and physical condition of the computer facilities.

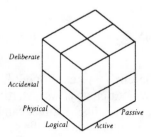

Figure 1.1 Classification of Threats

Deliberate, Active, Physical Threats

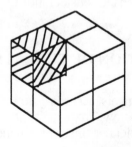

Figure 1.2 Classification of Threats

A simple example of a physical threat is fire. Since arson can totally destroy a computer installation, the materials used in the construction of the building are important contributory factors to this threat. As a basic requirement, the building housing a computer installation should be constructed from fire resistant materials, and the computer room(s) should not be located near areas which have a high fire risk. Backups should be kept of all programs and data.

Another deliberate, active physical threat is theft. To counteract this, it should be made difficult for an employee to obtain sensitive information, via printouts, floppy discs etc.

Deliberate, Active, Logical Threats

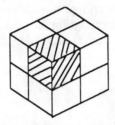

Figure 1.3 Classification of Threats

A logical threat is one which would directly affect data in the system, or the way in which that data is processed. There are two aspects to this:

- Unauthorised Access
- Unauthorised Modification

Unauthorised Access

This is a threat which has increased in importance over recent years, partly as a result of the growth of system networking. Traditionally, password mechanisms are used for legitimating access. However, there are a number of problems involved with this method, for example:

- people tend to use passwords which are easy to guess (e.g the name of the user's spouse).

- people are careless in the implementation and use of passwords, for example, the password is written down on paper

- in attempting to access the system from a PC, it is possible to write a password generator which will test each generated password against the names of authorised users

- the single state architecture in a PC is not capable of fully protecting its operating system.

- it is possible for a user to write a program which will simulate the host's part of the log-in sequence (this is known as spoofing). This program would store the user IDs and passwords.

- A more dramatic telecommunications example of unauthorised access occurs in unauthorised listening or monitoring as occurred recently by a private individual tape recording the secret conversations of UK's Princess of Wales with a friend (claimed by the popular press to be her lover)

Unauthorised modification

The perpetrator of a threat is not always someone who has accessed the system without authorisation. Here, the malicious user is an individual who abuses legitimate access rights. Therefore, unauthorised modification can occur either with or without unauthorised access. A simple example is that of a user gaining access to a sensitive file and changing its contents. Changing information in a payroll master file could lead the perpetrator to financial reward.

It is not only data, however, which is directly vulnerable. Code may be maliciously modified in such a way that it will fail to provide a service, or will perform in a slightly different fashion.

Clandestine code Code which is added or altered for use by a penetrator, without the knowledge of legitimate users or administrators, is termed a clandestine code. Sometimes its effect may be passive, for example copying information rather than changing it, but it is classed as active because its installation requires active attack. Examples of clandestine code are:

- virus
- worm
- logic bomb
- trojan horse
- trapdoor
- spoofing

A *virus* may be defined as a program that can infect other programs by modifying them to include a possibly evolved version of itself. With the infection property, a virus can spread throughout the system or network to infect other programs. Every program that becomes infected may then act as a carrier adding to the spread.

The computer *worm* is an independent section of code, which damages the files to which it has access. *Logic bombs* are pieces of code which lie dormant in a system until they are triggered by some event (for example, a date or time), and then render the system inoperable.

The *trojan horse* is a segment of code, usually placed in a common utility program, or embedded in a program of its own, which can be used to breach security in a number of ways. For example, it might cause damage to a file which the program reads or might copy information into a "back pocket" file to be read later.

A *trapdoor* is a piece of code which allows the penetrator to circumvent system security. For example, the code may allow the user to bypass the security aspects of a log-on procedure, thereby leaving the door wide open for a perpetrator with knowledge of the clandestine code or trapdoor.

Spoofing is a threat posed to the system operator or user and is intended to make him/her respond to a falsely generated system message. The simplest example of this is a dummy log-on screen which reads the ID and password of the next user to access a terminal, before passing control back to the legitimate log-on program. A second method is to use a falsely generated error report to gain information from the system operator.

As an example of deliberate, active, logical threats in practice, we now look at networked systems. The discussion is divided into '*threats to the host*' and '*threats to the subnet*'', and we touch briefly on some of the countermeasures which can be used to guard against such threats. These are included for the purposes of example only as the subject of security countermeasures is discussed in detail in Chapters 4 to 8.

Threats to the host

The host computer (or a major file-server or computer acting as a gateway) in a network is more vulnerable to threats than a standalone or multi-user machine as it is potentially accessible to a wider number of users who do not necessarily need physical access to the site.

PC network hosts (or file-servers) are particularly vulnerable. Unlike the majority of modern mainframe computers, these do not always provide hardware features with which to implement separate address spaces for the operating system and application programs (i.e. memory protection), nor do they always provide the distinct execution states that are necessary to prevent application programs from directly performing security-relevant functions.

In many networks having PCs as hosts, crucial network functions are implemented in the PC. Since the PC does not have a protected supervisor state there is no way of preventing a perpetrator from accessing these network functions and modifying them to allow violations of the network security policy. This is clearly an undesirable feature.

Threats to the subnet

Examples of deliberate, active, logical threats to the subnet are:
* Message stream modification: messages arrive but have been modified en route.
* Denial of service: messages do not arrive, or arrive late.
* Spurious connection initiation: messages arrive claiming false origins.

Message stream modification poses a very real threat to data on a network. It threatens the authenticity, integrity, and ordering of messages. Integrity implies that data should remain intact and unmodified; authenticity implies that the source of the message should be reliably determined; and ordering implies that messages should be received in the same sequence as they were sent.

Apart from physically protecting a line there is no other real way of preventing message stream modification. However, cryptography, with the use of a message authentication key (MAC, See Chapter 7), can be used so that all modifications can be detected with a very high probability. If the message has been encrypted it is usually almost impossible to change sensibly. A very small change to the cipher text would in most cases render the deciphered text meaningless.

Attack on authenticity may be made by modifying the protocol control information in the message so that it claims to be from a different sender. Such an attack can be successfully countered using digital signatures (See Chapter 7).

Attacks on message ordering involve disrupting the stream of PDUs (packet data unit) moving on the network. This includes deleting PDUs from the stream and altering their order.

The aim of a message ordering or message sequencing countermeasure is to detect such attacks and make it possible for the receiving entity to determine reliably the position of the PDU within the stream which is being sent. This is also relevant to the replay of messages, since a party could try to replay a message from one bank to another, telling the second bank to credit his/her account. To counteract a replay attack, all PDUs should have time stamps or sequence numbers.

Denial of service comprises attacks which may result either in the loss or in the delay of the message. The best countermeasure is to require (secure) acknowledgement of receipt of each message.

Spurious connection initiation poses a particularly dangerous threat. A spurious connection initiation is made by an intruder impersonating another user. Clearly, if an intruder were successful in establishing a connection while impersonating someone else, he/she would be in a very powerful position. To offset "false ID" attacks, a connection must be initiated in a fashion which supports the secure identification of the users.

Deliberate, Passive, Physical Threats

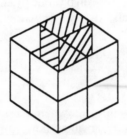

Figure 1.4 Deliberate, Passive, Phusical threats

As passive physical threats are directed against system components, but do not alter them in any way, they can only take the form of copying or simulation. The most basic form of this attack is key copying. Someone planning an attack on a communication network may try to physically make a copy of the key to the building or room where the communications equipment is kept. The key could be a plastic card with a coded magnetic strip, or it may simply be a traditional door key.

Deliberate, Passive, Logical Threats

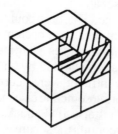

Figure 1. 5 Deliberate, Passive, Logical threats

Passive logical threats usually involve the unauthorised reading or copying of information. This can be done by *electronic eavesdropping* on communication channels, or by *accessing stored information* on a computer.

Electronic Eavesdropping

Electronic eavesdropping occurs when the information in a message is either leaked or stolen by an unauthorised party. As technology has advanced, the sophistication of electronic surveillance methods has increased considerably and is no longer restricted to the simple monitoring of data sent down the telephone line. Techniques include the following:

- emission monitoring
- bugging devices
- signal interception
- wire tapping.

Emission monitoring involves homing in to the stray electrical signals emitted from television or computer screens. These signals have two components: picture signals, which are relatively high-powered, and synchronising signals, which are weak but essential to the build-up of a comprehensive picture.

Bugging devices are widely available and are employed for listening to communications at system end nodes. An example would be a microphone radio transmitter disguised, perhaps, as a picture hanger.

Signal interception describes the use of specialised equipment to monitor transmissions from satellite broadcasts, microwave links and cordless and cellular telephones.

Wire tapping, which involves tampering with circuits and switching nodes, can be accomplished by someone with only modest technical training. Even local area networks, which should be the easiest to secure, are often unprotected and have exposed network terminations. The threat from wire tapping grows in proportion to the distance between the communicators.

When planning to eavesdrop , an intruder can use traffic analysis to deduce the best time and place for the operation. This will reveal when and where messages flow, their frequency, duration and level of importance.

Encryption To protect against electronic eavesdropping, encryption is often used. Thus, another important element of passive logical threats is cipher breaking or cryptanalysis. This illustrates the sometimes circular nature of threat and risk analysis. A countermeasure to eavesdropping is encryption. But a counter-countermeasure, which might then be used by the intruder, is cryptanalysis. All of this must be considered by the security designer.

Two approaches to cryptanalysis can be identified - Deterministic and Statistical. Using the deterministic approach, the cryptanalyst attempts to express the cipher operation in mathematical form. This can be used to break a linear system. Encryption brings with it its own problems: consider the case where a disgruntled employee encrypts some important files and blackmails the company into paying money in exchange for the secret key. The statistical approach attempts to exploit statistical relationships between characters of the plain text. Simple substitution ciphers are easily broken by this method. Both deterministic and statistical methods can be employed together.

Accessing Stored Information There are a number of different ways of gaining unauthorised access to information stored on a computer. Different types of systems, for example, single-user, multi-user or networked systems, are vulnerable in different ways. Protection is largely the domain of access control, addressed in detail in Chapter 4.

Some methods involve the use of a *clandestine code.* This is discussed in detail above, under Deliberate, Active, Logical Threats. Although, as we have seen the insertion of a clandestine code presents a physical threat, the result can sometimes be passive, e.g. the unauthorised copying of information.

Browsing is the activity of searching through directories and other data sets in the hope of finding interesting information. A powerful countermeasure, minimising the amount of information exposed to a browsing attack, is a multi-level secure system, possibly supported with file encryption.

Aggregation threats occur in databases where information contains different levels of sensitivity. The problem arises when individual objects with low classification are merged possibly resulting in a combination of information which should have a much higher aggregate classification. An example would be a bank's customer file (containing name and address details) and a file containing individual account balances, referenced only by a customer number. Each may possess a low classification, but when merged the result should have a higher classification. Strict procedures to ensure correct classification are the main countermeasure.

Inference threats are closely related to browsing and aggregation but involve a more sophisticated analysis of information. Database inference, for example, involves the analysis of information contained in a database to infer results not explicitly available or accessible to the user, though such a threat would be in the Deliberate, Active, Physical category.

Accidental, Active, Physical Threats

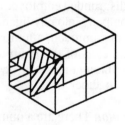

Figure 1.6 Accidental, Active, Physical threats

Hardware is vulnerable to accidental threats such as *fire*, *floods*, *earthquakes*, etc. Naturally the design of a building and the materials used in its construction will affect this threat. To offset the potential damage from physical elements it is therefore essential to keep offsite system backups.

Accidental, Active Logical Threats

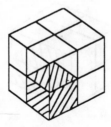

Figure 1.7 Accidental, Active Logical threats

It is possible for stored information to be *accidentally deleted*, although good software design can help to prevent this. This is especially true with PC systems where disc and/or software problems can cause the deletion of files. If a system backup is taken on a regular basis then accidental deletion does not pose a major threat but can still result in wasted labour. However, a very considerable threat is posed by *message stream modification* which can alter the authenticity and integrity of data. Data may be affected either by transmission errors or by a malfunctioning network component.

Accidental, Passive, Physical Threats

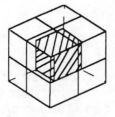

Figure 1.8 Accidental, Passive, Physical threats

There are very few examples of accidental, passive, physical threats. One possibility is that of a smart card being sent to the wrong address, potentially giving an unauthorised person a physical means of accessing the system.

Accidental, Passive, Logical Threats

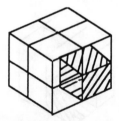

Figure 1.9 Accidental, Passive, Logical threats

Threats belonging to this category are realised when someone inadvertently obtains information. A common example is the crossed connection. Although usually a feature of telephone lines, it can also occur with radiowaves, microwaves, and satellite broadcasts. Obviously the threat compromises system credibility, causing loss of confidence if people feel that private information can be viewed or heard by others.

Further accidental, passive, logical threats may occur through:

- reading discarded information which has not been properly disposed of, or reading documents which have been left out in a careless fashion.
- accidentally reading screen output
- observing someone entering a PIN or password
- reading information which has been incorrectly delivered

1.3 CONCLUSION

This chapter has provided an overview of the threats facing computer installations and the consequences should they be realised. For convenience and clarity, we have made three broad distinctions:

- Deliberate and Accidental threats
- Active and Passive threats
- Logical and Physical threats

Other methods of classification could be used. For example, the combination of threats to which data in a system is vulnerable very much depends on the physical location of the data. Data on a network is often more vulnerable, especially if the telephone system is used. On a wide area network, it would be almost impossible to provide complete physical security.

The tables in Appendix A contain examples of threats under each of the main headings introduced in this chapter, analysing possible countermeasures for guarding against those threats. Neither the list of threats, nor the list of countermeasures are exhaustive. The intention is only to provide a list of examples.

2

Risk Management

2.1 INTRODUCTION

With the increasing computerisation of information, those who own or use computer systems are exposed daily to the risks of damage to or loss of their assets. Using risk management techniques, we are able to assess the likely occurrence of threats which face these assets, and determine the most cost-effective and pragmatic means of implementing security countermeasures. A major aspect of this is *Risk analysis*, which will be the subject of most of this chapter.

In today's complex business world, most computer systems are highly vulnerable and can only be termed 'secure' in the sense that they have not yet been challenged or compromised. Since threats to a system are manifold, an awareness of the problems involved should be brought to the attention of managers. If risks are to be effectively managed, the following questions need to be addressed:

- What is a risk?
- What impact would the materialisation of risks have on business objectives?
- To what extent should risk be accepted?
- How dependent is the organisation on its assets?
- What countermeasures are available to reduce unacceptable risks and what do they cost?
- What security safeguards provide the best return on investment?
- Who is responsible for the implementation of countermeasures?
- How and when will countermeasures be implemented?

2.2 THE STRUCTURE OF RISK MANAGEMENT

Risk management involves three processes - *Risk analysis, Decision management and Control.*

Risk analysis, which is discussed in detail in Section 2.3, involves examining the threats which have been identified, considering the countermeasures which can be used to guard against these threats, and analysing which countermeaures or combination of countermeasures (if any) are the most cost-effective.

Decision management involves using the figures, calculations and estimates resulting from Risk Analysis to decide whether to:

- make changes to the safeguards in order to control the risks
- accept losses resulting from insufficient countermeasures
- avoid risks by abandoning the activities
- diffuse the risk by delegating activities to several locations
- purchase insurance capable of compensating for any loss.

The *control function* relates to the implementation and verification of decisions agreed by Decision Management. This will apply both to procedural changes and to modifications in the system environment (e.g. the provision of new hardware and software).

Figure 2.1, shows the relationship between risk analysis, decision management and control.

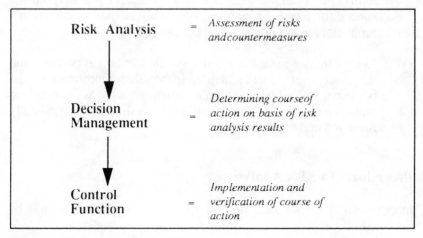

Figure 2.1 Processes in risk management

2.3 RISK ANALYSIS

The aim of risk analysis is twofold. Firstly, to obtain information expressing the total losses expected per timescale (usually a year), considering the use of the computer system and the application of possible countermeasures. Secondly, to establish the foundation on which management can decide whether or not to apply countermeasures.

For various reasons, companies are often reluctant to embark on a risk analysis project. It may be that management are satisfied with existing security arrangements and see no need for improvement. Or it may be that there are insufficient resources in terms of time, money and manpower to justify risk analysis. For those companies considering risk analysis, it is important that they first of all assess their needs carefully. The following points should be considered:

•   Estimate the expected lifetime of your computing assets. If extensive changes are about to be made to an organisation's computer facilities, in depth Risk Analysis procedures should be postponed.

•   Identify the assets worthy of protection

•   Be aware of the difficulties of quantifying loss in purely financial terms. For example, it is not easy to predict precisely how a successful attack on a bank would affect that organisation's reputation, assuming the news became public.

•   Realise that information within a system varies in importance and sensitivity over time. Fluctuations in the value of information must be accompanied by corresponding changes to the assessment and management of risk. Thus, Risk Analysis should be periodically reviewed and updated.

Procedures in Risk Analysis

In performing a risk analysis, the following procedures should be followed -

1. *Value assessment* - the evaluation of all information handled by the system.

2. *Threat assessment* - the analysis of all possible threats directed towards the organisation.

3. *Vulnerability assessment* - the identification of an organisation's vulnerabilities and an estimation of the consequences following a breach of security.

4. *Correlation of vulnerabilities and threats* - a synthesis designed to highlight which vulnerability is capable of being exploited by which threat.

5. *Consequence assessment* - an examination, following logically from Vulnerability Assessment, to determine possible countermeasures, their efficiency and cost.

The key point in the above process is that the cost of implementing and maintaining the countermeasures used should not be greater than the loss (financial or otherwise) which is likely to be incurred from any breach of security. Therefore, risk analysis involves a study of the cost-effectiveness of countermeasures, in addition to an assessment of which countermeasures are suitable.

The analysis of threats includes an assessment of their probability of occurrence. It is insufficient to quantify the damage should a threat be realised. This needs to be combined with knowledge of its probability of occurrence in order to decide on whether protection is worthwhile.

Approaches to Risk Analysis

There are two basic approaches to Risk Analysis - *Qualitative risk analysis* and *Quantitative risk analysis* (See Figure 2.2). These methods are introduced in this section and then examined individually in more detail.

Each method involves the risk analysis procedures. An assessment is made of the value of assets, the threats facing those assets, their probability of occurrence and the vulnerability of the assets to those threats. This is followed by a study of the suitability and the cost-effectiveness of countermeasures. It is in the way in which these assessments are made that the two activities differ.

In *Quantitative risk analysis*, all assets and resources are identified and valued in monetary terms. All potential threats are identified and their frequency of occurrence estimated. These threats are then compared with potential system vulnerabilities in order to reveal sensitive areas. Following this, the Annual Loss Expectancy (ALE) is calculated by multiplying the frequency of the threat occurrence by the asset's value or damage rating.

This gives management the opportunity to decide whether existing countermeasures are adequate or whether new safeguards are required. One drawback with quantification is that numerous calculations have to be performed and then reperformed if the parameters change. For this reason, many *Automated Quantitative Risk Analysis Tools* have been developed in recent years. A second drawback with quantification is its lack of precision. It is often very difficult to arrive at an exact figure for the loss or damage resulting from security breaches. Furthermore, this method is very time consuming with respect to exact value estimation. On the other hand, where exact values can be deduced, the approach provides a good basis for management to decide whether additional security resources are necessary.

In contrast, *Qualitative Risk Analysis* usually requires a smaller investment of resources. Instead of applying exact values in the assessment of the various threats and assets, this approach applies notions like high, low, and medium, which represent prices and the frequency of occurrence. Problem areas are usually identified fairly quickly. However, the weakness with this approach is in its foundation for decision making. The difficulty is in comparing the potential loss with the cost of implementing countermeasures to minimise that loss.

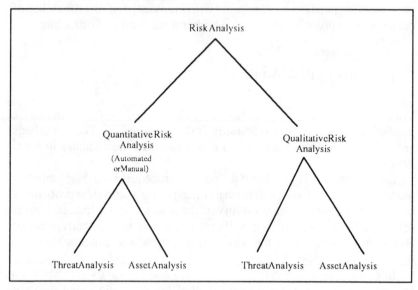

Figure 2.2 Approaches to risk analysis

Obviously an attractive 'middle' approach would be to combine the two methods by applying the qualitative approach in the preliminary estimate, thus covering wider and general aspects, and then using the quantitative approach to focus on the more specific and detailed aspects.

2.4 QUALITATIVE RISK ANALYSIS

Because risk analysis is an analytical procedure subject to many environmental variables, there is no single or universally accepted methodology. However, based upon the work of Campbell, 1983 [CAMP83], we can refer to a model designed to provide a framework suitable to most environments.

Campbell has designed a risk management approach which is modular, hierarchical, iterative, capable of assigning responsibilities to authorities, and predominantly qualitative. The Risk Analysis model is divided into two discrete activities, each described independently:

• Asset Analysis
• Threat Analysis

The two activities are strongly linked. The identity and value of assets must be known in order to quantify the threats facing the organisation. To know the full extent of all threats (if this were possible) would still not be sufficient to determine the cost effectiveness of countermeasures. It is necessary to know also, the loss which would be incurred if those threats were realised. Therefore, asset analysis forms the basis for threat analysis.

Each activity constitutes a task with a number of subtasks requiring greater or lesser analysis. These are discussed below.

Asset Analysis

Asset analysis establishes the financial foundation on which management will base its decisions; its purpose is to estimate the value to an organisation of possessing and using EDP facilities. The Asset Analysis procedure is comparatively independent of other activities undertaken during Risk analysis.

The result of this process is an estimated figure, expressed both in monetary terms and in terms of the organisation's computing assets. Three analytic subtasks are involved, as illustrated in Figure 2.3.

Sensitivity of Information

The first task is to determine the sensitivity level of the information contained on the system. Starting at the application level, and progressing through possible subsystems to the system level, a sensitivity rating is assigned to various pieces of software. In order to determine exactly the different degrees of sensitivity and the way data processing occurs, the information collected from the various types of software is aggregated in a base-up fashion, ending at the data processing level.

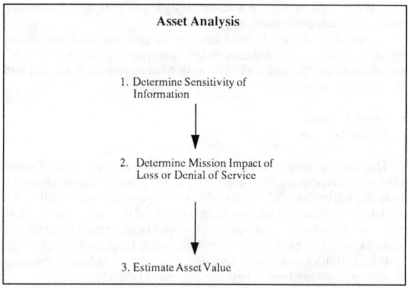

Figure 2.3 Steps in asset analysis

Impact of Loss or Denial of Service

This analysis is based on the previous one, and must estimate the loss resulting from a service being non-operational for a certain period of time. It produces an estimate of the impact to an organisation of being totally or partially non-operational due to faulty EDP facilities.

Asset Values

The estimation of asset values covers fixed assets, such as physical facilities, programs, manuals and so on. The end result will be a total figure for all fixed assets.

Threat Analysis

Threat analysis identifies possible threats, the vulnerability of an organisation to these threats, how the threats can materialise, and how they can be counteracted. The analysis can be subdivided into four tasks, as illustrated in Figure 2.4 below.

Threat Identification

Threat identification highlights and defines the threats which face the system. According to Campbell, threats can originate from the following broad categories:

- Environmental factors (flood, fire, earthquake etc.)
- Authorised users (programmers, operators etc.)
- Hostile Agents (any unauthorised user of the system, e.g. a hacker)

Vulnerability Analysis

This two part procedure identifies vulnerabilities in the system and estimates their potential for exploitation. The first process is vulnerability identification, which will highlight weaknesses in design, implementation, operation or security control. Secondly, vulnerabilities are weighted in order to determine their degree of seriousness.

Correlation of Vulnerabilities and Threats

Correlating vulnerabilities and threats is the logical outcome of the previous two subtasks and will provide information on the effects the various threats and vulnerabilities have on the system. Again, it is a two-part procedure involving synthesis and identification. With synthesis, the techniques or methods available to test the vulnerabilities are joined and the result is documented. Based on the synthesis, information regarding the identification of undesirable events is gathered.

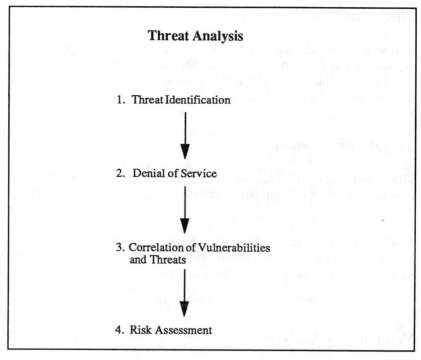

Figure 2.4 Steps in Threat Analysis

Risk Assessment

This task identifies the impact of attacks on the organisation's facilities, the information handled, the processing performed, the support provided and so on. It also identifies and evaluates appropriate countermeasures.

The risk assessment task is the single most important function since it is based on results from nearly all of the previous tasks. The aim is to produce a list of evaluated countermeasures based on the completion of six risk assessment procedures:

- Assignment of event weightings
- Determination of relative impacts
- Estimation of likelihood
- Ranking of acceptability/unacceptability
- Identification of countermeasures
- Evaluation of countermeasures

2.5 QUANTITATIVE RISK ANALYSIS

Quantitative risk analysis differs from qualitative risk analysis in that the aim is to collate much more detailed and exact estimates, using statistical and mathematical techniques. However, the basic structure is similar. An assessment has to be made of the assets of the company and of the identity of threats and likelihood of them being realised. Countermeasures need to be designed or identified and the cost of these compared with the probable loss to the organisation, should they not be implemented.

Using the quantitative approach, the assessment techniques illustrated in Figure 2.5 offer a structured way of estimating the occurrence of events.

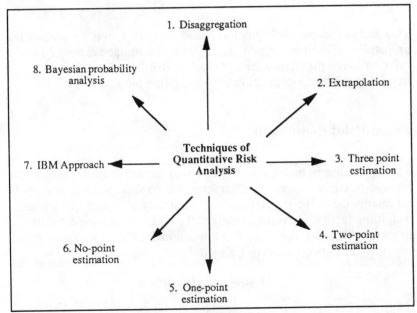

Figure 2.5 Techniques of Quantitative Risk Analysis

These techniques are used to determine the probability of threats being realised. A discussion of each is now given.

Disaggregation

It is often not possible to quantify as a whole, the threats facing the organisation. Disaggregation involves breaking the analysis down into smaller components. The probability of the occurence of each individual threat is analysed. If practical, this is further disaggregated. At the lowest level, every possibility is considered in isolation. Concatenation of the results gives an aggregate figure for the potential loss and the likelihood of a threat being realised.

Extrapolation

This technique uses information based on past events to predict the probability of their recurence in the future. Formulae are applied to the information on previous security breaches in order to identify a pattern or trend. On this basis, projections into the future are made.

Three-Point Estimation

This technique is based upon three parameters: alpha represents the highest possible value; ß represents the lowest possible value; M represents the value occurring most frequently. A fourth parameter, a weighting factor "'D', is used to adjust the outcome (the expected mean) towards either the upper or the lower limits. The expression which provides the expected mean (EX)is:

$$EX = \frac{alpha + MD + ß}{D + 2}$$

By varying the weighting factor and thereby generating different values for EX, it is possible to select the most suitable result.

Two-Point Estimation

In this estimation, only two points are available and these constitute the upper and lower limits. No knowledge is assumed of the most frequent value. Only the range between the extremes is available, so theoretically, in the case of a uniform distribution, each point in the range is equally likely. However, the best estimate would be the midpoint.

One point estimation

In risk analysis it is often sufficient to distinguish between orders of magnitude. Many analysts use tables which give an estimate of the probability of an attack occurring in a single year, calculated on the basis of the estimated frequency of the attack. The number of years increase by the power of ten to cover different orders of magnitude. In the following example each magnitude is multiplied by three:

Estimated Frequency (once every)	Likelihood Estimate (of occurence in next year):
3 years	0.3333
30 years	0.0333
300 years	0.0033
3000 years	0.0003

For example, in order to estimate the likelihood of power failure within the next year, the analyst has to determine the period between such failures e.g. three years, and then find the related likelihood in the other table; in this example, 0.3333.

No point estimation

This technique is based on the *Fuzzy Set Theory* where neither the upper/lower limits, the most frequent value, nor even the order of magnitude are known. In this approach, a prerequisite is a computer to calculate the probabilities derived from the beta function:

$$f(x) = \frac{\Gamma(\propto + \beta + 2)}{\Gamma(\propto + 1).\Gamma(\beta + 1)} . x \propto (1-X)\beta$$

($\propto$ and ß are shaping parameters)

The idea is to generate a number of different probability curves by varying $\propto$ and β, and then to choose the curve which seems most appropriate. Beta is obtained by random sampling the distributions preferred. Following this, the asset value (H), and likelihood (L), can be derived from the formulae:

$$H = \frac{1}{3} . 10^{6\beta + 2}$$

$$L = \frac{1}{3} . 10^{7\beta - 3}$$

This is surely the most imprecise approach, but still provides a foundation for a structured guess.

The IBM Approach

This is a variation of the one-point estimation method. It was developed by IBM and is based on the probability of threat occurence and the estimation of the related loss as expressed in the following table:

Threat occurrence rate (P)	Cost exposure value (V)
1 (Once in every 1000 years)	($10)
2 (Once in every 100 years)	($100)
3 (Once in every 10 years)	($1 000)
4 (Once in every 1 years)	($10 000)
5 (Once in every 0.1 years)	($100 000)
6 (Once in every 0.01 years)	($1 000 000)
7 (Once in every 0.001 years)	($10 000 000)
8 (Once in every 0.0001 years)	($100 000 000)

The annual expected loss (R) is then calculated using the formula:

$$R = \$10^{(P+V-4)}$$

For example, if it was estimated that a company may expect a system breakdown every fourth day (P = 6) due to a software error, and that the cost exposure (or loss) was approximately $1000 on each occasion, the expected annual cost related to the software error is determined by:

$$R = \$10^{(6+3-4)}$$
$$= \$10^5$$
$$= \$100,000$$

This method is quite crude but nevertheless enables the analyst to identify critical areas quickly.

The Bayesian Probabilistic Risk Analysis Method

This method compensates for the degree of uncertainty common to other methods; for example the difficulty in determining the likely occurence of potential threats, and the problem of determining the cost of a given threat. The method takes into account possible variations in threat occurence and cost exposure, and so minimises the uncertainty of the estimates. The risk arising from several threats to a single system vulnerability could be included in the calculation. For a full discussion of the principles involved in this form of analysis, see Ali Mosleh et al, 1985.

2.6 AUTOMATED QUANTITATIVE RISK ANALYSIS TOOLS

In order to obtain a complete picture of possible losses, numerous calculations must be performed. Every single asset must be measured against every potential threat. These analyses involve a huge amount of multiplication and are extremely time consuming if carried out manually. Consequently, *automated quantitative risk analysis tools* have been developed in the last few years. Using these, it is far easier to answer such questions as: "what will be the effect if we improve a specific countermeasure?" The use of such automated Quantitative risk analysis Tools will considerably reduce the analysis timescale. Nevertheless, a reasonable timescale is still required since a large quantity of data must be collected and input. During the 1980s, the market for automated risk analysis tools has developed and the trend has been towards implementing the software on microcomputers. The various packages available offer different features which tailor the process to a particular environment by removing superfluous questions.

2.7 CONCLUSION

It is only in recent years that attention has been given to risk analysis and its application to computer systems. There is still, however, a certain inertia amongst organisations in deciding whether to use the technique.

There is clear evidence to suggest that the majority of companies require more conclusive proof that Risk analysis will really save them money. However, it is very difficult to prove that it will. The immediate impression is that the technique increases company expenses if no adverse events occur. Also, in contrast to insurance cover, there is no compensation in the event of loss or damage. Additionally, there is a need for more information, especially as the Risk Analysis process is very complex.

Of the approaches developed for Risk analysis, the quantitative method is used most frequently. Although Qualitative risk analysis has the advantage of being descriptive, this benefit diminishes when compared to the automated versions of Quantitative risk analysis, which are faster, more flexible, and can be applied with greater ease.

Compared to the outlay and effort involved in manual risk analysis, the investment required to use automated tools seems small. Since increasingly sophisticated packages are now finding their way into the marketplace, there is probably little future for manually performed Risk analysis.

User Requirements

3.1 INTRODUCTION

A thorough study of user requirements is necessary, in order to know what we are trying to achieve in defining security measures. The user, in this case, is the organisation rather than the individual. The aim is to achieve an environment in which the system can be used efficiently for its legitimate purpose, but in which threats to the system (see Chapter 2) can be prevented from materialising.

Methodology and Structure

The methodology applied to determine user requirements is based largely on the following three elements (see also Figure 3.1):

- Existing literature relating to the security requirements of users
- Questionnaires sent to users
- Case studies of a number of organisations.

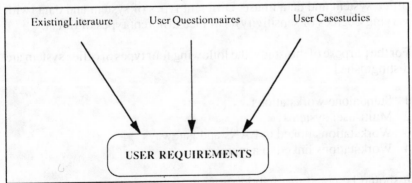

Figure 3.1 Methodology for user requirements study

The existing literature proved to be unhelpful in identifying user requirements, largely because the approach to the subject is predominantly theoretical. Little material is therefore offered on practical user requirements. Questionnaires and case studies were found to be useful in establishing a general framework and highlighting security issues. However, there was, understandably, a reluctance on the part of some of the organisations under study to discuss their present state of security.

In order to put the findings of the user requirements study into context, we begin this chapter with a general study of office systems. The MARS project focussed on the business world and the user requirements study looked at the commercial, financial and banking sectors and at the computing resources used by these.

We then move on, more specifically, to the results of the case studies and questionnaires mentioned above. This is followed by a brief discussion of legal requirements in EEC countries. Finally, we present a general framework for expressing user requirements. The latter includes what we consider to be the six primary security requirements and the constraints facing any organisation wishing to fulfil those requirements.

3.2 OFFICE SYSTEMS

In order to determine measures and requirements for security, we must first define the characteristics of the office environment. Threats, user requirements and suitable countermeasures are contingent upon the office system and data in use. Different types of system and data (with varying degrees of sensitivity) will face different types of threat.

For the purpose of this study, the following four types of office system are distinguished:

1   Standalone workstations
2   Multi-user systems
3   Workstations linked to LANs and gateways
4   Workstations linked to a mainframe.

It should be noted that hybrid systems, comprising two or more of the elements listed above often exist. In general, there is a scale, at opposite ends of which are centralised and distributed systems. In the middle is the mixed organisation, which consists of several centralised systems, communicating as components of a distributed system.

Standalone Workstations

A standalone workstation consists of a sophisticated microcomputer which is usually classified according to its price, capacity, or by the scope of the applications it is able to perform. The description "standalone" emphasises that tasks are performed in an isolated fashion by the single user. In the last few years, workstation technology has advanced rapidly with substantial increases in storage capacity, speed and overall performance. Additionally, the availability of integrated packages offering, amongst other features, spreadsheet, word processing and database facilities has underlined the importance of the standalone workstation.

Since standalone workstations are now commonplace, suitable protective measures should govern their use. Password assignment, password validation and isolation of particular subsystems (e.g. stocks information system, financial accounting), by means of specified access legitimation and by other means (e.g. manual log), should be implemented.

Multi-user systems

As office integration is not realised by standalones, there is a requirement for a multi-user system which can serve several users and perform various functions simultaneously, using time sharing. In an office, a multi-user system must be organised centrally, with each device connected to the central host by means of a dedicated line. The problems encountered are similar to those of a network since both have the following features:

multiple users
many peripheral devices (terminals, workstations, storage media, and output media)
data transfer from the central storage to the peripheral devices
the possibility of several users having access to the same files.

Multi-user systems require a significantly greater degree of security than standalone workstations. The major difference is that the operating system needs to be far more secure. In a system which is accessed simultaneously by a number of people, there are at least two important additional threats to consider. Firstly, one person may attempt to access files owned by another. Secondly, it may be possible for a user to access confidential information being used, and thus held in memory, by a different user. (The former threat also applies, although to a lesser extent, to standalone workstations, as different users may use the workstation at different times).

When considering multi-user systems, there are additional requirements for environmental security. The reason for this is that the terminals are often distributed and separate to the processor. All of these elements of the system need to be protected from physical and logical threats.

Workstations linked to Local Area Networks

The local area network (LAN) provides facilities for workstations (usually PCs or minis) to communicate with each other and to access centralised software and data, within a localised area (e.g. a building or a single room, or possibly a collection of buildings). The access of participating network users is controlled by various methods. Those widely used include Token and CSMA/CD procedures.

LANs may be connected via bridges to other LANs, or via gateways to other LANs, mainframes or wide area networks (WANs). Thus the range and diversity of network users presents particular problems. Additional security is required. For example, a clearing house service is necessary for the management of address tables controlling access rights to the connected workstations and servers.

Workstations linked to a mainframe

The fourth type of office system is that of a workstation, or set of workstations, linked to a mainframe, emulating terminals. This is different to the normal multi-user system, as the terminals have local intelligence and is different to a network as the workstations are acting in the manner of a normal mainframe terminal. However, because the workstations have local intelligence, they constitute a greater security risk than normal mainframe terminals.

3.3 THE CASE STUDIES

The use of case studies highlighted the relative importance of user requirements among various business institutions (commercial, financial sector, banking etc.). As an example, let us review some of the requirements stipulated for the banking environment.

Here a distinction can be made between front office and back office requirements; less emphasis being placed on data confidentiality within the back office. In this instance there is some conflict between the requirements of the bank and those of the customer. Customers obviously want restricted access to their transactions and account balances. They, therefore, attach great importance to data confidentiality. Meanwhile, the bank, wishing to minimise costs, might not place priority on the need for a highly secure system. However, if security becomes an issue in the drive towards competitiveness, a bank with good "read-only" access security may market this as an added feature to win custom.

Many of the banks under study strongly emphasised the need for secure communications. Generally speaking, sender/receiver authentication were identified as being of considerable importance. With regard to data integrity, since a large percentage of documents are in a high security bracket, a premium is placed on preventing "contamination". Of the banks interviewed, some regarded reliability of service as a crucial security requirement. Others felt that the importance of reliability varied according to the application and to the duration of any break of service. Denial of service for a long period would, of course, damage customer relations.

Based on case studies, the following tables compare the levels of security required in banking, financial and commercial organisations. Firstly, the participants were asked to specify the percentage of documents falling under each of the following categories: Secret, Internally Confidential, Non-Public, Public-Voluntary, Public-by-Law, or Other. Secondly, they were asked to rank each of the security requirements - Data Integrity, Data Confidentiality, Sender and Receiver authentication, Proof of Origin, Proof of Receipt and Reliability of service - as either high (H), medium (M) or low (L) in terms of their importance.

BANKS

Table 3.1 Confidentiality in banks

Type of Document	A %	B %	C %	D %
Secret		1.0	5.0	0.5
Internally Confidential	3.9	10.0	20.0	96.0
Non Public		96.0	87.0	65.0
Public Voluntary	1.0	5.0	5.0	1.0
Public by Law	1.0	5.0	5.0	1.0
Other				2.5

Table 3.2 Security requirements for banks

Security Requirements	A	B	C	D	E	F
Data Integrity	H	H	H	H	H	H
Data Confidentiality	H	H	H	H	H	H
Sender/Receiver Authentication	H	H	H	H	M	H
Proof Origination	H	H	H	H	M	H
Proof of Receipt	H	H	H	H	M	H
Reliability of Service	M/H		H	M/H	H	H

H = Rated highly important

M = Rated moderately important

FINANCIAL INSTITUTIONS

Table 3.3 Confidentiality in financial institutions

Type of Document	Financial Institution	
	A (%)	B (%)
Secret	90.0	20.0
Internally Confidential	-	75.0
Non-Public	10.0	5.0
Public-Voluntary	-	-
Public-by-Law	-	-
Other	-	-

Table 3.4 Security requirements for financial institutions

Security Requirements	Financial Institution			
	A	B	C	D
Data Integrity	H	-	H	H
Data Confidentiality	H	-	H	M
Sender/Receiver Authentication	M	-	H	M/H
Proof of Origination	-	-	-	-
Proof of Receipt	-	-	-	-
Reliability of Service	M	-	M/H	-

H = Rated highly important

M = Rated moderately important

COMMERCIAL ORGANISATIONS

Table 3.5 Confidentiality in commercial organisations

Type of Document	A %	B %
Secret	1.0	1.0
Internally Confidential	4.0	60.0
Non-Public	90.0	25.0
Public-Voluntary	4.0	4.0
Public-by Law	1.0	5.0
Other		

Table 3.6 Security requirements for commercial organisations

Security Requirements	Commercial Organisations	
	A	B
Data Integrity	H	H
Data Confidentiality	H	H
Sender Receiver Authentication	L	H
Proof of Origination	L	H
Proof of Receipt	L	H
Reliability of service	H	

H = Rated highly important

L = Rated low priority

Common to all of the organisations studied were the requirements for data confidentiality and integrity. Security of communications was also found to have a high priority. This includes the need for authentication, proof of origination and proof of receipt. A further area for concern was shown to be auditability. This can be defined as the ability of a competent and qualified auditor to independently establish the correct design and functioning of a system and its internal controls. Finally, one of the most interesting and emphatic responses to emerge from the studies was a widespread concern for the level of security available to protect data held on hard disk within PCs.

3.4 THE QUESTIONNAIRES

The questionnaires focused on asking organisations which automated methods they used and which level of security requirement they attached to each. The findings are summarised in the following tables on 'communications', 'document creation', 'information storage and retrieval', and 'banking automation'. The figures quoted under "percentage in use" refer to the proportion of respondents using a particular facility.

One area for concern, as revealed by the questionnaire responses, is the low level of security attached to PCs. The security arrangements for floppy disks ranged from low to average, although magnetic tape storage warranted a higher level of security. The hard disk was regarded as a very useful storage medium with a high level of security, though hard disks in micros did not attract the high security measures employed in mainframes and minis.

Table 3.7 Security requirements for office facilities: communications

Communications	% in Use	Security		
		Low	Medium	High
Facsimile	94	**	**	****
Telex	81	*	*	******
Teletext	25	*	*	******
Viewdata	69	****	*	**
In-House Viewdata	25	**	****	**
DT via PSTN	56		**	******
DT Via Leased line	81		*	******
DT via Public Network	62	*	*	*****
Tele-conferencing	19	****	****	
Video conferencing	12		**	******
Computer Conferencing	19	*****	***	
Electronic Mailbox	44	*	**	*****
In-House Electronic Mail	44	*	***	****
Micro-mainframe link	56	*	**	*****
Telephone Management	56	***	**	***

* = Security requirement rating to a maximum of eight stars

Table 3.8 Security requirements for office facilities: document creation

Document Creation	% in Use	Security		
		Low	Medium	High
OCR	31	***	***	**
MICR	50	**	***	***
Dictation Devices	81	******	*	*
Voice Recognition	0			
Handwriting Recognition	6			********
Document Reader	12	********		
Image Capture	0			
Memory Typewriter	75	*******		
Dedicated WP	87	*****	*	**
WP + added intelligence	50	***	***	**
WP + Voice input	0			
WP on PC	87	**	****	**
Typewriter	94	****		****
Matrix Printer	94	***	**	***
Letter Quality Printer	94	**	**	****
Laser Printer	87	*	**	*****
Plotter/graphics	87	***	**	***
Photo-composition device	19	***	*****	
Voice output	19		********	

* = Security requirement rating to a maximum of
eight stars

Table 3.9 Security requirements for office facilities: information storage and retrieval

Information Storage & Retrieval	% in Use	Security		
		Low	Medium	High
Floppy Diskettes	94	**	**	****
Hard Disks - Micro	87		**	******
Hard Disks - Mini	75			********
Hard Disks - Mainframe	75			********
Non-Erasable Storage	6		**	******
Microfiche	75	*	*	******
Microfilm	31	**		******
Image Storage	0			
Magnetic Tape/Streamer	94			********
VDU enquiries	94	*	*	******
Teletype	38	******		**
Data query language	69	**	*	*****
Multi-user file access	94		**	*****
Document search Facility	12		**	******
External database access	56		**	******

* = Security requirement rating to a maximum of
eight stars

Table 3.10 Security Requirements for Office Facilities: Banking Automation

Banking Automation	% in Use	Security		
		Low	Medium	High
SWIFT	44	********		
CHAPS	31	********		
BACS	31		*	*******
ATM - realtime	31	********		
ATM - online	31	********		
ATM - offline	19	********		
Homebanking	25		**	******
EFTPOS	19	********		
Intelligent Token	0			
Smartcard	0			

* = Security requirement rating to a maximum of
eight stars

3.5 SECURITY RELATED LEGISLATION

The growth of computer installations and computerised data has demonstrated a need for legislation to guarantee the privacy of the individual. Clearly there are legitimate reasons for maintaining large databases containing personal details (e.g. police, government and health service records), but it is important that individual rights should not be compromised.

To reach a suitable balance, it is essential to establish a framework of legislative and governmental control. The following section, therefore, outlines the current state of security and privacy legislation in Europe and North America. Much of this material was written in 1987/88 and has therefore been superceeded by more recent European Commission directives or regulations as well as new national legislation. It is important to remember, however, that security-related legislation can be a *constraint* to the satisfaction of security requirements, as it may restrict the extent to which data can be kept secret (see below).

International Legislation

The Council of Europe Convention

The Council of Europe Convention, signed in 1981, establishes a basis for co-operative data protection in the member states. It covers:

- modes of representation (plain/coded)
- storage medium (paper, disc etc.)
- method of transport (mail, PSSN etc.)
- Interface (computer to terminal, manual to computer etc.)
- Relations between the sender and recipient (within one organisation or different organisations).

OECD Guidelines on Data Protection

In 1980, the Council of the Organisation for Economic Co-operation and Development (OECD) - an international organisation comprising 23 states - published a set of guidelines for the protection of Privacy and Transborder Flows of Personal Data [OECD80]. These were adopted and became operational on 23rd September 1980.

Broadly, they attempted to establish a common purpose and interest in protecting privacy and individual liberties, while at the same time encouraging the free flow of information. Basic principles to be followed in national applications are stated, as well as the limits to be imposed on the collection of personal data.

National Legislation

There is now a vast body of legislation, both within the European Community and worldwide, covering all aspects of data security and privacy. This is likely to increase as new demands and pressures arise. At present, all countries with data protection legislation impose minimum security requirements on organisations in their own countries. These minimum requirements are:

- data integrity
- data confidentiality
- provision of controlled access to specified data.

United Kingdom

The Data Protection Act After being passed in 1984, the Data Protection Act became effective in Britain in November 1987. The Act stipulates that:

data users must register their personal data and outline its purpose

computer bureaux must register as such; they must not disclose data unless authorised by the user

accuracy or integrity must be safeguarded

data should be obtained fairly and should not be kept for any longer than required.

Information exempt from these provisions includes data held to prevent and detect crime and data related to payroll, pensions and accounts.

Sweden

The Data Act, 1973 This Act granted the right of citizens to gain access to government files concerning themselves, as well as files held within the public sector. It includes the right to request amendments to any inaccurate data. The Act also includes protection against access by unauthorised third parties.

West Germany

The Federal Data Protection Law, 1978 This legislation applies to all types of database in the private and public sectors, with the exception of legal information.

Under the terms of the Law, an individual has the right to see information regarding himself and have it corrected if appropriate. All companies with five or more people engaged in data processing must appoint a data protection controller to be responsible for implementing the requirements of the Law. More recently, regulations have been introduced outlining security and privacy requirements:

- entry control
- date of last issue control
- memory control
- access control
- transmit control
- input control
- order control
- transport control
- organisation control

France

The French Data Processing and Freedom Act, 1978 This act established the National Commission on Informatics and Freedom (CNIL). The law covers both manual and computerised data files in the private and public sectors and applies equally to data held for research and security. As with laws in other countries, there are provisions for the correction of inaccurate or misleading information, the onus of proof being placed on the organisation holding the record rather than the individual concerned.

The CNIL is consulted if any new laws which might affect data processing are proposed. It is recognised in France that the role of the CNIL will change as a result both of new technology becoming available, and present levels becoming more widely used.

French Encryption Legislation, 1986 This updates the previous legislation, applying new laws to govern the issue of encryption devices, their registration and transfer between users as well as their import and export.

Denmark

The Public Authorities Registers Act and the Private Registers Act These Acts cover the public and private sectors separately. Manually processed data is protected only in the private sector. Data held for scientific or statistical purposes is not covered. Very sensitive data may not be stored in private databases. It may, however, be stored in public databases provided consent has been given by the person concerned.

A Data Surveillance Authority, consisting of a council of seven and a secretariat of 25, is used to oversee the public and private sectors.

Luxembourg

The Personal Data Act This regulates the personal data of legal and non-legal persons in the public and private sectors. Authorisation by licence must be obtained for the establishment of a private database. Only those established in compliance with a statutory requirement are permitted in the public sector. Individuals must be informed if their personal details are stored.

The Ministry of Justice acts in the capacity of a data protection agency.

Spain

The Organic Law, 1982 Article one of this law states the fundamental right of an individual to have personal and family privacy and reputation protected from any kind of illegitimate interference. Article 7 refers to the unauthorised publication of information relating to the private lives of individuals, and also the publication of personal writing or private documentation. The law states that individuals have a right to compensation and to damages against whoever interferes in their private lives or publishes private papers.

The United States

The Privacy Act, 1974 As the federal government is not permitted to regulate the administration of the individual states except in designated areas, such as defence and foreign relations, the Privacy Act applies only to files held by the federal authority. The Act does not include legal persons. Although there is no data protection board and the onus of enforcement is placed largely upon the individual, the Act does grant very precise and legally enforceable rights. This means that individuals are allowed to sue the particular government agency involved if they feel their rights have been infringed. The CIA and FBI, however, are exempt from such actions.

Canada

The Human Rights Act - Protection of Personal Information, 1977
This act created the office of Privy Commissioner, to supervise the handling of personal data relating to persons in the public sector at the federal level. The Commissioner has investigatory powers and can inspect systems, but his powers of action are limited to making recommendations, publishing findings and compelling government bodies to reply to criticism. Regulatory powers are invested in a government minister who has the authority to exempt certain files from the provisions of the act on the basis of security, international relations, criminal intelligence etc.

3.6 A FRAMEWORK FOR EXPRESSING USER REQUIREMENTS

Based on the case studies, questionnaires and other research - including a thorough literature review - a set of six 'Primary Security Requirements' has been identified. These technology-independent requirements are outlined below. A number of Constraints (discussed later) are placed on their fulfilment. For example, the cost of some security countermeasures might exceed the value of their benefit. Such trade-offs need to be considered by the security designer; hence the need for Risk Management, as addressed in Chapter 2.

A distinction must be made between primary security requirements and the means of satisfying them. For example, access control is commonly regarded as a basic security requirement for any computing system. In fact, it is a means of satisfying the requirements for data integrity and data confidentiality. Means of satisfying primary security requirements are discussed in subsequent chapters.

This framework of primary security requirements, means of satisfying primary security requirements, and constraints, is represented in Figure 3.2. Constraints are divided into 'Functional Constraints' and 'Resource Constraints'.

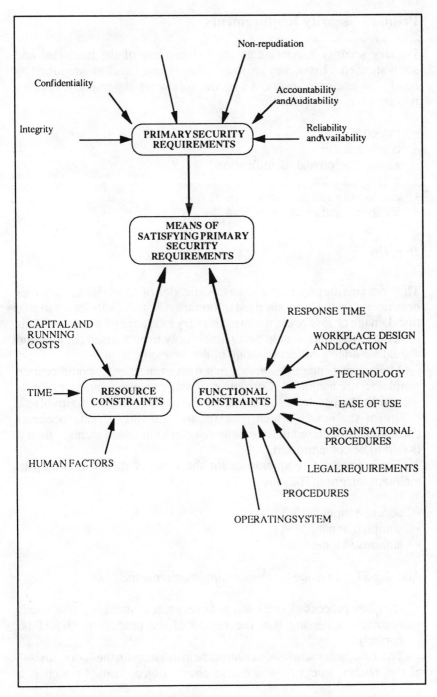

Figure 3.2 Framework of primary security requirements, means and constraints

Primary Security Requirements

Primary security requirements are independent of the hardware and software used. That is, they are standard operating conditions required by nearly all computer users. Thus, the following six primary security requirements were identified:

- integrity
- confidentiality
- authentication and identification
- non-repudiation
- auditability and accountability
- reliability and availability

Integrity

This concerns the prevention of the modification of information, resources or systems. Today, computerised information is such a valuable resource that damage or loss could threaten the very existence of a business. It is imperative that data should be available only to authorised persons and should accurately reflect the state of the company.

Maintaining integrity implies that data or messages should remain simple, secure and intact. Corruption of data can take a variety of forms - it can be deliberate or accidental. In the latter case it might involve a failure of the device which accesses the software. If data becomes corrupted, or is altered in an unauthorised or unintended manner, then it is said to be contaminated.

There are three requirements for the input of data which help to maintain integrity. They are:

- accurate input
- complete input
- authorised input.

Additionally, there are two processing requirements:

- complete processing (i.e. each and every record should be processed)
- accurate processing (i.e. the results of the processing should be correct).

These, together with other controls help to ascertain the "correctness" of the system. Integrity would also cover "object re-use" which is a requirement to ensure that resources such as memory and disk storage can be reused whilst preserving security.

Confidentiality

The requirement for confidentiality arises from the need to protect information, system assets and/or processes from disclosure to unauthorised parties. This is distinct from integrity as it is a requirement to guard against the passive threat of compromising secrecy, rather than the active threat of improper alteration.

The requirement for confidentiality varies widely for different types of entities. An example of highly confidential data would be that of information relating to a possible corporate takeover or merger. The disclosure of this information might be more serious than the interception and disclosure of electronic funds transfer transactions. In the latter case, the confidentiality of that data would not always be as important as its integrity, whereas in the former, confidentiality is of critical importance.

Authentication and Identification

This covers the identification of system entities and resources (eg users, processes, applications etc.) are as they claim they are or as they are perceived. In a secure system, the user must be required to prove his/her identity before commencing operation. In a communication system the sender and receiver of a message must provide mutual proof of identity. This process is termed authentication. In the former case it can be achieved, for example, by a password or, at a more secure level, by a smartcard. In the case of data communication, it is usually achieved using digital signatures known only to the two parties.

Non-Repudiation

Non-repudiation follows logically from sender/receiver authentication and involves preventing the denial that a message has been received, or denial that a message was sent. It is therefore important to be able to prove to a third party that the message was received, or was sent. This can be expanded to include the non-repudiable confirmation of the submission, delivery and receipt of such items as data. messages, commands, authority and so on.

Auditability and Accountability

Accountability is essentially a system of allocating responsibility. For example, accountability can ensure that an entity is held responsible for its actions so that violations or attempted violations of system security may be traced uniquely to it. For example in an EDI (electronic data interchange) system, maintenance of a secure audit log of messages sent and received enables the traceability of messages and message transfer auditing in the case of a compromise, a crash or as evidence in a dispute. Auditability is a basic precondition for auditing, permitting the objectives of an audit to be carried out speedily and effectively. These objectives are to determine whether a system:

- safeguards assets
- maintains data and system integrity
- achieves organisational goals effectively
- consumes resources efficiently

The system designer should be able to convince an auditor that the reviewed system is sound and under control. Furthermore, auditability requires that the auditor is able to re-perform satisfactorily, observe, check and test the system under review.

In order for reperformance to be possible, a system must have certain incorporated functions and specific features. Formal criteria for auditability comprise requirements for:

- re-performance of single transactions from their source document to the final records

- re-performance of the application programs such that a competent third party is able to evaluate the effectiveness of the control system in adequate time

- proof that documented application procedures have been used for each transaction.

For internal auditing, observation refers to the detailed and ongoing analysis of the following:

- business principles
- achievement of determined targets
- suitability and achievement of plans

- rules, guidelines and instructions
- regularity of guidelines
- profitability
- actuality
- quality of the organisational structure
- suitability of processes
- quality and functionality of information systems
- effectiveness of programs and their documentation.

Checking and testing are subfunctions of observation. Both are specific control techniques for auditing and are suitable to support the ongoing and detailed observation of the system.

Reliability of Service

There are two concepts.Firstly, availability is the prevention of the unauthorised witholding or denial of information or resource whether it be denial of access, denial of communications, deliberate suppression of information or messages or fabrication of new data, messages or traffic (ie to overload the system). Secondly, The service provided by an organisation must be both reliable and satisfactory. Usually there is no great problem with short service breaks. However, if a system were to go down for a number of days and no contingency plans had been made, then the consequences could be very serious. Secondly, when running, it is expected that a system will be reliable in its handling of data and programs.

It is imperative that business enterprises relying on computer technology provide for recovery plans and backup procedures in the event of system damage or failure. A disaster recovery plan is defined as a plan for transferring all data processing from one system to another following damage from fire, flood, electrical breakdown etc. Backup procedures include preparations for a course of action to be taken following the occurrence of machine failure - for example, sufficient capacity of key hardware and standby power.

Constraints

The following were identified as constraints imposed on the primary security requirements discussed above. They are divided into resource and functional constraints. The former apply to constraints arising from limited available resources - such as time, manpower and money. The latter relate to limitations arising from technology, the working environment and other factors.

Resource Constraints

Whatever the users' actual requirements, there is always a discrepancy between the ideal system and that which is most practical. Thus constraints, and in particular resource constraints, impose limitations on the means of satisfying primary requirements.

Capital and running costs together constitute a major constraint. Naturally, it is only worth spending money on establishing and using security measures if the expected benefits exceed the cost. Organisations must first determine, in financial terms, the risks involved from a particular type of breach in security. This is where a preliminary risk analysis can be used to advantage.

Estimating costs and benefits is not always an easy procedure. Equipment and consultancy costs, computer downtime during installation and person hours during and following installation are just some of the variables to be considered. The difficulty in making accurate assessments often discourages companies from purchasing and implementing security measures.

In addition to capital and running costs, a further consideration is the time taken to install security measures. Too often the priority is placed on installing or modifying software with little regard being given to security. In the rush to automate, the provision of adequate security measures is frequently seen as an inconvenience. Thus the constraint of installation time may cause an organisation to alter its choice between different available security measures. It may even prevent the introduction of security in certain key areas.

As a further resource constraint, we should also consider the human factor. Security management requires expertise and understanding. Skilled people are needed to design, implement, use and maintain a system. Human skills, often a scarce and expensive resource, are thus an important constraint on system security.

Other aspects of the human dimension involve productivity levels, quality of work and job satisfaction. The first, productivity, is of fundamental importance to the profitability of the work being done. Obviously time spent by the user in following security procedures and by staff in maintaining the security system can be damaging in terms of lost productivity. Quality of work and job satisfaction are similarly constrained. For example, a user who becomes preoccupied with employing system security measures may make mistakes or may work less efficiently than if his mind were focused purely on other work. Secondly, if the user is constantly frustrated by the security procedures required of him, then job satisfaction may suffer.

Functional Constraints

Functional constraints regardless of the monetary or other resouces available for security must be taken into account. Included in these are ease of use; response time; workplace design and location; legal requirements; technological advances; procedural requirements, and secure operating systems.

When planning and implementing any security measures in response to user demands, it is important to consider *ease of use*. For example, which would be more satisfactory for the user, logical or physical access control? The ease of use, flexibility and functionality of a security system are therefore important aspects of the overall security strategy.

Response time is a concern which is often treated as a primary constraint by many organisations. In some instances, for example, banking, it actually takes precedence over most security requirements. Since the response time is what the user experiences and values when interacting with the system, any procedure which occasions delay is viewed as an inconvenience. Thus the opinion held by many organisations is that the application of security measures may be unacceptable if they entail sacrifices in speed. Encryption is a possible example of this.

As far as *workplace design and location* are concerned, room layout and situation may prove a constraint on security factors such as fire protection and prevention. This constraint is generally only realised when relocation, renovation, or expansion of the workplace is under consideration. Other aspects of this problem may include the adequate provision of a power supply, air conditioning, and clear communication lines. The physical location of the computer system itself and its susceptibility to natural hazards should also be considered.

Legal requirements may impose constraints in a number of ways. While some legislation helps promote security policies, it can also restrict what measures can be taken or the way in which they can be introduced. For example, it is not uncommon for governments to impose legal requirements on the use and disclosure of encryption algorithms and keys, thus compromising the users' requirement for data confidentiality and traffic flow security.

When considering functional constraints, we should not forget the difficulties posed by on-going *technological* advance. Since developments are occurring rapidly, there is a problem in adjusting security requirements to meet new challenges. An example of this technological constraint occurs with user identification methods. As new techniques are developed to try to identify individuals, so accompanying ways are discovered to replicate the previously unique identifying characteristic, thus making the identification process unsuitable as a totally secure physical access control or authentication device.

Procedural constraints vary according to organisational, departmental or individual levels. They may also be imposed externally by legislative bodies. Since these procedures are usually designed to impose restrictions on certain actions, they may constrain what security requirements can be met, or, more likely, the way in which they can be met.

Finally, we should remember that security is, to greater or lesser extent, dependent on a *secure operating system*. If the security of the operating system is unsatisfactory, then there will be a constraint on the ease and success with which other security measures can be implemented.

3.7 CONCLUSION

The convergence of office systems, telecommunications and data processing presents both unrivalled opportunities and unprecedented threats. So far, few organisations have given sufficient consideration to the negative implications of the new information age. For this reason, we need to revise the way in which security requirements are assessed. Current approaches are technology-dependent and lead to an incomplete understanding of user requirements and appropriate safeguards.

Research has demonstrated that present security levels are often inadequate when confronted with the threats posed by converging technologies. Perhaps even more serious is the complacent attitude shown by many senior managers who believe that their security arrangements are satisfactory. With the pace of technological change, and the realisation of new demands and threats, this is clearly not so.

If we are to maximise the benefits of the information revolution, it is essential that an enlightened attitude is taken toward user requirements and the implementation of security measures. This necessitates co-operative research and a common understanding of the need to develop secure systems.

4

Access Control

4.1 INTRODUCTION

Access control refers either to the procedures and mechanisms used to restrict entry to the computer, or to software or data within the computer, and to those persons authorised to use such resources. It is most often considered in relation to initial access to a system, where passwords are commonly used to restrict access. However, this log-on process usually determines not only whether or not the potential user is to be allowed access to the computer, based on his/her User ID, but also which resources can be used subsequently during the session.

Two types of access control can be defined - 'logical access control' and 'physical access control'. Logical access control refers to the mediation of access using computer-based processes and procedures. The candidate user interacts with the computer in order that the system can establish and authenticate his/her identity. On this basis, access to the system is granted or denied. If granted, the activities of the user within the system may be further limited by logical access control measures. Physical access control usually precedes logical access control. It is the restriction of physical entry to the environment in which the computer is accomodated.

Sections 4.2 and 4.3 below examine logical access control and physical access control respectively. In Section 4.4, we list some of the desirable features of access control systems as defined by the MARS consortium.

4.2 LOGICAL ACCESS CONTROL

Procedures used in logical access control usually begin with the system prompting the user to declare his/her identity. This claimed identity has then to be authenticated. This can be done simply by entering a password, or where greater security is required, using, for example, either smartcards or biometric techniques. These methods are discussed in detail in the following chapter on user identification.

Logical access control is particularly important in distributed systems, especially those attached to public networks, where physical access control is often not practical or possible. In these circumstances, terminal identification and authentication becomes important. This subject is introduced briefly in Chapter 6, and in Chapter 7, protocols for user authentication in communications are examined in detail.

Access control involves much more than user identification and authentication. Although these are the most important prerequisites for access control, the main issues centre on what the user is permitted to do, given that he/she has been identified and authenticated. In multi-user systems, different users often need to be logically 'separated' so that they can only access particular programs or certain information. This is particularly the case where data of varying levels of sensitivity is held on disk and where users of the system have different levels of authorisation and clearance.

Logical access within the system should be governed according to a predetermined security policy. Where high security is required, users should be allowed access only to programs and data which they need to use. It is only by explicitly defining such a policy, that the security of the system can be designed and implemented efficiently and effectively. It should be noted at this point that an important concept is that of the trusted user or security supervisor. This person (or persons) is responsible for implementing and maintaining security and is therefore in a privileged position where trustworthiness is essential.

Logical access control thus entails allowing authorised users to access only those resources for which they have been granted clearance according to the security policy in operation. Ideally, methods for achieving this separation are built into the operating system. Secure operating systems are designed with this requirement in mind. This draws on the concept of the security *kernel*, where the security features of the system are embedded in the operating system. Alternatively, security can be introduced as an add-on to the basic operating system in use. This is the security *shell* approach.

With the shell approach, the security software acts as an interface between the user and the operating system. Sometimes 'emulation' is used so that, when interacting with the security module, the user appears to be accessing the operating system directly. The shell approach is less secure than the kernel approach because, if the user can break through the shell, the operating system is left unprotected.

A secure logical separation of users is a more complex task than might at first appear. This is because channels often exist allowing sensitive data to become accessible to lower clearance users. A classic example is where two users, A and B, are both allowed to access file X which has a low sensitivity level. User A has a low clearance level but User B has privileges which allow him to access highly sensitive data in file Y. If User B is allowed to read file Y and write to file X, then it is possible for sensitive data in file Y to 'migrate downwards' to file X, thus allowing it to be accessed by User A. Security policy and access privileges need to be planned very carefully if this type of breach is to be prevented. (Policies for the logical separation of users and their implementation are discussed in detail in Chapter 9 on Security Modelling.)

Finally, it should be stated that not only does access to a resource need to be controlled *per se*, but often the type of access needs to be restricted. For example, certain users may be given read-only access to a file, not permitting them to change its contents. A common method of achieving this is through the attachment of file attributes, giving the file characteritics such as 'read', 'write', 'execute', 'delete' etc. Different attributes can apply to different users or groups of users.

In more secure systems, it is often the case that the user is separated completely from the operating system and can access files only through applications. Similarly, users can be prevented from editing source code or accessing executable code in any way other than through running the application. Again the concept of the trusted user is important, for file maintenance tasks, software installation and upgrading etc.

4.3 PHYSICAL ACCESS CONTROL

Physical access control is used less commonly than logical access control. Although less emphasis is usually placed on this, it has been found during the course of the MARS project, that physical access control can be an extremely important tool. However, physical access control can be applied only to initial access and is therefore far less flexible. It can only be used to control entry into the physical environment in which the computer or terminal is kept.

Physical access control where used, precedes logical access control. If unauthorised persons can be prevented from entering the environment in which the workstation is housed, and only if the computer cannot be accessed from outside that environment, then the problem of computer security is immediately limited to the logical separation of legitimate users and to the protection of the system from unauthorised activity by any of those users.

Physical access control measures are far less useful in the case of multi-terminal and distributed systems. In the former, the more terminals which exist in separate locations (e.g. offices), the greater becomes the problem of restricting physical access and the greater is the potential for a security breach. In the case of distributed systems, physical access control is largely irrelevant. Where public networks are used, access control becomes purely a logical problem.

The remaining chapters in Part 1 often refer to issues where logical access control is involved. The importance of physical access control is stressed in Part 3 which describes the Guidelines for Workstation Security, developed by CIRU as part of the MARS project. However, some of the important methods of physical access control are introduced below.

Methods of Physical Access Control

The methods described here are used to restrict access to the room containing the workstation. If necessary, two or more of these methods can be used in combination. The workstation may or may not be in the same room as the CPU. If not, further physical security is needed for communications media and for the room containing the CPU. Methods for protecting cabling include concealment, segregation from other cables, electromagnetic radiation (EMR), proofing, tamper-protection, and the use of fibre-optics.

It is desirable to keep the workstation in a dedicated room if high security is required. Otherwise the usefulness of physical access controls is reduced and inconvenience will be placed on other users of the room. The simplest means of physical access control is for the room to be lockable with a physical key which is held only by authorised users. A slightly more sophisticated approach is to use a digital key pad on which the user types in a PIN or password number.

For a higher level of security, a magnetic stripe card can be used at the point of access. This is more secure than a physical key because it is harder to duplicate. For greater security still, a smartcard could be used. Cards are usually used in combination with a PIN. A full discussion of cards, which, of course, are also used to control access to the computer itself, is given in Chapter 5, User Identification and Authentication. For very high levels of security, biometric methods, also discussed in Chapter 5, can be used. Alternatively (or additionally) a human guard could be employed.

A further form of protection is needed against the threat of electromagnetic radiation (EMR) leakage. EMR emitted from a monitor can be received and interpreted remotely, using equipment which is quite readily available. To prevent this, EMR protection is needed. Alternatively, additional EMR can be transmitted to interfere with that emitted from the workstation. Finally, in order to prevent theft, the computing equipment itself can be secured to the desk or floor on which it is standing.

4.4 DESIRABLE FEATURES OF ACCESS CONTROL SYSTEMS

The following were identified by the MARS consortium as desirable features of any access control system (ACS):

Access Control Feature	Objectives
Complete protection of system	No tampering and resources
Protection by default	Flexibility
User-oriented architecture	Easy control
Adaptable system	No conversion if new resources
Efficient administration	Immediate intervention of security
Simple user procedures	Ease of use
Minimum effect on system performance	No downgrading of system performance
Possibility of centralised or decentralised implementation	Adaptability to security requirements
Possibility of auditing:	Monitoring and control • of users • of objects
Possibility of different audit logs:	Monitoring and control of: • Failed attempts • Successful attempts and objects requested • Modification of ACS databases • Use of non-authorised resources • Command and modify profiles
Possibility of ACS software backup with tamper-proof appendix files	Security of ACS
Possibility of database and user files backup	Security of data

4.5 CONCLUSION

There is a need to control access to the workstation and to the room in which the workstation is contained. The usefulness of physical access restrictions is often understated. For standalone workstations, or for systems whose components are contained within close locality to each other, physical access controls can reduce many of the problems which are usually addressed by logical access controls. This is achieved by eliminating all potential logical access attempts by users with no authorisation to use the system.

Although almost always necessary, the importance of logical access control is much greater in multi-user systems, where the logical separation of users and resources is required, and in systems which can be accessed remotely.

5

User Identification and Authentication

5.1 INTRODUCTION

The terms "user identification" and 'user authentication' are often, as in this chapter, used interchangeably. User identification refers to the action of the user claiming his/her identity when communicating with a device. Authentication is the process of proving that the claimed identity is genuine. In addition User identification is often used to cover both of these terms.

In this chapter, the general principles and methods of identification and authentication are examined. As an introduction, the three main generic methods of identification/authentication are briefly discussed, followed by an examination of the basic steps in accessing a system and the components of an identification/authentication system. Following this, in Sections 5.2 to 5.4, methods of identification/authentication are discussed in detail under the three main headings. Finally, in Section 5.5, we look at methods for providing permanent authentication.

Methods of Identification

The National Bureau of Standards (USA) outlines three generic methods of identification. The *first* method is based on the users' knowledge of a specific piece of information. The information itself need not be secret. It is only the fact that it is used for an authentication process which must be kept secret. This information can be a password, personal information, a numerical identifier (PIN or PIC), etc.

This method has several advantages:

* it is portable
* it does not require any possession of a physical object
* the checking process is simple.

61

It also has several disadvantages:

- the information is easily copied once discovered
- it can be discovered or disclosed without the user being aware of it
- the complexity of the information is limited by the human capacity to memorise.

The *second* method of identification is based on the user possessing a unique object.This object is usually called a token. Examples of tokens are cards, boxes, keys, etc.

This method has several benefits:

- the object can be very difficult or impossible to duplicate
- the object itself can include processing capabilities to increase the security level of the checks
  the theft of the object is easily discovered.

However:

- special devices are needed at the user location to read the token or the key
- the user cannot access the system without a token
- the complexity of the token must be sufficient to avoid duplication with the help of microcomputers and other commercially available equipment.

The *third* method of identification is based on analysing a specific characteristic of the user. This category is sometimes divided into two subclasses:

- the physical characteristic of a part of the human body: retinal and voice patterns, hand shape, finger print, etc.
- the dynamic characteristic of a human action: handwritten signature etc (e.g. pressure speed etc.)

This method is theoretically the most secure, but, in practice, it has a number of flaws:

- measurements are often difficult to obtain and are performed on mobile and evolving objects
- trade-offs have to be accepted between the security level of the

process and its complexity and speed

• several of these methods raise user objections.

Basic steps in accessing a system

The Login Procedure

This procedure is usually initiated by the actions of the candidate user: keystroke, "break", switch-on of the terminal, insertion of a card in a card reader etc. This action is transmitted to the host or, in the case of a local apparatus, to the processing unit .

Following this, the system activates the authentication process and obtains the identification information provided by the user. It verifies whether the candidate user has authorisation and checks his/her access rights to the system itself.

Depending upon the results of the checks, access to a specific set of resources is granted or denied.

Logged User Access Control to System Resources

In most systems, the results of the checks are valid during the whole session: the identification and authentication process is used only once. All access of the logged user to particular system resources will be controlled during the session.

More secure systems authenticate the user at regular or random intervals. However, it is not always an acceptable practice. In the case of ATMs, for example, it would be impractical for the PIN to be entered more than once during the session.

Components of an Identification System

The main components of an identification system are as follows:

1 The element on which the identification process relies (token, information, physical characteristic, etc.).

2 The reader: this is a peripheral transforming the above information into a coded message suitable for processing.

3 Programming tools: sometimes secret information has to be recorded on an object (card, key, etc.) before the object can be used. This is commonly termed "programming" or "personalising".

4 Checking units: these compare the information received from the readers with the original data.

5 Management unit: this performs all management functions such as generation, distribution, audit, etc.

These aspects can be combined in different ways to form access control or identification systems. There are three main categories of such systems:

• independent equipment combining a reader, a non-volatile memory and updating software
• on-line equipment combining a number of readers connected to a main unit, including checking and management facilities
• distributed systems combining a number of remote devices. Each will possess a checking unit and is connected through a network to a central processing unit for managing.

Figure 5.1 demonstrates the use of these components in a simple authentication scheme based on user passwords (the user information). Here, the programming tool is represented by the system manager who furnishes a password to the user and records it in the authorised user list of the checking unit. The user element of identification is the password and the reader is the terminal keyboard.

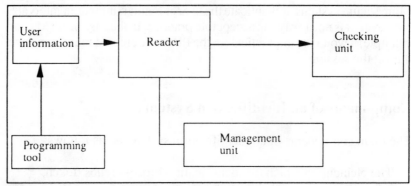

Figure 5.1 Components of an identification scheme

5.2 KNOWLEDGE-BASED IDENTIFICATION

With knowledge-based identification systems, each user is associated with a particular piece of information which is known only by him/her and the checking unit. This information can , for example, be a number or letter combination, a password, a PIN or any other information unknown by others.

The simplest way of using this method is for the individual to enter relevant personal information on the reader (keyboard, card reader, etc.). The checking unit compares this information with the original it has in store and, if the comparison is successful, gives access to the controlled system.

The most commonly used personal information is the password and this is often the only barrier raised against illegitimate use of a computer. Several recent events in various countries where timesharing networks have been abused prove how inefficient this is as a means of protection.

Whatever kind of information is involved (passwords, PINs, etc.), operational constraints and protection weaknesses are the same:

- the information must be kept secret by all parties concerned
- the information must be complex enough to discourage a systematic trial of all possibilities
- the information should be protected by appropriate means when exchanged between theterminal and a distant checking unit.

In this section, we concentrate on the characteristics and use of passwords. Following this, there is a brief discussion on the 'questionnaire' method of user identification.

The password method

The best-known example of identity verification using restricted or privileged information is the password. Since the introduction of time-sharing computers, many people have become used to the *login* or *logon* procedure with its characteristic questions, "Enter user ID:" and "Enter password:"

Characteristics of Passwords

Passwords usually comprise a short string of alphanumeric characters compatible with the character set of the computer in question. A combination of the following rules is possible:

- only alphabetic characters
- alphabetic and numeric characters
- special characters, authorised or otherwise
- distinctions made (or not) between upper and lower case characters
- variable or fixed length
- a minimum length, imposed by the security manager or system dependent.

These rules are important because they define the security features required to defend the system against a systematic search for the right password, or against a lucky guess. Great care should be taken in selecting a password. Either the security manager or the checking program itself should refuse proposed combinations which are too simple.

Lifetime of Passwords

Although passwords are secret, there is obviously a chance that they may become known to unauthorised parties. For this reason, a maximum time period should be imposed during which they are valid. In addition, other factors need to be considered, for example, the time needed to locate the password by hardware or software attack. Ideally, passwords should be changed or destroyed:

- at least once a month
- when the corresponding user has no more work to run on the computer
- when the service is terminated and, in particular, when the employee leaves the company.

When trying to access the system, a maximum number of attempts (say three) should be allowed to the user before he/she is refused access.

The Generation of Passwords

Passwords can be generated by either the user or the computer:

User-chosen passwords For a long time this was the only method used. Often there is no control by the computer over the "quality" of the password and it is the users' responsibility not to choose obvious passwords such as the name of their spouse.

An improvement is made when the computer checks some features of a proposed password, e.g. length, number of different characters, duplication with a previously used password etc.

Computer-generated passwords This is an effective means of providing simple and "strong" passwords, but it can present a major drawback if the passwords are randomly produced and therefore very difficult to memorise.

Distribution of passwords

All techniques involved in key distribution (see Chapter 7) are also operable for passwords. Here, we will describe some methods more specific to PINs or passwords, and highlight their drawbacks.

In the banking field, PINs are often associated with cards to be used in ATMs or EFTPOS. But a PIN without a corresponding card is useless. An appropriate method for disseminating passwords is letter distribution.

PINs are generated and printed on carbonless paper inside an already closed envelope so they cannot be read without opening the envelope. The card will not be distributed before the user has received the envelope undamaged. If this doesn't happen, the whole process is repeated with a new PIN. This method offers a modest level of security.

A second, and widely used method in computer time-sharing, is the distribution of passwords through a network. With this system, a provisional password is given to each new user, who has the responsibility of changing it to another one using a utility program.

This method provides little security against a deliberate attack and will only be effective against involuntary access attempts.

Storage of passwords

Memorising of passwords by the user For the user, the location of password 'storage' should be the human memory. However, a well known and surprisingly widely used PIN hiding-place is the address book.

A useful method of remembering passwords is to use various mnemonic devices. For example, establish a relation between digits and political, historical or personal events.

Storage of Passwords in the computer Since computers must not lose passwords when switched off, they have often used magnetic mass memory, tapes, or disks as a means of storage.

When time sharing networks were introduced, nobody imagined that a user could know the operating system well enough to gain unauthorised access to information. Consequently, passwords were stored unprotected in a table. This table merely contained the user ID and the corresponding password which used a simple identification mechanism, i.e. when a candidate user wanted to access the computer, he entered his ID and his password. The computer then referred to the password table to see if the password given was the correct one.

Historically, the first approach towards greater security was to use encryption algorithms to protect the passwords by enciphering them before file storage. However, the key must also be kept in the computer files, and the encryption algorithms used at the time were easy to invert.

Secure encryption algorithms have an important property: the knowledge of couples of cleartext and corresponding ciphertext is of no use in finding the key. Thus passwords are now used as keys to encipher a constant. The result of the encryption is stored in the password file.

Operating guidelines for password schemes

The knowledge gained from recent and widespread attacks has led to the production of guidelines for designing a good security identification system based on passwords. These guidelines include the following rules:

1   The whole control procedure must always be carried out until the final answer is entered , regardless of the validity of the first entries.

2   Once an authorised user is logged on, the system must inform him/her of the date and time of the previous successful or unsuccessful attempt to connect.

3   Password encryption is preferably done by a secure and hence slow encryption algorithm.

4   If possible, the system must invalidate the connecting line after a few unsuccessful attempts in a given time.

5   All attempts, successful or not, must be recorded for audit.

6   If the encryption process depends on the computer hardware, duplication of files will be useless.

The Questionnaire Method

The questionnaire method can best be explained using the following analogy. In a film, the hero (who is claiming a false identity) is asked a question which, were he not an impostor, he would know the answer to. For example, "is Smith still living in London?" , or something similar. Being an impostor, he can only guess at the truth and is therefore likely to be caught out. This questionnaire process can be adapted for computers.

An appropriate set of questions is prepared, preferably irrelevant to the users' everyday life so as to avoid a search by the potential intruders. Questions such as date of birth, marriage, birth place of parents, etc. should be rejected. This technique should not be used in systems requiring a high level of security.

5.3 BIOMETRIC IDENTIFICATION METHODS

Biometric methods of identification are based on measuring the physiological characteristics unique to each and every individual. The following are examples of these characteristics:

- voice
- finger prints
- body contours
- handwriting style (as an extension of the physiological and psychological make-up of the individual).

Biometric methods generally involve performing some human action. This could be, for example:

- drawing a few signatures so that the system can analyse and record their characteristics
- looking into a scanning apparatus in order to record retinal patterns
- intonating words for the analysis and recording of voice patterns.

These methods have, with some success, been adapted to computerised identification. However, the complexity of measuring physical attributes, their variation with time, and the cost of identification apparatus explain why so few devices have thus far been used. Additionally, they are often treated with some suspicion.

All biometric techniques are based on similar concepts and employ common features and functions, the most important being the procedures for enrolment and access. Usually, the identification system is used in conjunction with other information, such as a PIN. In this inspection, a reference pattern which is known to be secure is compared with freshly recorded identifying data.

The common techniques of recognition are picture analysis, shape recognition, signal processing, algorithms, 2-D and 3-D geometry as well as microelectronics. For example, identification using retinal or shape recognition is performed in the following way. An electronic picture is taken with a camera (usually CCD) in infra-red or visible wavelengths. This picture is then digitised and processed so that the least possible amount of information has to be stored and compared. The result of these calculations is then compared with the original one. This may involve either a bit-by-bit comparison or very sophisticated algorithms.

Dynamic handwritten signatures and voice recognition are similar but require different readers: mechanical transducers for the former and microphones for the latter. Voice recognition algorithms are based on linear prediction parameters of speech or on proprietary technologies.

One of the main weaknesses with the biometric method is that physiological characteristics do not always remain constant. In some cases, major differences from the expected value can be encountered in very short periods of time, e.g. voices can change with a cold, fingerprints by humidity.

One convenient method for evaluating the relative efficiency of identification devices is by comparing the following values:

- the False Accept Rate (FAR) which is the proportion of unauthorised people accepted compared with the total number of person checked (also termed type II errors)

- the False Reject Rate (FRR) which is the proportion of authorised people rejected compared with the total number of persons checked (also termed type I errors)

- the checking delay which is the time required by the apparatus in a typical application to do all the computations and make a decision. The larger the enrolees file, the more time will be needed.

Examples of existing systems using the different biometric techniques available are now considered.

The retinal scan

This technique uses the blood vessels at the fundus of the eye as a distinguishing feature of the individual. These vessels can be observed relatively easily if the fundus of the eye is illuminated. In a two-step process, an ultra-low intensity light source first scans a part of the retina. Following this, the sample is digitised and transformed with a sophisticated mathematical algorithm.

An example is Eyedentification System 7.5 and Eyenet System 8600, both marketed by Eyedentify Inc.:

> FAR < 0.0001 per cent
> FRR < 5 per cent
> Checking time < 2 seconds

The FRR high value is a major drawback because many people will take exception to being falsely denied access.

Another system is produced by Altema International.

The fingerprint

There are two approaches to fingerprint identification. The first involves pattern recognition and image processing techniques. Here, the system obtains an image of the fingerprint by the combination of electronic sensors and an optical light source. This image is then compared to the originals which are stored on suitable media. In the second approach, a mechanism extracts various information on, for example, ridge endings, waves and splits. This information follows a unique pattern for each individual.

An example is Ridge Reader Physical by Fingermatrix, Inc.

> FAR: .001 per cent
> FRR < .5 per cent
> Checking time: 4 seconds

There are three models available, P100 network unit with PC host, P200 standalone, P300 smart card system. Other models are produced by Comparator Systems Corporation and Identix.

Handwritten signatures

Handwritten signature methods can be either static or dynamic. With the former, visual processing techniques are used to identify signatures. However, since duplication is relatively easy for a competent forger, this method is very unreliable. A far greater measure of reliability can be achieved using the second technique which measures the writing process rather than the signature itself. An example is Dynamic Signature Verification System by Thomas de la Rue Inc.:

FAR: 3 per cent
FRR: 0.7 per cent
Checking time: 5 seconds

The user enters up to nine signatures to find six sufficiently similar to the archived ones. The storage capacity is limited to eight hundred signatures. Other models are produced by Inforite Corporation, IBM and the Stanford Research Institute.

Voice recognition

The voice recognition method uses the distinguishing features of the individual human voice: pitch, accent and intonation. Early computerised methods, based on frequency analysis, were not entirely satisfactory. However, the most recent method, which is based on recognising the vocal features associated with the permanent structures of the throat, is more reliable. Advances in voice synthesis will increase the accuracy of this method.

An example is Voice Key by ECCO Industries Inc.:

FAR: 0.1 to 2 per cent
FRR: 0.25 to 5 per cent
Checking time: 3 seconds

The effects of daily variations and illness are taken into account to automatically update the user reference profiles. Other models are produced by Vaxtron Systems Inc., Interstate Voice Products and Vecsys.

Hand shape

Since each individual's hand is unique, techniques which can recognise differences in shape and size offer a useful means of user identification. One method is based on image processing and geometrical recording. Another focuses on the translucent quality of fingertips. Using the latter, the system utilises an intense light source and measures the light transmission through the fingertips.

An example is ID 2000 T1 by Stellar Systems Inc.:

> FAR: < 1 per cent
> FAR: 1 to 3 per cent
> Checking time: < 6 seconds

Another model is produced by Mitsubushi Electric Sales America Inc.

5.4 POSSESSION METHODS (HARDWARE-BASED)

Possession methods are access procedures that involve physical objects such as a mechanical keyboard key, magnetic or punched card or a PIN pad. Security procedures are located in two places: the host and the device hardware. These consist of:

- cards: smart cards, key-holders and cards with encryption methods
- keyboard keys and plug-in modules
- handheld password generators.

This concentration of information in a single object has one major flaw; from the device hardware an intruder may obtain information about the authenticating protocols (password, PIN, etc.) and at the same time about the access rights of the user.

As with most methods, the authentication process is often preceded by an identification one: the candidate user claims his identity by means of a name or code. The objects concerned are:

- cards with PIN
- objects with a keypad including handheld password generators.

We will first examine the different types of card available, under the following headings:

- simple cards
- embedded cards
- magnetic cards
- memory chip cards
- simple electronic cards
- smart cards
- laser cards

Following this, we will discuss the use of other hand-held objects. (Note: there are other types of cards such as a paper-based cards with encoded printed information contained within them. But we will only discuss those in the above list).

Simple cards

Included here are printed symbol cards, hollerith cards and embossed cards.

With printed *symbol cards*, information is represented in a sequence of parallel lines of different widths. Several codes have been standardised (e.g. Universal Product Code) and are commonly used in various commercial activities for product identification. The *hollerith card* stores information using small square holes. This is no longer used for computer programming since more advanced magnetic media are now available.

As it's name suggests, the *embossed card* possesses raised data on the card surface. These cards, technically very simple, have a number of flaws:

- the encoded information is visible and can therefore be read and consequently duplicated
- the cards can only store a limited amount of information
- they are read-only.

Embedded cards

Embedded cards may be electrical matrix or magnetic-based. With the *matrix based cards*, the card contains an electrical printed circuit on which diodes are connected to generate a unique code. The printed circuit is buried in the plastic and so is not visible. The authentication process implies that an electrical connection is established between the card and the decoding circuitry in the reader.

Magnetic cards come in three different types:

- magnetic slug cards
- capacitor cards
- wiegand cards.

Today, only cards based on Wiegand technology are of any real value in the industrial sector. The Wiegand effect is produced using processed wires that react uniquely to magnetic field changes. Each bit of data is encoded in a wire that has a magnetic snap action under tension. The small wires are embedded into positions in the plastic card where they will react to a change in the intensity and polarity of the magnetic field.

Magnetic cards

Magnetic cards can be either sandwich or magnetic strip. *Sandwich cards* are a relatively inexpensive form of technology comprising bundles of barium-ferrite material inserted between two plastic layers to form individual codes. Small spots on the magnetic sheet may or may not be magnetised, thus forming a code that is read by a row of magnetic sensing heads.

In *magnetic strip cards* the code is recorded magnetically on a strip by equipment using magnetic tape recording technology. The encoded strip is then placed on the back of the plastic card. One or several tracks contain a limited amount of information. The information in embossed lettering on the card is duplicated on the tracks, together with other information (for example, last transaction). Since this information is easily duplicated, cards are often used in combination with an additional PIN.

Several organisations (for example, VISA) have introduced a further barrier against unauthorised duplication by incorporating holograms on the card surface.

Memory Chip Cards

Memory chip cards are designed to serve as memory vaults. They contain a non-volatile memory of a few hundred bits and two write-protected areas where a serial number and an application-dependent code are recorded. The information is stored in the memory which does not permit access. Thus, modification, deletion, or data reading is not possible. Processing functions are limited to a mutual identification procedure between the card and the terminal.

Simple electronic cards

Simple electronic cards include a memory of a few thousand bits and a custom processing unit. They will typically feature:

- protection of the users' identification code
- protection of confidential information recorded at the time of manufacture
- protection and storage of external information.

The validation and authentication functions are not performed by these cards.

Smart cards

A wide range of functions are offered by smart cards. They contain programmable microprocessor-type chips and are designed for complex applications. Their capability is extended if a means of network communication is integrated in the reader.

Essentially, the cards function as miniature computers, capable of being field programmed and possessing far more processing power than single electronic cards. Several different technologies based on galvanic contacts, microwaves and photovoltaic cells are used. The most efficient, simple and inexpensive means of transferring signals and power is through standard gold contacts.

The main applications of smart cards are:

- identification
- access control
- electronic file
- financial operations
- information processing.

Laser Cards

The basic material used in laser cards is a light-sensitive layer of very high definition. During the manufacturing process, data can be recorded on the layer using photolithographic techniques. Data is read optically, with light reflected differently according to the bit value. This pre-recorded layer is laid on a plastic card which is dust and scratch protected by an acrylic layer. In certain designs, new information can be written on it with a laser. The process is called DRAW (Direct Read after Write).

Laser cards are read-only and have the following applications:

- portable databases
- physical support for computer or robot software
- electronic books.

The main characteristics of laser cards are:

- very high capacity
- low cost archival support
- individual recorded information cannot be modified
- there is no restriction on the information format. Data can be protected by encryption
- card authentication can be achieved by various means: pre-recording of marks, geometrical patterns, security combinations, etc.

DRAW cards can be used as:

- payment cards
- archival cards
- identity cards
- access control cards with internal audit trails.

Other hand-held objects

The techniques described here are essentially based on the idea that a secret element, generally a PIN, is stored in one, two or three places: host, device and users' memory. To have access to the protected system, up to three keys may be concerned: a users' key or a PIN, a device key and a host key. This may involve the physical presence of the candidate user and may require an additional reader connected to the terminal as well as software implemented algorithms to generate new passwords.

Hand-held objects use the technology of smart cards. They contain a microprocessor, ROM and RAM, a replaceable battery and an eight-digit LCD display. Additionally, they can include a small keypad. The user identification number is stored in a protected area of a memory chip. Each protected device has its own key access. The access control operates in a time-shared mode.

During the manufacturing process a secret numeric code or key, associated with the host or the application, initialises the device through a series of keypad operations. Then a secret key (or PIN) is chosen by the security officer or the user. It is then stored in the handheld object.

The authentication process works in the following way: The candidate user sends a PIN to the system, and the system returns a random number, data code or sequence number which is displayed on the terminal. A one-time, device-derived password is determined by combining the numerical code entered by the user. The user enters the generated code on the keypad.

The Safeword Key (manufactured by Enigma Logic)

This key is extremely small, consisting simply of a proprietary microchip which is coded in order to identify each device. Another portable hand-held unit is required - the Enigma LOGIC Standard Decoder - which can be mounted on the access terminal. The key is inserted into the decoder area and connected to it through galvanic contacts. At authentication time, the key is inserted into the decoder. The decoder calculates a unique one-time password based on the random keyword generated by the proprietary algorithm. Then the user communicates this password displayed on the decoder to the system via the terminal keyboard.

The PFX Passport (Manufactured by Sytek)

The passport is the size of a pocket calculator and, indeed, can also function as a four-function calculator with memory. Another unit is needed: the authentication server, which is connected in series with the host.

At initialisation, the PIN used for access is recorded on the passport by the security officer or by the user. At authentication time, the user logs on with a PIN or a user code. The authentication server sends an acknowledgement message to the user on the terminal display. If a valid PIN has been entered, the host system generates a one-time password which the user has to enter on the keyboard. Access is granted if the password is validated by the security server.

Colour-Based Protection Device (manufactured by British Technology Group)

This system is based on the comparison of colour combinations generated by the polarising properties of several layers of plastic. The decoder contains four buttons allowing the user to select a combination of numbers, depending on the particular device. Applications include the protection of low cost programs and the protection of data in data storage media.

Emitting devices

Emitting devices are usually used for access control to restricted areas but can also be used for computer access. The major advantages of these objects is that they do not require physical contact between the device and the checking reader. Small, medium-frequency emitters are contained in the device, which can send messages to a receiver located at a short distance.

Personal emitting bracelet:

The electronic bracelet is an identifying device which does not require actions like keyboard entry. All the operations are fully automated and initiated by the receiving device, the only requirement being that the checking unit is not far from the receiving point. In highly sensitive areas, the receiving point generally resembles an airlock.

The identification process is based upon several pieces of information: the person's weight, an identification code, changed each time the bracelet is put on, and an encryption algorithm. The person's weight is measured at enrolment time and again at each check-point where a weighing apparatus is integrated in the airlock. The bracelet is sent a random value by radio at each receiving point and responds with a value calculated with the encryption algorithm and secret parameters. All this information is checked after decryption. The system comprises the following components:

- the emitting receiver bracelet
- the emitting/receiving checking unit
- a central controller.

5.5 PERMANENT AUTHENTICATION

In most identification/authentication schemes, a single authentication process occurs at the beginning of a work session. Sometimes, however, a permanent or almost permanent control may be necessary. There are various means of achieving this:

- permanent authentication using encryption
- permanant authentication using passwords
- permanent authentication using passwords and encryption.

Permanent authentication using encryption

In communications systems permanent identifying action can easily be achieved using encryption utilities (see Chapter 7). Since any transmitted data is supposed to be meaningful, encryption and decryption must use the same key (or pair of associated keys in the case of public-key cryptosystems) to avoid unintelligible data being received. The candidate user obviously cannot work if he does not own the correct key.

Permanent authentication using passwords

Entering passwords repeatedly at short-time intervals is, of course, a method which users will not readily submit to. However, the job can be performed by automatic password generators. This method is similar to time-stamped authentication schemes (See Chapter 7).

Permanent authentication using passwords and encryption

With this method, again used in communications systems (See Chapter time or sequence number validation using a password generator that guarantees the unique quality of any piece of data exchanged between two entities. In particular, identical messages sent at different times will be enciphered differently. This prevents the replay of old enciphered sequences that an intruder may have recorded through tampering.

5.6 CONCLUSION

As the computerised storage of data increases and computer systems are accessed by larger numbers of people, the need for secure user identification becomes increasingly important. This chapter has outlined the present state of technology in this field and outlined some of the developments which are likely to be refined in the future (for example, biometric methods). We should be aware however, of the difficulties involved in creating methods of identification and authentication which balance acceptability and practicality with effective levels of security.

6

Terminal Identification and Authentication

6.1 INTRODUCTION

In this chapter we discuss terminal identification and authentication, which is usually used in conjunction with user identification and authentication. This procedure is designed to verify the location of users attempting to access a system, and thereby establish whether or not they possess authorisation. We will discuss two major approaches - the leased line approach, and callback systems.

6.2 THE LEASED LINE APPROACH

Normal time sharing networks provide easy access to hackers since a modem is all that is required to call the host through public networks. One straightforward countermeasure is to communicate through private networks (if allowed by national legislation) or leased lines. This will block unauthorised access. However, the major disdvantage of this approach is its high installation cost (in the case of a private network) or charges (with leased lines).

6.3 CALLBACK (OR DIALBACK) SYSTEMS

Callback systems allow access to the "system" only after testing and verifying the origin of the call. Traditionally, this is the technique used for secure voice communications by telephone; both correspondents hang up and the person receiving the call then dials back the number the caller has given. The receiver can, in the meantime, check the number in a directory.

Procedures

When a user attempts to start communicating with the computer or database, the call is first received by the callback system, which is placed between the receiving modem and the host computer. The procedure is as follows:

1   The user tries to enter into communication with the computer or database, either by dialling manually or by calling through a smart modem.

2   The access request is received by the callback device, which asks for personal identification number (PIN) or access number (Location Identification Number or LIN) or password.

3   The user enters the requested information and waits to continue. Step 4:

4   While the user waits, the callback system disconnects the line and then consults its user directories or libraries to validate the information the user has given.

5   The callback system dials back the number corresponding to the user's access code, but only if the information actually corresponds to an authorised user. Failing this, the contact is not re- established.

6   The user who answers the call then indicates that he was actually expecting the call, to avoid validating a link that was not requested in the first place.

7   Once this acknowledgement is received the modem hands over access to the user and becomes transparent for the user until the next access request comes in.

Advantages of callback systems

1   Since the callback system allows a connection only after the above conditions are fulfilled, a potential intruder cannot even attempt to communicate with the computer

2   Dual protection is possible:
   • physical identification of the terminal by the call number
   • user identification by the PIN or the optional callback system password

3   The system can be used only to check the password and not to go through the whole callback procedure

4   By using an audit trail, the security system records each call or attempted call

5   The system is relatively inexpensive (particularly in comparison to encryption devices or leased lines).

Disadvantages of callback systems

1   Telephone charges are increased

2   The time spent waiting for the return call can range from approximately two to fifteen seconds (depending partly on traffic), and can be more for long distance calls.

Design of callback systems

Two types of callback system exist: analog and digital. An analog callback system is located between the user's modem and the telephone system (see Figure 6.1). Some commercially available devices include 'Backus', 'Optimum Electronics' and 'Wall Data'. A digital callback system is located on the host computer side of the modem (see Figure 6.2). Commercially available devices include 'TACT' and 'Digital Pathways'.

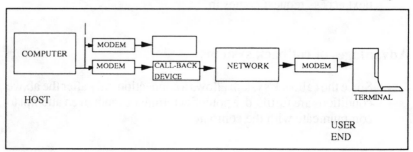

Figure 6.1 Analog callback system

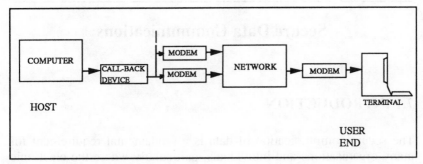

Figure 6.2 Digital Callback System

Analog and digital callback systems compared

Analog callback systems can be configured to protect both the telecommunication system and the host computer, with protection at the destination end. Analog callback systems are compatible with almost all existing hardware and software. They are transparent to the digital signals from the computer. This is not true for the digital callback which requires the use of specific modems on the computer side.

6.4 CONCLUSION

Terminal identification and authentication offers a useful and necessary supplement to user identification and authentication. Because of the distributed nature of many computer systems and their ability to be accessed from remote locations, it is important to verify whether an access point is authorised or not. Without terminal identification and authentication, it would be very difficult to isolate hackers. However, since it is always possible to duplicate hardware components, terminal identification and authentication should be considered as only one aspect of a security system.

7

Secure Data Communications

7.1 INTRODUCTION

The secure communication of data is a fundamental requirement for many organisations and individuals, particularly where the electronic transfer of money is involved. This is pertinent not only to the financial sector but, as electronic retail payment and home banking increase in importance, it directly affects a wider set of people. A good example is that of treasury management systems, used by companies to communicate with their banks (see Part 3). The requirement for secure communications is not limited to the field of financial transactions. Other sensitive information flows also need to be protected.

The security required in data communications is much greater when open networks are being used. Where there is greater access to the network, the possibilities for fraud increase. This is not to say that security is not required for dedicated networks or local area networks, but the need to protect information using public networks is greater and it is this area to which the methods of this chapter are most applicable.

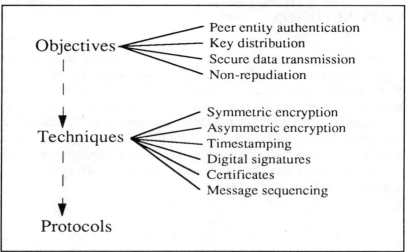

Figure 7.1 Aspects of data communications security

The chapter is divided into three main sections: 'Objectives in Communications Security', 'Techniques' and 'Protocols'. There are four main objectives in providing secure communications. The first is the authentication of communicating parties, the second is the distribution of keys, the third is secure data transmission and the fourth is non-repudiation. Techniques include asymmetric encryption, symmetric encryption, digital signatures, certificates, message sequencing and timestamping. Protocols for achieving the four objectives, using these techniques, are examined in the third section of the chapter.

7.2 OBJECTIVES IN COMMUNICATIONS SECURITY

Authentication

Peer-entity authentication

In data communications, peer-entity authentication is the mutual proof of identity of two communicating parties. This is sometimes termed sender-receiver authentication. The sender must be sure that data is being sent to the correct address and that the second communicating entity is not an intruder. Similarly, the receiver must be convinced of the correct identity of the sender. (Usually, in a session, the receiver subsequently becomes a sender and vice-versa.)

There are often two aspects to authentication - mutual authentication of the computer itself with the other communicating party, and authentication of the *user* of the computer to the other communicating party. For example, in an on-line ATM system, when a cardholder uses a terminal, the identity of the cardholder must be proved to the bank's server, but before that, the terminal itself needs to be authenticated to the bank's server. Furthermore, the terminal must have proof that it is communicating with the bank and not with an illegal third party.

It is arguable whether the first stage in communications security is authentication or whether it is key distribution. Mutual knowledge of keys, or at least of some secret information, is needed in order to authenticate. However, in order to distribute keys, authentication needs to have taken place. Methods of solving this problem are discussed in the section on 'Protocols' below. Most assume an initial, once-only, manual distribution of master keys.

Data origin authentication

Data origin authentication is a concept related to peer-entity authentication. It relates to the provision of assurance that data does originate from the claimed sender.

Key Distribution

The most important tools in communications security are keys for the encryption and decryption of messages, or of parts of messages. Usually, these keys need to be kept secret and be known by only the two communicating parties. However, there is obviously a requirement to distribute the keys to the two communicating parties and often this will be performed over the network. There is, therefore, a problem in protecting the information transmitted (the keys), when that information itself is needed in order to communicate securely.

Usually, many different keys are used. These are said to be at different 'levels'. Different keys may be used for peer entity authentication, key distribution, message authentication, message confidentiality etc. Clearly, there must be some initial distribution of master keys used for peer entity authentication or key distribution. Once this has been done, the keys used for message authentication and confidentiality can be distributed over the network, regularly, under the protection of the master keys.

In the case of master keys, *manual key distribution* is often performed. These keys are obviously not changed frequently. Additionally, many of the schemes for key distribution and for the provision of communications security use an independent, trusted, *key distribution centre* or *key management centre (KMC)*.

The section below on 'Protocols for Secure Data Communications' describes schemes for using the available techniques to facilitate key distribution.

Secure Data Transmission

There are two important aspects to secure data transmission - *data confidentiality* and *data integrity*. The confidentiality requirement is the need to protect data from disclosure to unauthorised parties. Integrity is the need to ensure that the message contents have not been changed in any way .

Non-repudiation

Non-repudiation is the requirement by means of which the receiving party can prove to a third party that the message was received and that it was sent by the sending party; and the requirement that the sending party can prove to a third party that the message was sent and that it was received by the receiving party.

7.3 TECHNIQUES IN COMMUNICATIONS SECURITY

In this section, the techniques of encipherment (or encryption), timestamping and digital signatures are described.

Encipherment

Two distinctions can be made in classifying the methods and schemes of encipherment or encryption. The first is between link encipherment and end-to-end encipherment. The second, regarding the type of algorithms used, is between symmetric encryption and asymmetric encryption.

Link encipherment

In a typical link encipherment scheme, a link encipherment device is placed between each participating station and the communications medium, as illustrated in Figure 7.2. In this case, all data transmitted and received by each station on the network pass through the device, typically consisting of a high throughput hardware module. The module performs the encipherment and decipherment functions on the data, using a predetermined cryptographic key.

Because of the physical location of the link encipherment device, all transmitted information is enciphered before reaching the communications medium, including such information as the network addresses which are added by the various protocol layers. This type of scheme, therefore, requires that all adjacent network stations are fitted with a compatible device, configured to enable the decipherment of the transmitted information. This is necessary even if the next network station is not the final recipient since the protocol information must be deciphered for interpretation by the various protocol layers, for example to enable message routing by the intermediate stations.

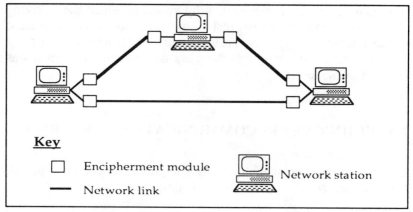

Figure 7.2 A link encipherment scheme

The main advantages afforded by a link encipherment scheme are that the use of the device can be completely transparent to the user and that the installation and management of the equipment can be simple for a small network.

End-to-end encipherment

The other main category of encipherment for use in communications systems, is the end-to-end encipherment scheme, so called because it is the two communication endpoints which control the operation of the encipherment mechanism. Whereas the link encipherment scheme performs encipherment on all transmitted data, the end-to-end scheme can use encipherment for the protection of selected portions of data.

For example, information can be enciphered before the routing protocol information is added, and in this way will, therefore, be transmitted in clear form, and be intelligible to all network stations regardless of their ability to decipher the protected information. This enables the enciphered data to pass through any number of intermediate stations without decipherment before reaching their final destination.

The management of encipherment keys is usually more complicated in this type of scheme than in link encipherment schemes, resulting in the formulation of a number of sophisticated procedures for the distribution and management of keys.

Link vs. end-to-end encipherment

One of the main advantages of end-to-end encipherment schemes over link encipherment schemes is that of greater flexibility. This has enabled a range of services to be described based on the use of end-to-end encipherment. For example, some of the services which may be offered include: data confidentiality, data integrity, user authentication, and signature services. Greater flexibility, however comes at the expense of added complexity in the management of encipherment keys, and link encipherment schemes allow for a simple key management scheme on point-to-point networks. In terms of the protection provided by the two types of scheme, again there are advantages and disadvantages to both types of scheme. Since the link encipherment scheme treats user data and protocol information equally, when the decipherment operation is applied at a network node in order to interpret the address information, the user data is also revealed. Thus the data are protected only during transmission and not during routing within the network nodes. End-to-end schemes provide protection both within the network nodes and during transmission, but the protection applies only to the user data and not to the protocol information. This may provide an opportunity for some types of attacks, such as those based on traffic analysis. The choice of scheme depends upon the network architecture, the application and the level of protection required. In a simple point-to-point network, the most cost effective approach would be to provide link encipherment devices for those nodes and connections which are seen to be at greatest risk. For a network architecture in which messages are routed through an unknown number of nodes before reaching their destination, an end-to-end scheme may be the preferred solution so as to prevent the disclosure of information within the intermediate nodes themselves. Increased security may be provided by a combination of the two techniques. In a broadcast network architecture, however, the use of link encipherment devices would prevent the correct interpretation of the address information, and so can not be used.

Symmetric encryption

A symmetric encryption method is one whereby both communicating parties hold an identical key (or, at least, one key is easily determined from the other) , i.e. the same key is used to encrypt the data as is used to decrypt it. The best known symmetric encryption algorithm is the Data Encryption Standard (DES) created by the United States National Bureau of Standards. DES enciphers 64-bit blocks of data using a 56-bit key.

Symmetric algorithms are used widely for the encryption of communicated data. Until recently, all crypto-systems were symmetric. Asymmetric algorithms also now exist. There are advantages to both methods, symmetric encryption is faster and requires less computing power.

Asymmetric encryption

In asymmetric crypto-systems the keys used for encryption and decryption are different. The difference is to the extent that at least one key cannot feasibly be determined by knowledge of the other. Therefore, it is possible to reveal one of the keys without the other being determinable. The two keys are termed the 'public key' and the 'secret' or 'private key'.

Asymmetric crypto-systems can have considerable advantages over symmetric systems. Firstly, they can be of considerable assistance in key distribution and authentication. The public key of the sender can be freely distributed over the network. The receiver can then be sure that any information which can be deciphered using that key must have been encrypted by the holder of the secret key, the sender (note: this, in itself, is not sufficient to provide authentication because it must also be proved that the original distributer of the public key is who he/she claims to be). The holder of the public key can encipher information and be sure that it can only be deciphered by the holder of the secret key.

The best known asymmetric algorithm is RSA (Rivest-Shamir-Adleman scheme [RIVE78b]). This relies on the use of a one-way function, where it is infeasible to compute $f^{-1}(y)$ even if y is known in the formula $y=f(x)$. The scheme is based on the difficulty of factoring large numbers.

Timestamping

Timestamps are usually used to allow the replay of messages to be detectable, or as part of a certificate for non-repudiation (see below). A timestamp consists of several fields - for example, year, month, day, hour - and is bound to a message to specify the time the message was sent.

Any replay can be detected by examining the timestamp. Each network user can operate a simple quartz clock which provides a timing standard maintainable with sufficient accuracy. However, it should be remembered that the use of timestamps may not be suitable for all types of connections, e.g. connections where there is no network-wide reliable source of time.

Digital Signatures

The concept of digital signatures forms the basis for the design of data origin authentication protocols. A digital signature cannot be imitated, is message and sender-dependent, and provides more protection against fraud than normal handwritten signatures. Many cryptography-based methods have been produced to provide digital signatures. These methods utilise both symmetric and asymmetric crypto-systems. In some protocols, message secrecy is also provided. The signature and secrecy transformations can be integrated together or they can be kept separate.

Asymmetric crypto-systems provide a particularly useful basis for creating digital signatures. One approach is to perform a function on the message being sent, i.e. to create a short message authentication code (MAC). This, along with a message identifier (MID) is encrypted using the secret key of the sender, This is sent with the message and message identifier. When the message is received, the receiving party decrypts it using the public key of the sender and verifies its validity by comparing the two MIDs and by performing the same function on the message and then comparing the MACs. If these match then it is known that the message came from the sender, because only the sender has knowledge of its secret key.

Certificates

Certificates are used in protocols for the non-repudiation of messages. A certificate is used to prove, at a later point in time, that a message sent to a party was received by that party, or that a message received from a party was sent by that party. Digital signatures, using asymmetric keys, are useful for *authentication* because it is clear that a signature encrypted under the secret key of a sender A must have come from A, unless that key has been compromised. However, this is not sufficient to provide for *non-repudiation* because a message sender, wishing to deny having sent the message, could deliberately disclose the secret key by broadcasting it over the network, thus removing the possibility of proof of message origin.

Thus, certificates are used to provide some additional security. This usually involves the use of an independent arbitrator, which, for example, uses its secret key to encrypt the signature of the sender, along with a timestamp to prove when the message was sent. The resulting 'certificate' is then sent to the receiver.

Message sequencing

Message sequencing is usually used to prevent the possibility of message replay by an intruder. This is a fairly simple technique, whereby a sequence number is attached to each message, usually encrypted, thus making it obvious if the same message is received twice.

7.4 PROTOCOLS FOR SECURE DATA COMMUNICATION

Many schemes have been proposed, using the above techniques, to achieve authentication, Key distribution, secure data transmission and non-repudiation. The more successful of these have become or will become standards. Schemes are described below for each of the following:

- peer entity authentication
- data origin authentication
- non-repudiation

Many of the schemes described also include mechanism for ensuring data integrity and data confidentiality. Many rely on the use of a third party Key management Centre (KMC) which is usually able to facilitate easier key distribution and a higher level of security. The assumption being that the KMC can be trusted.

Peer Entity Authentication

A peer entity authentication service that will provide a high level of authentication involves a key establishment stage and an authentication stage.

To begin, we will describe protocols based on both symmetric and asymmetric ciphers. The availability of a KMC is assumed. The calling or source entity is denoted A while the recipient or destination entity is denoted B. We will assume that A and B are identified in messages by their unique identifier Id_A and Id_B.

Peer Entity Authentication Using Symmetric Encryption

Needham and Schroeder, '78 [NEED78], present a scheme using *symmetric* encryption and a KMC. Both A and B have a key-encrypting key, KK , known only to itself and to the KMC (these will have been manually distributed). This key is used to encipher the data-encrypting key, KD, whenever it is transmitted through the network. The process is illustrated in Figure 7.3 and described below.

1   A sends a request to the KMC when he wants to communicate with B. This message contains his identity, the identity of B and a random number used only once (denoted r1).

2   The KMC computes a data-encrypting key, KD, and sends a message =back to A, encrypted under KK_A. This contains the session key KD that A and B must use for their communication, the random number r1 and the identity of B (to prevent replay of a previous message). Also contained in the message is information for B, enciphered with KK_B. This includes KD and the identification of A.

3   Only A can decipher the message and check the information. If everything is in order, A keeps the key KD and sends to B only that part of the message encrypted under B's key-encrypting Key KK_B

4   Only B will be able to decipher the message to obtain KD and A's identity. The key establishment stage is now completed and both A and B are in possession of the data-encrypting key KD. B sends A another randomly generated number, r2, enciphered under KD.

5   A deciphers the message and sends back to B some function, f, of r2, enciphered under KD. B then deciphers the message, computes with the inverse function and compares the result with the number r2. If the reply is satisfactory, the communication encrypted under KD can begin.

If B obtains the correct value, he knows that the entity at the other end is certainly A. In contrast, A does not know for sure whether the entity called is B. Indeed, some intruder, say Z, may masquerade as B and establish a normal conversation with A. Such a situation, however, can be prevented by insisting on a mutual authentication before any data messages are sent.

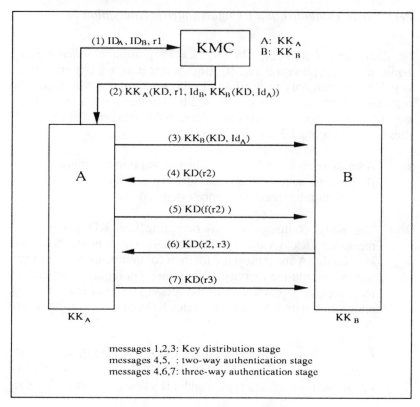

Figure 7.3 Peer Entity Authentication - Needham and Schroeder (1978)

6   Mutual authentication is based on a three-way handshake between A and B. Thus, for A to establish B's authenticity as well as providing proof of its own authenticity to B, (5) is replaced by $KD(r2, r3)$ where r3 is a random number generated by A.

7   B authenticates A by comparing r2 with the relayed value and authenticates itself by sending $KD(r3)$.

Peer Entity Authentication Using Asymmetric Encryption

Pope and Kline ('79) [POPE79] present a protocol which uses *asymmetric* ciphers. The key management centre in this example is called an authentication server (AS). Assume that A and B have their public keys, P_A and P_B, known by the server (again manual distribution is assumed). Their secret keys are S_A and S_B. The authentication server, AS, has its own public key P_{AS} (Known by A and B) and secret key S_{AS}. The scheme is illustrated in Figure 7.4 and described below.

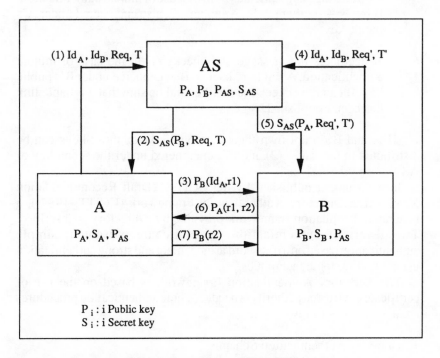

Figure 7.4 Peer entity authentication - Pope and Kline ('79)

1   A sends the server a timestamped message requesting communication with B.

2   AS sends A the public key of B, a copy of A's request and the timestamp. The whole message is enciphered under the secret key of AS.

3   A deciphers the message using the public key of AS. This

authenticates the source of the message. A confirms with the timestamp that it is not an old (replayed) message and verifies with the copy of request that his original message has not been altered. A extracts the public key of B. A sends it's identity to B, along with a random number r1, both enciphered under B's public key.

4   and (5) B performs the steps 1 and 2 to retrieve A's public key.

5   B sends the number r1 back to A, enciphered under A's public key. This message authenticates B. In the case of mutual authentication, B sends A another random number, r2, also enciphered under A's public key.

6   A deciphers the message and checks r1. In the case of mutual authentication, A sends r2 back to B, enciphered under B's public key. B can now check the number and be sure that a reliable link has been established.

(If A and B do not own their own public keys, those keys can be distributed in messages (2) and (5), enciphered under the secret key of AS.).

In a document published by the CCITT (Draft Recommendation X.ds7 - The Directory Authentication Framework (CCITT, 1987)), a general authentication framework provided by a directory is described. Two levels of authentication procedure are presented: simple authentication based on a password arrangement and strong authentication using cryptographic techniques.

The Directory Authentication Framework is based on the use of certificates. A trusted authority is needed. Three authentication procedures are described as follows:

1. One-way Authentication Scheme

Two users A and B wish to authenticate each other. It is assumed that user A has obtained certificates and public keys beforehand. The different steps are:

(i)   A generates a random number r1.

(ii)   A sends a signed message to B and a certificate containing A's identity and A's public key. The signed message contains r1, a timestamp and the identity of B, encrypted under B's public key.

(iii) B obtains the public key of A from the certificate, verifies the signature of the message and checks the certificate, the timestamp and the random number to verify that the message has not been replayed and that the certificate has not expired.

2. Two-Way Authentication

In the two-way authentication scheme, there is a reply from B to A to establish:

- integrity and originality of the authentication tokens
- mutual secrecy of the tokens.

3 Three-Way Authentication

In the three-way authentication scheme, there is another message exchange from A to B, allowing the same controls as the two-way scheme but without the need for timestamping.

User Authentication

Williams' 'See-Through Authentication System' proposes a general model for an authenticated mechanism that unequivocally establishes the identity of the user, regardless of user location or system/network configuration. The specific constraints of this system are as follows:

- the user must be present and is actively involved in the sign-on process
- each sign-on is unique
- the user cannot unilaterally circumvent his/her authentication process.

The scheme is constructed so as to associate two of the identification principles using something the user knows and something the user owns.

User Device

Each user receives a personal physical device. A secret element which is known by the authenticating system is stored in the device. The device is able to compute and generate a one-time password each time it is used. This generation is done by a complex algorithm and is a function of the secret element .

User PIN

Each user will also receive a personal identification number. The scenario is as follows:

1   The user sends his PIN to the host.
2   The host responds with a code called a "challenge."
3   The user enters the challenge into the device.
4   The device computes a password using secret information and the challenge.
5   The host then selects the secret information associated with the user and computes its own version of the password using the challenge.

Additional security can be added with:

* invulnerable technology in the user device
* no physical connection between the device and the terminal
* additional mutual authentication between the user device and the user by, for example, applying another PIN or using biometric techniques.

Data Origin Authentication

The concept of digital signatures forms the basis for the design of many data origin authentication protocols. Three examples of this are given here. The second and third involve the use of certificates. The first does not.

Example 1

To sign a message, the sender i first computes the Message Authentication Code, MAC, a function of the message, M and the Message Identifier, MID. The next step is encipherment of the pair (MAC, MID) under the sender's secret key, offering as the signature: $\text{Sig}i(M) = S_i(MAC, MID)$

If secrecy is required as well, then the message M is enciphered prior to transmission. At the receiving end, the recipient obtains (MAC, MID) and the message M by decipherment and also computes MAC. If this value matches the value of MAC sent by i, then i is authenticated as the sender of message M.

An intruder may record the signature for the purpose of masquerading as i, but the chances of successfully binding the signature to another message are very slim indeed. This method of separating the signature transformation from the secrecy transformation has a number of advantages over the combined secrecy-signature transformation:

- the signature can be implemented using a public key system while a conventional method like the DES can be used for secrecy. Thus the advantages of both crypto-systems can be exploited

- storing the signature in case of disputes places no heavy demand on storage space as the signature is only one block in size

- no redundancy is required in the message because it is extremely difficult to find another that will produce the same MAC.

Example 2

This protocol uses public key certificates but does not provide message secrecy.

The source entity is denoted by A and the destination entity by B. These have unique identifiers Id_A and Id_B respectively. To provide B with proof of data origin, A forms a signature of the message M, $Sig_A(M)$. A requests a certificate, C_A, from the Authentication Server, AS, and sends the following to B: CA, $Sig_A(M)$, M

B checks that the timestamp, T, in C_A is valid. B uses P_A to obtain (MAC, MID) which is enciphered under A's private key. B then computes a new MAC and if this value matches the value of the MAC from A, then B is satisfied that message M originated from A. The fact that anyone in possession of A's public key can obtain the pair (MAC, MID) is in no way a weakness of the protocol because the MAC is computed with a one-way function. Therefore it is not possible to obtain M from MAC.

Example 3

This protocol provides both data origin authentication and message secrecy services. The signature transformation involved is separated from the secrecy transformation.

A obtains its certificate, C_A from the AS. For secrecy, a conventional method like DES is used to encipher the message M. A generates a random 56-bit value, say KD_M and uses it as a key for the DES encipherment operation. Since B must also know KD_M in order to recover M, A enciphers KD_M using B's public key and sends it together with A's certificate, C_A, A's signature, $Sig_A(M)$ and the enciphered message, $KD_M(M)$ to B: C_A, $Sig_A(M)$, $KD_M(M)$

The strength of the protocols given in the above three examples depends to a large extent on the assumption that none of the private keys are compromised, and also on the properties of the MAC. One condition which must be satisfied is the absence of an inverse property for the function used to compute the MAC. Secondly, given a MAC for a message M, it must not be possible to find another message, M1, such that the MAC computed for M1 is equal to that computed for M. If the first condition fails, then the secrecy of messages can no longer be guaranteed, while failure of the second condition might allow an intruder to bind bogus messages to a previously recorded message.

Non-Repudiation

Protocols for Non-Repudiation (Origin) Services

Protocols providing a non-repudiation (origin) service are very similar to the protocols providing a data origin authentication service. In the latter, the signature of the source entity, though providing proof of data origin to the destination entity, cannot provide a non-repudiation (origin) service. The reason for this can be explained using the following scenario.

Suppose that some time after having sent a signed message, the source entity A decides, for whatever reason, to deny having sent the message. Knowing that the destination entity B is in possession of its signature $Sig_A(M)$ for that message, A must find a way to free itself from any binding signatures in which its private key S_A is used. An easy way for A to achieve this is to disclose its private key by broadcasting it over the network. A compromise is deemed to have occurred when the KMC is in possession of the key. The KMC will keep a record of any compromise as well as the time it was detected. Now A can argue that $Sig_A(M)$ has in fact been generated by some other entity in possession of the compromised private key, since there is nothing to verify when the key was created. Thus A can deny having sent the message in question.

To guard against such an eventuality, the signature has to be made more binding by recording the time it was created. One method is to use signature certificates. This is similar to public key certificates which provide a guarantee of the integrity of public keys. If SigA(M) is the signature of entity A for a certain message M, then the signature certificate for A is: $SCA = S_{KMC} (T, Sig_A(M), Id_A, P_A)$

A requests such a certificate from the KMC by passing on its request together with its signature $Sig_A(M)$ and its unique identifier, Id_A. The KDC appends a timestamp T and also A's public key to $Sig_A(M)$ and A, and certifies all the variables by encipherment under its private key. The timestamp acts as a deterrent against deliberate key disclosures (typified by the scenario above) because the holder of the signature will now be able to determine whether a message was signed before the key disclosure

Protocols for non-Repudiation (Destination) Services

Providing a non-repudiation (destination) service requires a slightly more complicated protocol than the one for non-repudiation (origin) service. The same principle is involved but there is greater involvement on the part of the KMC. As with the other protocols which have been described, the KMC must be secure as well as trusted by both the source and the destination entities. We will refer to it as the arbitrator AS.

There now follow three examples of non-repudiation (destination) schemes. Example 1 uses symmetric crypto-systems. Examples 2 and 3 use asymmetric systems. From a functional point of view, asymmetric systems seem to provide the ideal method of implementation for a non-repudiation (destination) service mechanism.

Example 1 - Using Symmetric Crypto-systems A typical arbitrated signature scheme based upon symmetric crypto-systems would be as follows (See Diagram 7.5):

The arbitrator AS shares a key KK_A for secure communications with a user A and a key KK_B for secure communications with a second user, B. If A wishes to send a signed message to B, the sequence would be:

1   A computes a message identification code (MID), composed of the sender's name, the receiver's name and the message sequence number: MID = (IdA, IdB, Seq)

2   A creates the message M with the MID and the actual data to be transmitted: M = (MID, Data).

3   A computes a Message Authentication Code MAC: MAC = f(M)

4   A computes his signature: the concatenation of MID and MAC encrypted under KKA: SigA(M) = KKA(MID, MAC)

5   A sends to AS his signature SigA(M) and the message M.

6   The arbitrator AS computes the MAC from M, reads M, deciphers SigA(M) to recover the MAC and MID and compares the two MACs and two MIDs to authenticate and validate the message.

7   AS creates a new message M': M = M, SigA(M), (time/date of receipt), MVI (MVI is a message verification indicator that the arbitrator uses to indicate to the receiver whether he considers the message to be genuine or not).

8   AS sends to B the message M', encrypted under KK_B.

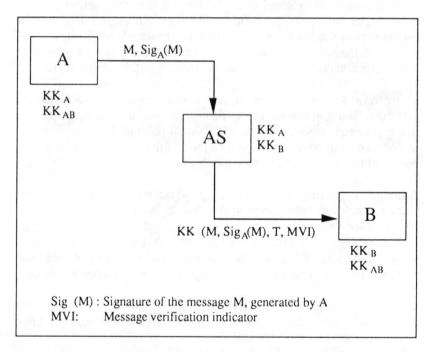

Figure 7.5 Scheme for non-repudiation (sender) using symmetric crypto-systems

In this scheme, the receiver cannot modify the sender's digital signature SigA(M) because B is ignorant of KK_A. He cannot modify the message itself because he has no capability for forging a digital signature in place of A. When a message has to be hidden from the arbitrator a variant of this scheme uses a secret key, KKA_B , shared by A and B, to encrypt the message. The arbitrator still receives sufficient authentication and validation information. The security of such a system, however, depends on the trustworthiness of the arbitrator.

Example 2 - Using Asymmetric Crypto-systems Without Certificates
This example is illustrated in Figure 7.6 and described below.

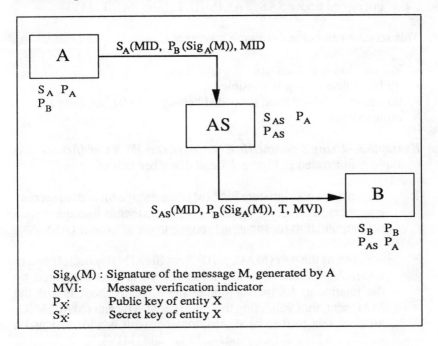

Figure 7.6 Non-repudiation using asymmetric crypto-systems without certificates

Assume SX is the secret key of X, P_x is it's public key and M the actual data to be transmitted.

1   The sender, A, computes a signed message by encrypting the message, M, the MAC and the MID, under his secret key: SigA(M) = S_A(M, MAC, MID)

2   The sender enciphers the signed message under the receiver's public key: PB(Sig_A(M))

3   The result of (2), along with the MID, is then encrypted under the secret key of the sender: SA (MID, P_B(Sig_A(M))

4   The result of (3) is sent, with the MID, to the arbitrator, AS: SA (MID, $P_B(Sig_A(M))$), MID

5   The arbitrator, using A's public key PA, extracts MID and compares the two MIDs in order to authenticate and validate the message.

6   The arbitrator creates a new message with the time/date of receipt, T, and MVI, a message verification indicator, and sends it to B, encrypted under SAS: SAS (MID, $P_B(Sig_A(M)$, T, MVI)

This scheme offers the following guarantees:

• information is hidden from the arbitrator
• no fraudulent dating is possible
• no common information is needed between sender, receiver and arbitrator.

Example 3 - Using Asymmetric Crypto-systems With Certificates This example is illustrated in Figure 7.7 and described below.

1   A computes it's signature SigA(M) for message M, and for secrecy enciphers M under AS's public key. A then sends its request for a non-repudiation (destination) service to the arbitrator (AS)

2   AS obtains the pair (MAC, MID) from SigA(M) by decipherment under A's public key. The message, M, is also recovered by decipherment. AS then computes the MAC to check it with the MAC sent, thus validating the message, M. The pair (MAC, MID) are then sent to B to be signed, together with A's identity and a message telling B that message M is valid (MIV).

3   B is assured that message (2) originated from the arbitrator AS, because of its encipherment under AS's private key. AS, in the message, informs B that AS is in possession of a message from A and is waiting for B's signature before delivering the message. B therefore sends back SigB(M) to AS.

4   AS checks that (MAC, MID) is correct and, if so, delivers PB(M) to B.

5   In addition, the arbitrator, AS, forms the signature certificate for B, SCB, and sends it to A as proof of the delivery of message M.

On receiving message (4), B can validate M by checking the MAC. A validates SC_B by checking the timestamp and also whether the value of MAC from $Sig_B(M)$ is equal to the one initially computed by A. If SC_B is valid, then A knows that M has been delivered to the intended destination entity. A then stores SC_B, in case B later falsely denies receiving M or its contents.

6   For a non-repudiation service (both origin and destination), the arbitrator, AS, forms the signature certificate for A and sends it to B, together with the enciphered message, M. Thus SCA is appended to message (4). B stores SC_A as proof that message M was sent by A.

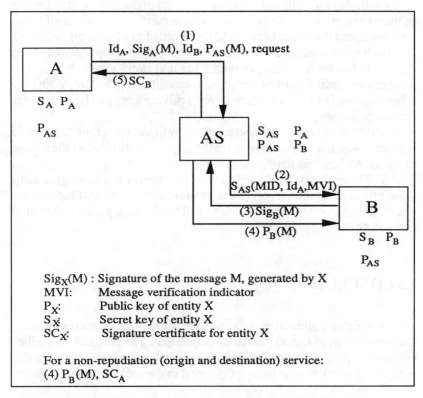

$Sig_X(M)$: Signature of the message M, generated by X
MVI: Message verification indicator
P_X: Public key of entity X
S_X: Secret key of entity X
SC_X: Signature certificate for entity X

For a non-repudiation (origin and destination) service:
(4) $P_B(M)$, SC_A

Figure 7.7 Non-repudiation using asymmetric crypto-systems with certificates

On-line Certificate Log

The protocols described above for non-repudiation services are assumed to operate in an open systems environment. If sufficient precaution and care are taken in the storage and use of private keys, the possibility of a compromise is remote. However, to ensure a high level of network security, provision should be made for such an eventuality.

If the private key of the Server is compromised, the intruder in possession of that key can masquerade as the Server and produce fake public key certificates. Off-line publication of public keys will allow detection of such a compromise. An even more serious situation arises if, in addition to knowing the server's private key, the intruder also possesses the private key of some entity. The intruder will now be able to create signature certificates that are legally binding to that entity. Detecting fake signature certificates is not as straightforward as the detection of fake public keys.

Certificates alone do not solve the problem of disclosure of the server or user's private keys. Thus, as an added security measure, certificates, signatures and disclosed keys could be recorded in a log or an audit trail.

This log is stored on a write-once device such as an optical disk. Only the server has write-privileges on the log and every user can read it. A recovery procedure must be provided in case of server failure. With such a log, disclosure of a user's or a server's private keys can be detected in the following way:

If an intruder is able to masquerade as A to the server, he can forge a signature which will be registered in the log. A can then detect the misuse of his secret key and notify the server.

An intruder, knowing the secret key of the server and having the same write privilege as the server, might attempt to record certificates in the log. If he is successful, the disclosure will be detected by the server after comparing the log with the last version.

7.5 CONCLUSION

This chapter has outlined the objectives, techniques and protocols involved in the provision of secure data communications. The protocols described represent only a small proportion of the work which has been done in this area. Much work is now being performed in the area of standardisation.

8

Auditing Techniques

8.1 INTRODUCTION

The difference between auditing a computer based system and auditing a manual one is greater than is often realised. This is true even of a simple computerised ledger system, but when the complexities of production control, stock control, management information systems etc. are taken into account, it becomes extremely important to use efficient and effective techniques.

According to one definition (IFAC,1982, Auditing in an EDP-Environment [IFAC82]), "An audit is the independent examination of any entity, whether profit-oriented or not, and irrespective of its size, or legal form, when such an examination is conducted with a view to express an opinion thereon. Compliance with basic principles requires application and reporting practices appropriate to the particular circumstances"

The overall objectives of auditing in an EDP/EDI environment are the same as in a non-automated organisation. Accordingly, Weber, 82 [WEBE82], defines EDI-auditing as "...the process of collecting and evaluating evidence to determine whether a computer system safeguards assets, maintains data integrity, achieves organisational goals effectively, and consumes resources efficiently." However, whereas the objectives of auditing remain constant, the techniques used in an EDI system differ considerably from traditional methods.

This chapter examines the components involved in auditing, before looking more specifically at EDI auditing approaches, methods and tasks. A section is then included on computer auditing tools. Finally, events accounting and auditing, and database auditing are discussed.

However, one change which effects the EDP auditing environment is the switch from mainframe computing to PCs and workstations in both standalone mode and as part of local area networks.

8.2 COMPONENTS OF AUDITING

Different types of audit can be classified according to the subjects who perform the audit (for example internal/external auditor), the object being audited (for example annual balance sheet) and the rules and principles which are checked for compliance with the auditing objects (for example rules for the rendering of accounts, law or data protection).

For our purposes, we will restrict the discussion to internal and external auditors as auditing subjects, and an EDI system as the auditing object. We define the major components of the audit system as the internal auditor, the external auditor, the internal control system and the audit trail.

The internal auditor

The internal auditor is a component of both the auditing function and the object being audited (i.e. because he is a member of the organisation which is subject to external audit). The objectives of an internal audit are primarily data integrity, system effectiveness and system efficiency.

First of all, the auditor must determine whether the controls applied comply with the respective internal guidelines or legal regulations. Additionally, the internal auditor should have a more active function. His involvement in the planning of the EDI-system and its internal controls would contribute to the achievement of the overall object.

The external auditor

The task of the external auditor can be defined as an independent appraisal of internal controls established in an organisation. In contrast to the internal auditor, the external auditor is not a member of the company which is subject to his review.

The overall objective of an external audit is to vouchsafe the aims and polices of an organisation. Furthermore, an external audit must prove that the interests of the participants (for example the shareholders of a public company) and those of third parties (for example the public or creditors) are taken into account and satisfied by the organisation. Since auditability is a significant security requirement, auditing must also be regarded as a security measure. A system can only be considered secure if auditability is realised and auditing satisfactorily performed.In general, an external audit is required by law. This will demonstrate the degree to which the auditing objects comply with specified legal regulations. Naturally, these will depend on the nature of the business and the country where it is located.

In order to evaluate the orderly operation of a company's accounting system, the external auditor has to check the EDI-system, which is the basis for the production of the accounting system in a computerised environment. To achieve this satisfactorily, is is essential for the auditor to maintain an independent status.

The Internal Control System (ICS)

Auditing is assisted by the Internal Control System (ICS), a set of measures and techniques established by the management within a business to safeguard its assets, ensure the reliability of its records, promote operational efficiency and encourage adherence to established policies.

The techniques applied are either manual or automated. The most significant manual technique is the use of checklists to investigate appropriate controls. Automated electronic checklists also exist on microcomputers. These are easier to use and can be adjusted more quickly to the specific EDI-system to be audited.

For both the internal and external auditors, one of the first considerations in auditing a company's EDI-system is to check the relevant parts of the internal control system. If weaknesses are detected in the internal control system, the audit can be intensified in these areas.

In the EDI environment, two questions arise concerning the internal control system. Firstly, how far can internal controls themselves be automated and the EDI-system be used as a tool for control? Secondly, what special internal controls are necessary in the area of DP-applications to ensure correct system performance?

Specific internal EDI controls focus on the system procedures and can be grouped into three different categories:

- organisational controls
- programmed controls
- machine-integrated controls.

The internal and external auditors will concentrate on the organisational and programmed controls, since machine-integrated ones are mostly provided by the manufacturers.

A system which obviates the role of the auditor is known as self-controlling. This will have no requirement for auditing since all the necessary internal control and auditing functions are already incorporated. However, the automated auditing functions themselves must be auditable. Only if this is possible can we say that self-controlling systems are trustworthy.

The Audit Trail

Some ambiguity surrounds the definition and purpose of an audit trail. However, taking the U.S. Department of Defence's comprehensive definition, we can describe it as "a set of records that collectively provide documentary evidence of processing used to assist in tracing from original transactions forward to related records and reports, and/or backwards from records and reports to their component source transactions" [DoD 83]. This definition is influenced by a technical view of audit trails. More generally, they are chronological lists of events which occurred to an entity.

Computerised systems comprise two different audit trails. An accounting audit trail shows events and operations upon data items within a database system (examples would be the creation, modification and deletion of transactions). Secondly, an operations audit trail provides information about events in relation to application procedures. It is maintained by the operating system and by utilities for the system's management, for example logging of resource consumption.

8.3 THE IMPACT OF ELECTRONIC DATA INTERCHANGE (EDI) ON AUDITING

The impact of EDI auditing can be characterised in the following ways:

1   The auditing object changes. An increase in the number of EDI systems in use can be observed over recent years. They are employed by companies to guarantee and secure objectives.

2   The increasing use of computer-based information systems requires the application of particular auditing methods and auditing instruments in order to be able to design an efficient audit.

3   The legal rules and financial reports on which the audit is based are

changing. For example, the adjustment of accounting to the EEC directives has lead to specific requirements for security which have to be taken into account by the auditor and by organisations which use EDI-systems.

8.4 APPROACHES TO COMPUTER AUDITING

Types of audit

Various approaches relating to the audit of a computer-supported system can be distinguished. These approaches differ with regard to the auditing instrument, the computer and the auditing object, and the system. The auditing approach is therefore determined according to the components included in the audit. The options are:

• verification approach, i.e. audit of single items of data, components and incidents
• systems auditing, i.e. auditing of complete procedures
• vouching approach

The verification approach involves the audit of single items of data, components and incidents. The auditor devises independent means of verifying the existence, ownership and valuation of assets. The systems approach is oriented more towards the objectives of the enterprise. Questions such as whether procedures will be appropriate or which assets will be safeguarded in the future are tackled. The vouching approach is an audit around the computer. The orderly and correct processing of a number of transactions is checked without integrating the computer itself. The computer is a "black box". The processscan be performed with or without the use of a computer. The computer can be used as a support or, to some extent, substitute for the auditor. Alternatively, a verification, vouching or systems audit can be performed without using technical instruments.

Around versus through the computer

In the field of EDI auditing, two general approaches for handling the auditing object, the computer, can be distinguished:

- auditing around the computer
- auditing through the computer

Auditing around the computer excludes the computer from the audit process. Auditing objects are the input and output of the application systems and the internal control system for the computer installation. The auditor assesses the quality of processing by examining the quality of the input and output. Systems which allow for the successful application of an audit around the computer are, however, relatively few in number.

Auditing through the computer of a modern complex DP-information system is in many cases the only means of assuring correct system performance. Large volumes of input and output cannot be checked in a direct way. To assure the completeness and the accuracy of the processing, the logic and controls existing within the system - as well as the records produced by the system - must be audited. The advantage of auditing through the computer is the increased scope and breadth of testing, which therefore promotes confidence in the accuracy of the processing.

8.5 COMPUTER ASSISTED AUDITING TASKS

Computer assisted preparation of an audit

The preparation of an audit can be undertaken using computer-supported application procedures to plan auditing activities and design the auditing environment. The employment of workstations for audit support is appropriate, especially if time and personnel planning as well as the production of accompanying documentation are considerations. There are many PC-based packages available which fulfil these requirements.

The advantages of such packages are the system-supported standardisation of reporting, enhancement of optical presentation by means of graphics, easy integration of tables and calculation results, time saving and access to stored data as well as an improvement of auditing quality by means of machine-stored checklists and questionnaires.

Computer assisted systems audit

Auditing techniques for a systems audit of EDI-based systems can be grouped into those which are documentation-oriented and those which are function-oriented.

Documentation-oriented techniques are:
- questionnaires and interviews
- generation of compiler-listings
- flow-chart generation.

These techniques aim to verify whether the system actually complies with its original documentation. But, more importantly, they allow evaluation of the consistency and accuracy of the documentation itself and the contents of the programs.

Function-oriented techniques are aimed at proving the ability of a system to function as intended. Two techniques are involved in this approach. Isolated methods use:

- test decks
- mapping
- tagging and tracing
- snapshot
- program code comparison
- source code review
- parallel simulation and controlled simulation;

Concurrently usable methods use, for example:

- Integrated Test Facility (ITF)
- Job Accounting Facilities (JAF)
- System Control Audit Review File (SCARF).

Techniques which are used in an isolated way do not co-operate with application software or operating systems. Concurrently usable methods co-operate closely with the application or system software and are therefore to a certain extent capable of proving program integrity. These methods are also known as Concurrent Audit Techniques.

8.6 COMPUTER AUDITING TOOLS

The following discussion, on computer auditing tools, is divided into tools used for *systems* auditing and tools used for *verification* and *vouching* auditing. Although many of these tools were developed for a mainframe environment some can be carried over to a more distributed computing environment.

Tools for systems auditing

A classification of computer-assisted systems auditing techniques can be made according to the propriety and availability of the auditing tools. Here, we must distinguish between *client-owned* and *auditor-owned* tools. The former are installed in the system of the auditing object, while the latter are specific audit instruments belonging to the auditor.

Methods that Work with Client-Owned Tools

Test Facilities This method uses test data, which is input into the computer outside the usual data flow. The processed results are compared with manually produced results obtained in advance. If desired, trace instructions for the automatic logging and controlling of the test run can be implemented.

Client-owned decision table techniques can be incorporated in the source code of the the application programs. They can be interpreted by means of specific software and are employed for the determination of particular data constellations. One practical example is the decision table processor VORELLE from the company Mathematischer Beratungs und Programmierdienst. This so called source code review is a technique which proves the functionality of software in an isolated way without using test data.

The Integrated Test Facility (ITF) This method involves processing fictitious events together with the real company data. In order to prevent collision between test data and real data, the ITF should be installed in a dedicated subsection of the system. It is established and treated as a subsection of the "real" processing system and can prove program integrity for specific sections of software. Furthermore, it allows control of the processing sequences in real-time systems.

Work Reperformance/Controlled Reprocessing This is the repetition of program sequences for single but consistent sections of work. Compliance of the repeated results with the real results is verified. To a limited extent this can qualify program integrity. The method meets its limitations in systems with integrated data storage and complex program and file systems. Like parallel simulation, controlled reprocessing is a function-oriented technique, usable in an isolated way.

Flowcharting Software Using flowcharting software, the program code is retranslated into a program flowchart. A prerequisite of this method is access to the source code, which is not delivered with the program. An example of flowcharting software is AUTOFLOW. The generation of flowcharts is a document-oriented technique.

Source-code comparison software To prove the identity of documented and used software, program versions are compared. The audit states whether the authorised software and the software employed correspond.

Data Dictionaries Extended database systems have a complete documentation of the stored data material, including information such as filename, fieldname, format and range of values. The data dictionary promotes an understanding of data structures and provides references for the mental reperformance of the data flow within application programs. Used in this fashion, the data dictionary can be regarded as a tool for documentation-oriented techniques.

System management facilities/Job accounting facilities Large systems are supervised by hardware and software monitors. System management facilities, such as those integrated in IBM OS/VS or SIEMENS BS 2000, deliver the necessary overview of run duration and the frequency and execution time of programs. This helps to establish information on unauthorised program usage. In large systems, access control is realised in system programs. The audit aims at verifying the effectiveness of these control mechanisms.

Job Accounting Facilities belong to the group of concurrent audit techniques. They co-operate with the software and may be used to prove program integrity.

Monitoring facilities Monitor facilities like SCARF (System Control Audit Review File) can be used to select audit-relevant data according to specified criteria. This data is then stored in a separate file and can be prepared and used as audit evidence.

The implementation of this technique should be planned during system development. The employment of monitoring facilities would be particularly useful if the auditor could program the necessary instructions himself and thus hide the selection criteria he intends to apply. This concurrent auditing technique co-operates with system and application software.

Methods that work with auditor-owned tools

Auditor-owned tools can be very useful, but must be compatible with the existing hardware and software. This can be a problem because of the range of different clients an auditing firm has. This section examines EPSOS-D, a minicomputer package and then goes on to look at the use of the microcomputer by the external auditor.

EPSOS-D This is an example of a dialogue-oriented auditing system, used with COBOL, C and DBASE III, which assesses the auditability of programs. In addition to this, it supports the selection of an auditing technique and the promotion of software aids methods for DP management. Primarily, EPSOS-D qualifies formal security features as follows:

- size of modules
- module sequence
- number of modules per page of the assembly list
- visibility of the data structure
- groupings of data fields
- observance of format in the data definition section
- assignments of and optical separation of groups
- number of statements per program line
- number of operators in one COMPUTE-statement
- visibility of comment lines
- separation of COBOL words
- cyclomatic number
- module entrance and exit
- number of GOTO-statements
- number of GOTO-statements outside of modules
- nesting of conditional statements
- number of conditions of an IF-instruction
- span
- non-reachable instructions
- loop-independent instructions in a loop.

From the list above, the auditor can select the particular characteristics which are relevant according to the objectives of the audit. In a dialogue with the computer, the auditor can additionally select additional criteria for auditing, for example the correct use of variable names, sensible positioning of brackets, headings and comments, etc.

Microcomputer tools Audit support by microcomputers is an increasingly used technique since their storage and calculation capabilities are advancing rapidly. The auditor can use the micro for the reperformance and checking of programs and data files that have been transferred to the micro. The micro can also be used to monitor the data-flow or obtain statistical samples. A further advantage of the micro is the emulation of operating systems. For example, IBM-PCs are now capable of emulating the VMS-operating system. This affords the auditor the opportunity to employ all existing mainframe-oriented auditing packages or system management facilities.

It should be borne in mind that all leading companies have now developed software packages to be used by auditors on portable micros. These include modules for planning and preparing an audit, performing word processing and producing single and consolidated financial statements.

Tools for computer-assisted verification and vouching audit

To audit data, verification and vouching approaches are used. Again, a distinction can be made between client and auditor-owned tools.

Methods that work with Client-Owned Tools

General Utilities The use of general utilities allows the auditor to merge, separate, combine, sort, select or compare data files. The advantage of these facilities is the constant availability for auditing. However, the drawback is the large number of different computer languages, with instructions varying from system to system. Furthermore, the general utilities are not sufficiently equipped with auditing features.

Database Utilities A database management system (DBMS) incorporates a data manipulation language (DML) which uses DBMS user-enquiries. A distinction between host language and self-contained DMLs is made. The DML is a straight interface between an auditor and a DBMS. For auditing purposes, the self-contained DML is the most appropriate alternative to auditor-owned tools. Even PC-oriented and simplified DBMS's allow the auditor to directly interrogate any user data.

Methods that Work with Auditor-Owned Tools

Specific Auditing Software Specific software is developed to solve individual questions. The auditor takes the hardware/software environment of the auditing object into account and uses the software for a special task.

Generalised Auditing Software The first versions of generalised audit software packages were created in the late 1960s. They work with files which have to be extracted from existing data files. When dealing with complex data structures, there is a need for the easy transferral of files since the auditor must create temporary files in a readable and auditable format.

Generator and Interpreter Auditing Software The auditor uses a generator that permits the development of single task-oriented programs. The generator contains an interpreter which executes the commands.

Current Developments Examples are given below of major developments in the field of auditor tools for computer-assisted verification and vouching. These examples are primarily German as they were researched by the University of Köln. Similar examples are available in other countries. This provides the reader with an idea of what may be on offer with various other languages.

1. Audit Command Language (ACL)

The ACL was intentionally developed to obtain one common language for auditors. It is an interactive program that runs on the Michigan Terminal System and SIEMENS BS 2000 and is now available for IBM PCs. Although this relates to a specific product, others are available which offer similar facilities.

The application consists of a dialogue with masks for the enhancement of existing procedures (RUNS), data descriptions (FORMATS) and computing (WORKSPACES). To re-calculate data, several functions and demands are defined in the WORKSPACES, for example LIST, TOTAL, SUMMARISE, FIND, CALCULATE or UPDATE. For the characterisation and analysis of data some special commands have been set up, for example STATISTICS, REGRESSION, COMPARE, VERIFY, STRATIFY or HISTOGRAPH.

Portability is achieved by the command TRANSFER, which accomplishes the transfer of several database systems into a universal system based on a common schema processor. Management and control are executed by monitoring system commands such as COPY. This guarantees protection against the destruction of original files. Another useful facility is the SUPERVISOR which allows the reperformance of the specified data and the subsequent re-arrangement of the audit. SUPERVISOR can restrict users, user-groups, departments or time-periods.

2.   Allgemeine Portable Prufersprache (APS)

Since 1982, the German Ministry for Research and Technology has funded the development of an interactive "Common Portable Auditor" language (APS). The APS language is programmed in COBOL and runs on SIEMENS BS200 under UTM/TRANSDATA DMBS as well as on DEC-VAX under UNIX.

In contrast to ACL, the APS language is more complex. The federation of auditors evaluated the two different auditing languages as follows:

i)   ACL is too insecure because it is easy to use and has some commands which guide the auditor.

ii)   APS appears to be more secure and has more features than ACL. Thus the development of APS as a further prototype of ACL is recommended.

3.   The Internal Control Model (TICOM)

TICOM is a computer-assisted method for designing, analysing and evaluating internal control systems (ICS). With TICOM, the auditor has a computer-based analytical tool that first helps to model the internal control system and then to query the model.

TICOM is based on the concept of artificial intelligence. It helps to describe office information systems while emphasising internal accounting controls. When compared with traditional evaluation methods, the advantage of TICOM is that the evaluation can be more rigorous and exhaustive.

TICOM contains two sets of interrelated computer programs (a) the Internal Control Description Language (ICDL) and (b) the query-processor. The ICDL works in a similar way to flowcharting concepts. It allows the description of the system by means of a formal language. The computer then compiles the system into a graph representation, where the nodes represent actions and the arcs represent precedent conditions. The approach closely resembles the construction of an expert system.

8.7 EVENTS ACCOUNTING AND AUDITING

As we have seen, EDI-auditing depends to a large extent on the system which has to be audited and on the purpose of the individual audit.

The theory of events accounting forms the basis for a new approach to accounting information systems. Use of these systems would lead to different auditing demands and pressures which influence the techniques to be employed.

Events Accounting Models

Events accounting is an alternative to the traditional value accounting approach. Value accounting systems consist of aggregated values which are the processed results of economic transactions. Events accounting systems only store the original economic event. This event consists of the transaction itself as well as all relevant evidence for the transaction.

Events accounting systems are characterised by their ability to store the maximum amount of information in order to serve a wide range of users and information purposes. Furthermore, they do not allow the matching or deletion of events. Problems can be encountered with the definition of events and the kind and extent of permissible summation.

Events will form part of an audit trail. In summary, the operational audit trail records all machine events that occur. These are authentic, complete and accurate representations of real-world events. The audit trail contains many items that are used to image events; for example:

- transaction amount (the value of a data item, in the database, to be updated)
- before image (the prior value of a data item, in the database, to be updated)
- after image (the new value of a data item in the database)
- time stamp (the unique identification of the time a transaction updated a data item in the database)
- user identifier (the unique identifier of the person who initiated the transaction)

The accounting audit trail, containing specific data items, stores the events and serves an existing accounting system by specifying the accounting objectives. To meet these objectives, data are extracted from the events file, sorted into the required order and the results presented. For many smaller businesses, a more complete record of events or transactions allows a better information system as well as one which may be easier to audit.

Recent research has concentrated on the design of generalised approaches to events-based accounting models, which can satisfy a very wide range of information needs. The REA-accounting model, for example, promotes a generalised accounting information framework to be used in a shared data environment. It consists of sets representing economic resources (R), economic events (E) and economic agents (A), and the relationships between these sets.

8.8 DATABASE AUDITING

As we have demonstrated, events-based accounting models require database approaches. Let us now consider how auditing is affected in a database environment.

Loosely defined, the term database refers to a collection of data items which are administered through a database management system to facilitate more than one application. The familiar characteristics of a database are high complexity, the storage of large amounts of information serving as a common basis for all users, no data redundancy, the integration of data and processing, specific administrative functions; data independence and data dictionaries, flexibility and user friendliness.

The centralised planning and control of databases by the database administrator impinges on auditing in several ways. For a start, it will highlight the strengths and weaknesses of the system and provide technical and administrative information and tools for the audit. As a support tool of the database administrator, the data dictionary will contain information regarding the definition of all the data collected in the database.

The purpose of a data dictionary is to organise, update and maintain the so-called meta-data. The meta-data contain a precise definition of each entity, attribute and relationship within the data model of the respective database. The data dictionary is therefore at once an auditing object and an auditing tool.

We can then, conclude that a computer-assisted systems audit is essential in a database environment.

The auditing areas are as follows:

• general organisational measures

- documentation system
- processing system
- control system.

The audit of general organisational measures must prove the functionality of a database system and the efficiency of data processing. As with any EDI-system, the organisational structure, the assignment of tasks, work instructions, documentation, archiving and the segregation of duties have to be checked. In database systems, the control of administration and system development is also necessary.

The audit of the documentation system involves the data dictionary in addition to the usual components of documentation. The data dictionary contains information about the definition of data, its origin and use, access rights and conditions of integrity.

The audit of the processing system poses specific difficulties, because in a true database, programs and data are independent of each other. The audit of the programs alone does not lead to a complete audit trail, since they do not contain the access paths through the different data levels. In order to create a complete audit trail, the database administration system has be included. Thus, a transaction trail can be created which contains all elementary operations of the administration system and the processing rules of the application programs.

The transaction trail can be audited by means of system control programs which produce transaction-logs. The control system must guarantee the accuracy (or integrity) as well as completeness of the data.

8.9 CONCLUSION

The description of EDI-auditing reveals that only a computer-assisted systems audit is able to produce reliable evaluations of the performance of computerised information. Manual reperformance of a complex EDI-system within the restricted time schedule of an external audit is impossible. Furthermore, the client regularly requires an efficient audit, which can no longer be achieved with an audit around the computer using traditional auditing methods.

An audit around the computer is, for a number of reasons, inappropriate for office systems which require a considerably high degree of integration. Firstly, these systems often lack documentation of all the processing steps, which is necessary for a manual reperformance of operations. Secondly, even if such documentation were available, the amount of operations carried out would be too great to permit a thorough audit.

The selection of an adequate statistical sample for a manual verification audit will pose severe problems for the auditor. These are compounded by the need to audit the samples in a given time. In addition to a computer-assisted systems audit, a computer-assisted verification audit is necessary.

The present extent and variety of office information systems necessitates considerable knowledge on the part of the auditor. With the rapid advances in technology, it is often difficult to keep abreast of developments in the area of EDI systems. Members of the auditing profession must therefore be flexible enough to adjust their expert knowledge to meet new demands and challenges.

Although we are fully aware of the problems posed by highly automated office systems and have developed advanced auditing techniques, current approaches are still weak in many areas. For example, techniques are often limited as far as application to different EDI environments is concerned. Only ACL and APS are designed to be adjustable to any system. Greater compatibility is therefore required. Furthermore, the auditing profession lacks common criteria for audit software. This can be attributed to the differing requirements of clients, competition between firms, and the variety of auditing approaches. On this basis, we can identify at least two requirements for the auditing profession:

- further education in EDI auditing
- compatible audit interfaces and techniques.

Steps are now being taken to meet these requirements. For example, with regard to further education, large auditing companies now provide courses for their employees to overcome their knowledge gap. However, for the majority of auditors a considerable lack of DP expertise must be assumed. In the area of audit interfaces and techniques, some auditing firms as well as national and international professional bodies are working on the creation of flexible tools and techniques. In this context, the idea of the expert system as an auditing tool is under discussion. Indeed, some prototypes have already been designed. Another concept which is also being pursued is remote and/or permanent auditing.

Underlying much of the research and discussion in this field is the realisation that a common auditing strategy is required. Such a strategic approach should be supported by suitable standards on an international level. Apart from audit interfaces and techniques, auditability as a basic system requirement would benefit from standardisation. Similarly, this could be extended to a common audit language and document layout.

9

Security Modelling

9.1 INTRODUCTION

In this chapter, we present the results of a state-of-the-art study made by the Consortium, of theoretical models for secure systems. In looking at such models it is as well to remind ourselves that they can provide us with not only a means of defining exactly what security is and which security requirements exist but also a means of verification, when the system is put into practice, that security has been achieved. Additionally, they provide a means by which systems designers can demonstrate to a third party that their system is secure, a tried and tested basis for implementing security, a means of meeting the fundamental point that security must be designed and implemented as an integral part of the system and ensures that the user gains a simplified overview for the user of the system as a whole. Modelling is, however, an extremely difficult process and requires a balance to be struck between the creation of a model which is applicable to the real world and one which is abstract enough to be useful on a more general and wide-ranging basis

Security Models

The examples discussed in this chapter represent a sample of the research that has been undertaken to devise formal security models for computer systems. In general, the models enforce controls which are more rigid than those of the actual implementations, so actions that are deemed to be secure in the 'real' environment may be prohibited by the security model. Although this ensures a rigorous testing process, it is sometimes the case that models are too restrictive to be practical for intended users.

All the models discussed require correct identification and authentication. Without authentication, user identification has no credibility. Without reliable identification neither mandatory nor discretionary security policies can be properly invoked since there is no assurance that proper authorisation can be made.

The following classification has been devised for assessing security models.

1   Access-matrix models
2   High-water-mark models
3   Information flow models
4   Network security models

Examples of models relating to each of the above categories are discussed in Sections 9.2 to 9.5 below.

Implementation issues

In Section 9.6 we will describe two fundamentally different ways of implementing a security system - the security *kernel* and the security *shell*. The kernel is implemented in software and/or hardware. It is embedded within the operating system and in some sense dominates and controls that system. In this instance, the operating system may have to be written around the kernel. In the second approach, the operating system remains intact, and a shell built around it enforces the security.

A further important implementation issue is the concept of trusted subjects - high privileged users who will usually access the system via an exclusive set of interfaces. This is necessary, for example, for system maintenance or to perform certain actions not permitted by the access checks built into the normal kernel functions.

Verification

Verification, discussed in Section 9.7, is a very important concept in security modelling. Security modelling assists in creating a specification. When the secure system is implemented, both designers and users must be confident that it fulfills its specification, that it does what it is meant to do and no more, and that it has not been tampered with in any way. Verification involves a methodology applied to evaluate this.

9.2 ACCESS MATRIX MODELS

The access matrix consists of three principal components - a set of passive objects such as files, terminals, devices and other entities implemented by an operating system; a set of active subjects which manipulate those objects; and a set of rules concerning the ways in which the subjects may modify the objects. Any subject can also be an object and vice versa.

The access matrix is a two-dimensional array containing information about the access rights and privileges which each subject has to each object. One column exists for each object and one row for each subject. Access is controlled by a reference monitor which reads the appropriate entry in the access matrix each time a subject attempts to access an object and then allows or prevents access accordingly. Four examples are given in this section of access matrix models. All of these are capability based models.

Capability-Based Models

The access matrix forms the basis of most capability-based models. The capability approach offers a means of implementing data security. Using a list, this method defines which objects a subject can access. Capabilities are listed according to the recorded security policy of the organisation. The policy will also include rules on which objects are allowed to pass or what privileges to rescind.

Often, a security kernel is used and the system produces a capability list for each user ID. The capability acts as a pass, granting the user permission to access certain files and processes (objects). In many examples, each object has an owner; the owner of an object can pass or revoke privileges.

The capability approach can be used to implement security on a multi-user workstation. For instance, users could be authorised to access only those files or processes relevant to their needs or for which they have the appropriate security clearance.

The capability approach was originally developed as a prototype security kernel, implemented in a Plessey System 250 in England, in 1975, and in various PDP 11 environments, using the UNIX operating system. The foundations were laid by Popek, Walker *et al* at UCLA in the seventies.

The Bell and LaPadula Model

Based on the capabilities concept, the Bell and LaPadula model is one of the most valuable access matrix models. It is a formal model for computer security, prepared by the MITRE corporation and endorsed by the American Air Force. The model applies the concept of the finite-state machine, which views a computer system as a finite set of states, together with a transition function to determine what the next state will be, based on the current value of the input. The transition function may also dictate an output value.

Using the conventional access matrix concept, the Bell and LaPadula model consists of a set of passive objects such as files, terminals, devices and other entities implemented by an operating system, a set of active subjects which manipulate the objects and a set of rules relating to the way in which the subjects can modify the objects (subjects can also be objects and vice versa). Each subject has a clearance while each object has a classification. Furthermore, each subject also possesses a current security level which may not surpass the subject's clearance. Capabilities are determined according to the classification of each object and the clearance of the subject.

The access matrix is defined and four modes of access are presented and specified as follows:

Read-only: a subject can read but not modify an object
Append: a subject can append to an object but cannot read it
Execute: a subject can execute an object but has no read or write access directly
Read-write: a subject can both read and write an object.

Additionally, a control attribute, which is similar to an ownership flag, is defined. This offers the subject the flexibility to transfer to other subjects some or all of the access modes it possesses for the controlled object. However, the controlled object itself cannot be transferred to other objects.

The creation of objects is completed following a two-part operation:

1 The inclusion of a new inactive object to the existing set of objects.
2 The activation of an inactive object.

The so called 'tranquillity principle' ensures that no operation may alter the classification of an active object. Security in the bell and LaPadula model is achieved by applying two fundamental properties:

1.   *The Simple Security Property*

This dictates that no subject has 'read' access to any object with a classification greater than the clearance of the subject. This means that no user may read information classified above his/her clearance level. For example, a user who has a clearance of 'secret' would be denied access to a file classified 'top secret', but would, however, be able to access a file classified as secret.

The simple security property fulfils the basic requirement of preventing unauthorised users from accessing sensitive information. Alone, however, it does not achieve complete data security. It would still, for example, be possible for a hostile program to transfer data from one file to another with a lower security classification. This means that a Trojan horse attack is still possible. For this reason, a further security property (*-property) is included.

2.   *The *-Property (star-property)*

The inclusion of this property ensures that no subject has 'append' access to an object whose security is not at least the current security level of the subject. Additionally, no subject has 'read'/'write' access to an object whose security level is not equal to the current security level of the subject; and no subject possesses 'read' access to an object whose security level is not at most the current security level of the subject. The star-property regulations distinguish the model from other access matrix models, meaning that no user may lower the classification of information. For example, a user with a clearance of 'secret' would be denied 'read/write' access to an 'unclassified' file, but would be permitted 'read'/'write' access to a file with a classification of 'secret'. The *-property prevents the subject from modifying an object possessing lower access class than itself. Thus, a program operating on behalf of one user cannot be used to pass information to any user having a lower access class.

One criticism of the Bell and LaPadula model is that its rules are perhaps too restrictive. Users are very limited in what they can do. They are permitted to 'write' to but not 'read' objects with a higher classification and can read but not write to objects with a lower classification. 'Read/write' access is only permitted to objects with the same classification as the clearance of the user.

The model also includes a discretionary protection policy which may be used to differentiate users within the same class. Discretionary policy allows a user to grant or revoke access to a document, according to the stipulations outlined above (for example the owner of a document is still allowed to revoke access to someone who is permitted, by non-discretionary policy, to access that document).

The discretionary rules do not, however, overcome the criticism that the model is possibly too limiting. As indicated, discretionary rules can only be implemented under the provisions of the non-discretionary rules. Thus, although the opportunity is provided to improve security in particular areas on a discretionary basis, it is not possible to relax security where it is believed to be unacceptably restrictive on the operations that need to be performed. In fact, for the honest user, such discretionary rules may make the model even more rigid and limiting.

As defined so far, the model represents a system with security but not integrity protection. 'Read' access is not permitted to objects with a higher classification than the clearance of the subject. However, since 'write' access is permitted to objects with a higher classification, integrity of data is not guaranteed. The * property exists only to prevent information being written to objects of a lower classification and does not exclude the possibility of a hostile user maliciously altering information contained in files of the same or higher security classification. For this reason, the model was extended by the MITRE corporation in 1977 to include the concept of integrity.

An integrity lattice is constructed in the same way as the security lattice, with integrity levels defined for the purpose of preventing the direct and indirect modification of information. A subject cannot 'read' an object with a lower integrity classification than its own, or 'write' to an object possessing a higher integrity classification.

The Bell and LaPadula model, which we will return to later in this chapter, owes some of its importance to the fact that it was the first major model to construct rules on the basis of the access control matrix. It also formed the framework for the highly secure SCOMP mainframe operating system, which has been given the highest possible security ranking (A1) by the US Department of Defence.

The Take-Grant technique

Capability systems can be modelled using the Take-Grant technique (see Landwehr, 1981 [LAND81]). This modelling technique uses graph theory but could equally well be represented on an access matrix.

The protection state of the system is described on a graph. There are two types of node - one type representing objects, the other subjects. Arcs connecting the nodes show any access rights the subjects have to the objects. The arcs are labelled with the set of these access rights. Possible access rights are 'read' (r) 'write' (w) 'take' (t) and 'grant' (g). If a node has a 'take' access to another node then this means that it can take that node's access rights to any other node. 'Grant' access enables the first node to give its access rights to the second node.

The model also includes a set of rules for adding and deleting nodes and arcs to the graph. The 'take' and 'grant' facilities are two of these rules. There is a 'create' rule which enables new nodes to be added to the graph. When a subject creates a node then the two are linked on the graph by an arc which can contain any subset of the possible access rights. There is also a 'remove' rule which allows removal of access rights from an arc. If all access rights are removed, then the arc disappears. Other rules can be added if required. For example, a 'call' rule could be added to model invocation of a program as a separate process. An example is given in Landwehr (1981). This is illustrated in Figure 9.1.

The graph method of modelling has the advantage that information can be presented in a more compact way than on an access matrix. This is because arcs need only be included where there would be non-null entries in the matrix. However, where large numbers of access rights exist the graph will become complicated.

There are a number of disadvantages to the basic Take-Grant model. For example, information can be copied from one object to another via a third object, all without the receiving object having taken or been granted access rights to the source object. This can occur if any information is copied by the third object. A further disadvantage is that the model does not include security classes. Subjects and objects are not distinguished according to clearance levels or security levels, though this could be achieved by labelling nodes and restricting access rights accordingly.

Finally, the Take-Grant model has been criticised on the grounds that it is too weak to be usefully applied to real systems. The argument is that in many systems the result would be a fully connected graph where all subjects can gain access to all objects.

The Feirtag-Levitt-Robinson (FLR) model

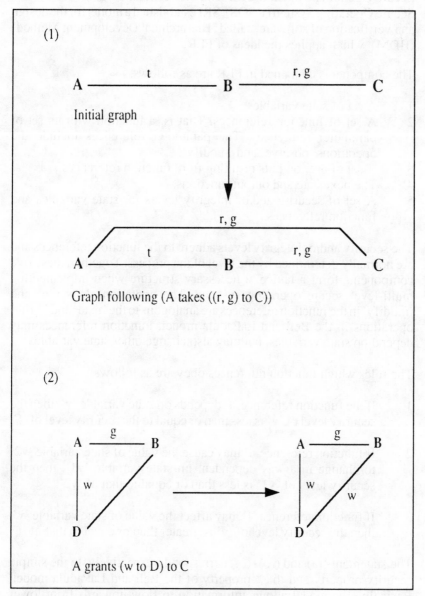

Figure 9.1 Examples of Take-Grant graph technique

Based on experience obtained during the specification of the Provably Secure Operating System (PSOS) and the verification of the Kernalised Secure Operating System (KSOS), SRI established a model for the design and verification of software, called 'Hierarchical Development Method' (HDM), which applies the ideas of FLR.

The components contained in FLR are as follows:

1   A set of state variables.
2   A set of function references. That is, a function with its set of parameter references. The parameter references include the operations 'observe' and 'modify'.
3   A set of user outputs resulting from function references.
4   The next state and output functions.
5   A set of security and/or integrity levels for state variables and function references.

The security and/or integrity levels adhere to the function references and are normally determined by the level of the process. Together, these five components form a lattice, a necessary structure when implementing multi-level secure operating systems. The operations 'observe' and 'modify' in the function references are analogous to the 'read' and 'write' operations in the Bell and LaPadula model. Function references may depend on state variables, but may also change other state variables.

The rules which function references obey are as follows:

1   If the function reference 'f' depends on state variable 'v', then the security level of 'v' is less than or equal to the security level of 'f'.

2   If function reference 'f' may cause the value of state variable 'v2' to change in a way dependent on state variable 'v1', then the security level of 'v1' is less than or equal to that of 'v2'.

3   If function reference 'f' may affect the value of state variable 'v', then the security level of 'v' is greater than or equal to that of 'f'.

The statements (a) and ((b)+(c)) correspond, respectively, to the simple security property and the *-property of the Bell and LaPadula model. Basically, the model allows information to flow upwards from lower security levels to higher ones.
    To demonstrate the efficiency of this model an example from Haig,

84, is outlined below. This compares the capabilities of Bell and LaPadula with those of FLR. Using a value at the secret level, a user (subject) at the confidential level wishes to modify a state variable at the top-secret level (see Figure 9.2). In the Bell and LaPadula model, the user must first read the value specified at secret level and afterwards use this value to modify the object at the top-secret level. The read operation is forbidden in accordance with the simple security property. With FLR, the transaction can be accomplished if there is a function which applies the value at secret level in order to modify the state variable at the top-secret level (without knowledge of the contents of the state variable on secret level).

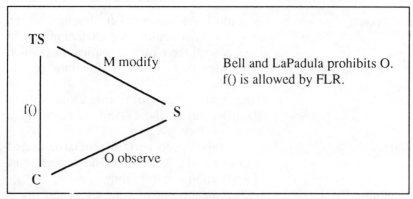

Figure 9.2 Example of Fiertag-Levitt-Robinson model

The concept of the FLR model provides the basis upon which security implementations can be specified. The structure allows the proofs of security to be factorised into smaller units (variables). Systems such as KSOS, PSOS and SCOMP have applied variants of the FLR model in an effort to provide multi-level security.

Military Message System (MMS)

Drawing on research and implementation experience, Carl E. Landwehr, Constance L. Heitmeyer, and John McLean [LAND83a] developed a new security model with the intention that it should be based on a specific application rather than attempting to mould applications to fit. In visualising an application-independent abstraction for a secure computer system, they addressed the problems encountered in different projects (for example SIGMA and GUARD), applied the Bell and LaPadula approach, and included trusted processes.

The MMS model was basically developed for military purposes, but nonetheless represents an interesting approach to secure, multi-level systems. By focusing on the actual application's functional and security-related requirements, and thereby deriving the constraints to which the system must be liable, it is possible to produce a system which enforces a uniform security policy on all parts of system software, yet is non-rigid and suits the end users.

The components of the model use concepts which are applicable to other models. Some of the main features are as follows:

Entity:	An object or container.
Container:	A multi-level information structure which carries a classification. A container may hold objects with their own classifications which can differ from the classifications of the container.
Object:	The smallest unit of information with a classification in the system. It is purely a single-level entity.
Role:	A user privilege to perform special dedicated operations like distribution, downgrading of classification and re-routing of messages.
Container Clearance Required	CCR is an attribute of some containers. Its purpose is to solve theproblem that Containers may hold objects having different classifications within a narrow range, such that a given user, with a clearance below some of the objects' classifications, may gain access to information which he/she is not intended to see.
Direct Reference:	A reference applying the entity's ID directly.
Indirect Reference:	A reference applying multiple parameters, where the first may be the ID and the subsequent an offset.
Access Set:	A set of triples (user ID or role, operation, operand index) that is associated with an entity.

A significant aspect here is the introduction of multi-level objects in the concept 'container'. Apart from some basic security assumptions regarding user behaviour, a valid user is expected not to compromise sensitive data to which he has legitimate access. The model consists of the following ten security assertions:

1   *Authorisation*: a user can only invoke an entity if the user's ID or current role appears in the entity's access set along with that operation, and an index value corresponding to the operand position in which the entity is referred to in the requested operation.

2   *Classification hierarchy*: the classification of any container is always at least as high as the maximum classification of the entity it contains.

3   *Changes to objects*: information removed from an object inherits the classification of that object. Information inserted into an object must not have a classification higher than the classification of that object.

4   *Viewing*: a user can only view (on some output medium) an entity with a classification less than or equal to the user's clearance and the classification of the output medium.

5   *Access to CCR entities*: a user can have access to an indirectly-referenced entity within a container, marked 'Container Clearance Required', only if the user's clearance is greater than or equal to the classification of the model.6. Translating Indirect References: A user can obtain the ID for an entity that he referred to indirectly only if he is authorised to view that entity via that reference.

6   *Translating indirect references* a user can obtain the ID for an entity that he has referred to indirectly, only if he is authorised to view that entity via that reference.

7   *Labelling requirement*: any entity viewed by a user must be labelled with its classification.

8   *Setting clearance, role sets, device levels*: only a user with the role of system security officer can set the clearance for a user or the classification assigned to a device. A user's current role set can be altered only by that user or by a user with the role of the operating system security officer.

9   *Downgrading*: no classification markings can be downgraded except by a user with the role of 'releaser'. The user ID of the releaser must be recorded in the 'releaser' field of the draft message.

10   *Releasing*: no draft message can be released except by a user with the role of releaser. The user ID of the releaser must be recorded in the 'releaser' field of the draft message.

(Assertions (9) and (10) address functional aspects in the military area.)

An example will show the effect of some of these assertions. A container marked 'CCR = SECRET' contains 4 objects, each identified as confidential (see Figure 9.3).

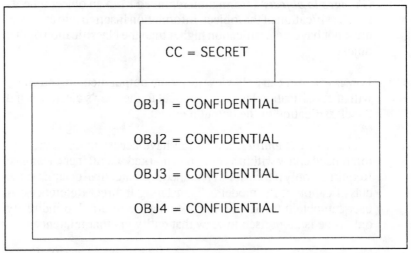

Figure 9.3 Example of objects within container

A user with a clearance 'confidential' is able to view OBJ4, a single object, if he uses direct reference. On the other hand, if he uses indirect reference he will not obtain access to the file in accordance with assertions 4 and 5. A general condition which is always in force is assertion 1, so the user ID has to be present in the access set of the object requested.

9.3 HIGH-WATER-MARK MODELS

High-water-mark models work on the principle of recording the history of an object in terms of the security levels and categories which are assigned to it, as well as to other objects it has accessed, and then controlling access to the object on the basis of this. The high-water-mark represents the highest level of data sensitivity that the object could contain.

This approach differs to that of the access matrix model because, in the latter, the contents of the access matrix are pre-determined according to security policy, and, although they can easily be changed, this is not done dynamically by the system. In this respect the access matrix model is less flexible. The possibilities have to be assessed before implementation in order to determine the access matrix, whereas the access rules of the high-water-mark model are determined on a continual basis according to the histories of the subjects and objects in question.

An example of a high-water-mark model was implemented in the Adept-50 time sharing system constructed at the System Development Corporation in the late 1960s. The system uses four types of objects - users, terminals, jobs and files. Each object is described by the following three properties:

- Authority (A)
- Category (C)
- Franchise (F)

The authority property contains the sensitivity level of the object; the second, the category property gives the current access categories, and the franchise property, consists of a set of user designations. Franchise sets are used to implement discretionary need-to-know controls. A history function is present to record the highest authority assigned to the object and the combination of all categories assigned to the object since its creation. This constitutes the high-water-mark of the object. The authority, category and franchise properties are used to determine which properties are assigned to new objects as well as to control access to and by the object.

Users wishing to access the system identify themselves and give a password. The system first checks the franchise set for the terminal to determine whether the user is authorised to use it. After this the password is verified. The user's ID is then assigned to the job servicing the user's terminal, and following this the job is then given authority and category properties according to the category and authority properties of the user and terminal authorities. The authority selected will be the lower of user and terminal; the category is the intersection of their category sets.

Authorisation for a job to access a file is granted only if the level of the job in the lattice A, C and F is at least that of the file. When access to a file is given, the history functions are updated according to the authority and category set for the file.

New files resulting from this job are assigned an authority and category designation based on the history functions of the job. The authority property is set to the highest file accessed by this job since log-on. The category is the combination of all the category sets of all the files accessed since log-on. The franchise is set to that of the job.

The system can be applied equally to workstations in a standalone environment or on a network. Access to files on a multi-user workstation can be strictly monitored and the use of the workstation within a network can also be controlled using the high-water-mark system.

The high-water-mark approach is, in fact, quite suitable for application to a network system. Information unclassified in one branch may become confidential in another branch at a different point in time. Obviously, it would be undesirable for the first branch still to refer to this as unclassified. If an access control matrix were in use, then it would be necessary to update the access matrix continuously. This updating process renders the access matrix vulnerable to attack, whereas the high-water-mark system has the advantage of automatically amending security classifications where necessary.

Although not in widespread use, the high-water-mark approach is very thorough, since in controlling information flows it takes account of all objects accessed in the past by an object, as well as effectively eliminating the possibility of unauthorised access to a file. The 'Trojan horse' threat is eliminated and the system is fairly flexible as it determines access policy on a continuous basis.

9.4 INFORMATION FLOW MODELS

Information flow models focus on the actual transfer of information between objects, rather than on the access allowed between objects. This affords a more detailed security program to be implemented as well as eliminating some possible weaknesses in the access matrix approach.

The difference between this and the access matrix approach is that the latter will restrict access to any object with a higher security classification than the subject. Thus, for example, a subject will be prevented from accessing even non-sensitive data if it is contained within the same file as more highly sensitive data. This problem is avoided in information flow models because they operate by restricting the flow of information from one object to another. Therefore, a subject may be allowed access to a file containing sensitive data but may only be allowed to copy non-sensitive data to an object with a lower classification. The security model focuses on the transfer of data rather than the more general concept of access.

It is possible for individual items of data within a file to be protected. Their movement to another file can be prevented without the same protection specifications being applied to the whole of the file. We can see, then, that the information flow approach offers a greater level of precision than many other models.

It has been suggested that access matrix methods, such as those used by the Bell and LaPadula model, could still contain information channels. In the Bell and LaPadula system, for example, this could be done by inserting the channels in the return code provided when a request to apply a rule is denied. However, the information flow approach prevents this because it actually supervises the operations which transfer information between objects.

Denning and Denning, 1979, provide a useful introduction to the concept of information flow models. The model is described in very simple terms with just two classes of information being defined: confidential (C) and non-confidential (N). All flows are allowed except those from class C to class N. This escapes the problem of controlling the flow of sensitive and non-sensitive data contained within a single file. For example, a service program handling customer data may contain confidential information. It may retain some or all of the non-confidential data but must not retain or release to its owner any of the confidential data.

More complex flow controls could be used, for example, in government or military systems. Each security class may be represented by an authority level and a category. These could be represented by (i,x), where 'i' denotes the authority level and 'x' denotes the compartments the data belongs to. If there are m compartments then there will be '2^m' categories, each relating to a possible combination of compartments.

In order for information to be allowed to flow from one security class to another, the receiving object must have the same or an equivalent authority level as the information and must possess all the security compartments of the information. This framework for implementing the information flow model is very similar to the Bell and LaPadula approach. However, the model is less limiting since it is the flow of information from object to object which is being controlled. The emphasis, then, is placed on restricting the flow of highly classified information rather than restricting the flow of any information from an object which contains some highly classified data.

The information flow model can be applied by assigning a security class or clearance to each running program. The program is only allowed to read memory segments with the same or a lower security class and is only allowed to write to segments with the same or a higher security class.

However, this is very difficult to accomplish without encountering the basic limitations of the Bell and LaPadula model. The assignment of a security class would therefore need to be very flexible and complex in order to achieve the full advantages of the information flow approach. One criticism is that overclassification of data will occur and data will only be allowed to flow upwards to segments with a higher classification. This problem is particularly apparent if, before starting its job, the program is given the security class of the highest segment it will access. An alternative approach is to change the security class during the running of the program according to the highest segment it has accessed at that juncture. The model then becomes very similar to the high-water-mark model.

Denning and Denning, 1979, give an example of the limitations arising from the approach described above. A program may handle customer data, some of which is confidential. An income-tax computing service, for instance, might be allowed to retain a customer's address and bill for services rendered (classified as non-confidential), but not the customer's income or deductions (classified as confidential). Using the method described above, the program used to handle the data would have to be classified either as confidential or non-confidential. If classified as confidential, it would be forbidden to write non-confidential data into any of its files; If classified as non-confidential, it would be forbidden to process confidential customer data.

As a result of this limitation, the only way such a program could be run would be to give confidential status to customer information which is normally non-considered non-confidential. Generally, outputs from any program must have a security classification at least equal to inputs. The confidentiality of each output must be as high or higher than the confidentiality of each input.

The problem of overclassification can be reduced either by allowing the manual downgrading of information by an authorised person, or by permitting downward flows through programs which remove information inputs of a higher confidentiality. Such methods are not, as yet, widely developed and may be very difficult to implement.

In order to avoid the overclassification problem, a more complicated approach may be necessary. The system must be capable of analysing the precise relationship between inputs and outputs if information flows are to be monitored effectively. As Denning and Denning observe, this is by no means a simple process. For example, the following statement might be executed whilst the value of 'x' is 1 or 0:

```
IF x=0 THEN y=0 ELSE y=1
```

This statement implicitly copies the value of 'x' to 'y'. Some information is transmitted to 'y' even if the value of 'x' is not 1 or 0. More complex methods than this can be implemented to breach security.

Approaches which attempt to solve this problem include traditional formal verification methods. However, most of these methods are based on static analysis. The program is verified prior to execution, and if the security classification of variables is to alter during execution, then a combination of run-time checking and static analysis is necessary.

9.5 NETWORK SECURITY MODELS

Most of the models described in the previous sections can be applied to network systems. However, some researchers have designed models specifically for application to networks, either because a separate treatment has been considered necessary, or in order to exploit the opportunities for security implementation that distributed systems provide.

By their nature, distributed systems provide the opportunity to separate data from certain system users. For example, a workstation could be separated from a local area network by trusted software or hardware devices which limit access to authorised system users. If physical or logical access to the actual workstation can be controlled in addition to control of access through the network, then a secure system can be achieved.

Rushby and Randall - A Distributed Secure System

Rushby and Randall, 1983 [Rush83], have designed a model which uses a distributed system to enforce security. Their paper outlines the problems of the controlled sharing of secret information, mentioning the multi-level security policy employed in military and government environments. It points out that conventional computer systems are incapable of enforcing these policies and that they are vulnerable to outside penetration and to the 'Trojan horse' attack.

Some crude approaches for solving this problem are described. These include 'period processing' (in which a single system is dedicated to particular security partitions at different times, and is cleared of all information belonging to one partition before it is allocated to a different one), and the 'system high' (which requires all users to be cleared to the level of the most highly classified information that the system contains). The necessity for verification and the problem of performance degradation are also mentioned.

Rushby and Randall then go on to give a detailed description of a security system which they developed on a distributed system called UNIX united. They argue that their approach solves or reduces most of the problems mentioned above. They also claim that the system is secure, efficient, cost effective and convenient to use.

The aim is to build a distributed secure system rather than a secure operating system. It involves inter-connecting small, specialised, demonstrably trustworthy systems and a number of larger, untrustworthy host machines. The trustworthy machines mediate access to and communications between the untrusted hosts. The latter each provide services to a single security partition and continue to run at full speed. The trustworthy machines also provide other security-related services such as a means of changing the security partition to which a given host belongs.

The main advantages of the system are that the untrusted machines can be used without the constraint of security mechanisms which may cause performance degradation, while the trusted machines are used purely for security purposes, thus making verification simpler as well as performance, cost and ease-of-use more attractive. The system uses four different separation mechanisms:

- physical
- temporal
- logical
- cryptographic.

Physical separation is achieved by allocating physically different resources to each security partition and function. Trustworthy monitors are required to control communications between the distributed components. Temporal separation allows the untrusted host machines to be used for activities in different security partitions by separating those activities in time. Logical separation of functions is achieved by means of a separation kernel. Cryptographical separation uses encryption and related techniques to separate different uses of shared communications and storage media.

Wood and Barnes - A Practical Distributed Secure System

Wood and Barnes, 1985, apply the Rushby and Randall approach in their 'Practical Distributed Secure System'. Both had contributed to the Distributed Secure Systems project for the Networks Division of the Royal Signals and Radar Establishment, MoD.

The system is divided into security compartments with data being partitioned into disjointed sets, one for each security compartment. Access to this data is controlled by trusted hardware and software which implement a clearly prescribed security policy. The basis for this system rests on first achieving sufficient separation between security compartments and then adding a trusted controlled sharing mechanism to implement the security policy. Isolation is accomplished by using the methods laid down by Rushby and Randall - physical, logical, temporal and cryptographic separation.

By applying these, Wood and Barnes argue that only relatively small amounts of trusted hardware and software need to be used. They describe an implementation based on a conventional local area network system, connecting single-user intelligent workstations and a variety of servers. A trusted hardware device, which can be relied on to enforce the necessary security policy, is interposed between each end-system. This is known as a Trustworthy Network Interface Unit (TNIU).

Each end-system is assigned to one or more security compartments, and this association is stored in the associated TNIU. The TNIU is then used to ensure that data can be transferred between end-systems sharing a common security compartment. This is achieved by identifying the security compartment of all data flowing on to the network. Data is only passed from the network to an end-system if its identity corresponds to the security compartments allocated to the end-system. Usually the TNIU will also encrypt and decrypt data flowing through the LAN, and in this instance the security label operates as an identifier for the crypto key to be used.

For an end-system allocated to a single security compartment, the TNIU ensures that only data in this security compartment can enter or leave. In consequence, it is not necessary for the software in a single-level end-system to be trusted.

Flexibility is obtained through an Access Control Centre (ACC). This is a trusted system component which offers greater facilities for enforcing a security policy than TNIU. It is, in effect, the master trusted unit of the system. The ACC has several purposes. For example, a user at a single level workstation can log into a particular security compartment by presenting his name, password and desired security compartment to the ACC via the workstation TNIU. Additionally, the ACC can record an audit trail of security-relevant system activity, and provide a terminal for the system security officer to carry out tasks such as examining the audit trail, maintaining a list of valid users and controlling crypto-key management.

Jones - A Secure Distributed Machine as a Formal Object in Design

Jones, 1985 [Jones85], presents a network security model and uses an example from the banking world to illustrate it. He defines one of the major goals of the data processing industry as being "able to use a network to implement several systems which are completely separate and sufficiently secure from their users' point of view". Furthermore, he states "it must be possible to introduce a new system and to modify or remove an existing one easily, interfering with other users only to the extent that they may see some acceptable change in performance".

In order to achieve this, Jones suggests that we should identify logical objects in terms of which systems may be designed and built. He describes such a logical object as a "generalisation of a machine". Jones applied the model to an example from the banking world (see Figure 9.4). Area A1 is seen by the customers A and B. This is the automated teller machine. Area A2 is seen by the manager and used to authorise payments, record transactions and send transactions to another location, A3. Area A3 is the location where information is kept for the general manger. The arrows flowing from 'x' to 'y' mean that 'x' has the authority to use 'y'.

The security requirements are given as:

- Decomposition into resources: access control requirements are made explicit by describing the system in terms of resources and showing their authorisation to connect to each other
- Data Privacy and Integrity
- Authentication
- Constraining users' actions
- Resource sharing
- Creation of resources at an end-system: if A2 is installed as a general purpose computing system, the resources, such as 'customer authentication', must be created securely from the basic resources of the system. The same is true for A3
- Supply of resources between end-systems: A mechanism is needed to allow, for example, 'General Manager's reports' to be used by 'General Manager's service', 'Manager's customer service' and 'account handler'.

Jones suggests that the requirements be satisfied by means of the security mechanisms summarised below:

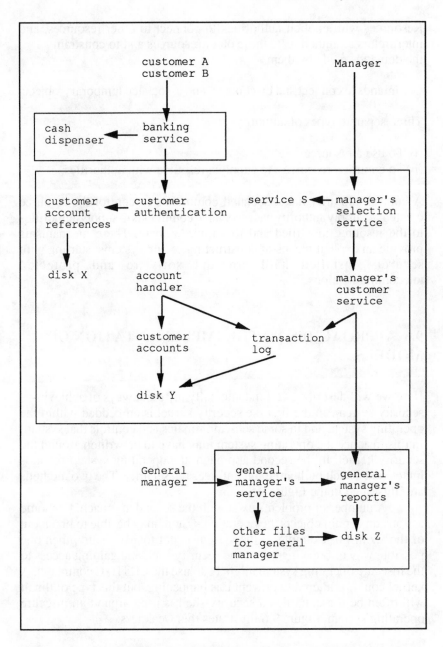

Figure 9.4 A Secure Networked Banking System (Jones, 1985)

Resources with explicit authorities to connect to other resources, and interpreters to authenticate these other resources and to constrain the demands made by them

Commands to connect and disconnect, and associated temporary objects

Three separate types of authority:

(i) To use a resource
(ii) To control a resource - to supply a resource with authorities.

A control authority has associated commands to control the resource created. A supply authority has associated commands to supply authorities to the resource identified and to withdraw them. These mechanisms provide an explicit means of constructing secure systems, starting with securely installed hardware and software and protected telecommunications.

9.6 APPROACHES TO THE IMPLEMENTATION OF MODELS

Here we will describe two fundamentally different ways of achieving a security system. In the first the security kernel is embedded within the operating system and in some sense dominates and controls that system. In this instance the operating system may have to be written around the security kernel. In the second approach, the operating system remains intact, and a shell built around it enforces the security. The two methods are illustrated in the Figure 9.5.

A number of problems exist with the second approach. For some actions on certain objects the operating system may be able to break out of the shell. For example, if the system is not totally secure, then one possible way of breaking out of the security shell and gaining access to the insecure operating system might be to use the CRTL+C command. A kernel could be altered to prevent this happening, but this type of threat will often be present when a security shell is used around an insecure operating system. Figure 9.6 illustrates this weakness.

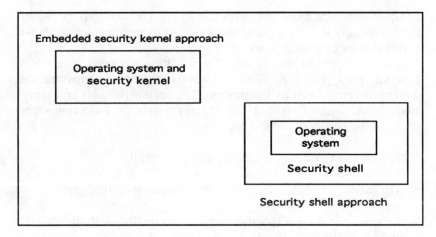

Figure 9.5 Embedded security kernel approach

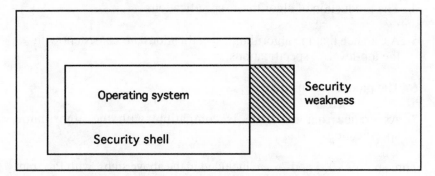

Figure 9.6 Security shell method including possible weaknesses

9.7 VERIFICATION

When a secure system is implemented, both designers and users must be confident of three things:

- that it fulfills its specifications
- that it does what it is meant to and no more
- that it has not been tampered with in any way.

Verification, then, is an important and integral part of secure system modelling. It implies that software must be measured against the properties and qualities stated by its formal specifications. The code must be proved to be consistent with its specifications. The software must also be shown to do no more than what is specified.

The development and object of verification has been covered by Bonyun, 1984 [BONY84], who addresses current problems and the directions being taken by the process. The review includes an excerpt from the Anderson Report, 1972, which presents the following seven steps for the design of a reference monitor:

1   The creation of a mathematical model of security

2   The production of top-level (non-procedural) specifications

3   Assurance that these specifications are compatible with the model and hence the security policy

4   The production of algorithmic specifications

5   Assurance that the algorithmic specifications are consistent with the top-level   specifications

6   The production of code

7   Assurance that the code is compatible with the algorithmic specifications.

Three proofs - 3, 5 and 7 - are included in the above steps, with Program verification referring to 3, 5 and probably 7 as well. It is essential to be able to verify that the reference monitor does exactly what it is intended to do.

Bonyun, 1984, identifies three advances in the technological world which have changed the nature of the verification problem:

1   The increasing use of microcomputers and the growth of micro-technology which is now impinging on all aspects of our daily lives.

2   The twin realisation that, on certain occasions, the basic rules of security need to be broken, and that mechanisms should exist to permit necessary violations to occur in a controlled manner.

3   A more thorough understanding of the character, role and problems of the languages which are used to express requirements, formal specifications and high level code.

Verification that a formal specification obeys a security model can be complex and difficult to achieve. If it can be demonstrated that the design implements the requirements stipulated by the model, then the aims should have been accomplished. However, this is not a simple matter. One difficulty is that automated verification of the security properties of large amounts of source code is, at present, beyond the state-of-the-art.

Ames et al, 1983, note some of the current problems with verification. They state that:

> "Formal verification of a kernel involves problems of program correctness, and we are still quite a long way from being able to prove the correctness of a large computer program. Because formal verification technology has not fully matured, we need to understand its current capabilities before defining requirements for a major kernel development. Unrealistic expectations for verification can turn a practical development effort, fully within the bounds of current technology, into a research effort that could consume unlimited resources"

It should therefore be appreciated that difficulties in verification may be a serious handicap in system design. The limitations in this area should be borne in mind, because they may inhibit the practical development of security proposals. Nonetheless, Ames *et al*, 1983, note that traditional techniques such as structured design and testing can improve confidence in a system.

Furthermore, Bonyun, 1984, highlights an on-going problem in the field of verification which arises from the nature of the subject, *viz.* verification systems take so long to develop and implement that the job concurrently being worked on becomes outdated.

9.8 CONCLUSION

Within a single-user workstation context, the operating system is important in that it controls all the activities of the user, including those associated with data storage and integrity. The security models developed to date concentrate on the operating system as the key element in the provision of control and countermeasures that enable a security system to function.

Three basic approaches exist: access matrix models, high-water-mark models and information flow models. Access matrix models define a set of subjects which can manipulate objects. In practice, this is usually defined by a matrix which contains the information giving the access rights and privileges which each subject has to each object.

High-water-mark models reflect the importance of the data (or objects); the so-called high-water-mark indicating the highest level of data sensitivity that the object can contain. No subsequent provision is made for the security classification of the object or for data to be changed (downwards).

Information flow models focus on the transfer of data and divide objects (e.g files) into finer granularity than the access control matrix. Hence a subject that is granted access to a file containing data may be only allowed to copy non-sensitive information.

Of these models, it appears that the access matrix one has the greatest theoretical value. By extending it, allowing it to be modified over time and making the objects finer and responsive to an event (i.e. an information flow), the access control model is suitable for analysing the inherent qualities and properties of the other, more complex models. There is a further reason for closely examining the role of the access matrix model. The U S Department of Defence Computer Security Evaluation Centre has developed criteria (known as the 'Orange Book') for evaluating the suitability of computer hardware/software systems for processing classified information.

Most of the major operating systems with high DoD security classifications (for example SCOMP) are based on a modified Bell LaPadula approach to the access control matrix. If these models can meet the highest means of classifying an operating system, there is no reason why the same principles should not apply to the more basic workstation.

However, it is likely that many of the models discussed have too stringent security protection for the commercial workstation environment. They have been designed for the purposes of military security, and clearly there are important differences between military and civil applications. The requirements for military security will almost always be greater than those for civilian security.

The security needs of commercial workstations are more flexible than military needs. An example of this can be seen by looking at the high-water-mark model. There is no provision in the model for the security classification of an object to be changed downwards and a consequent process of overclassification may occur. In an office workstation this can lead to an undesirable situation where it becomes unnecessarily difficult to use the system properly. Downward classification then becomes desirable. In the military situation, downward classification to facilitate more efficient use would not be considered.

One of the consequences of the military nature of the models is that the trade-off between user requirements and constraints is not considered. There is virtually no constraint when considering essential military security, whereas in the commercial situation, where profit is an important goal, the cost of installing and running a security system must be compared with the benefits derived from the improved security. Other constraints such as user-friendliness, ease of use, response time etc., important in the commercial environment, are not considered in the design of of military security models.

Another drawback with the models is that they are fairly old and therefore do not fully take into account current technology and requirements. For example, the Bell and LaPadula and high-water-mark models date back to the early 1970s. Modifications to existing models thus seems necessary before they can be successfully applied to office workstations. However, the basic principles may remain the same. For example, the access matrix approach, perhaps with a little modification, seems appropriate for application to an office workstation.

Network security is another area in which many of the existing models fail to fulfil the requirements of an office workstation. As yet, the models have not been sufficiently developed to be applied to networked workstations.

Implementation of the models has probably been achieved most satisfactorily by using the approach of restructuring the operating system to include the security kernel. If security is implemented as a shell, the possibility remains that an intruder could break through the shell and interact directly with the unprotected operating system.

If the model is to be implemented in a shell, then the most desirable system will probably include full emulation of the operating system. If this is achieved, then the user is given the impression that he is interacting directly with the operating system, with the shell becoming invisible. An invisible shell is harder to detect and thus harder to break through.

10

Communications Security Model (MoSel)

10.1 INTRODUCTION

In Phase 2 of the MARS Project, models were designed by the consortium for communications security and for workstation security. This chapter describes the communications security model, MoSel (MOdel for Security devELopment).

The MoSel model provides both a systematic approach to security design and testing and a medium for expressing the results of that activity. It is an approach which is more abstract and is therefore not to everyone's taste. A process model provides the essential methodological framework for security design and a product model guides the activity of designing and testing security aspects of communications systems. It is based on an analogy with the model for software development presented by Ould and Unwin (1986). Therefore, design of security aspects of a communications system is treated like development of a software design specification. Threats are related by analogy with tests of a software design, and vulnerabilities are treated like design faults. The product model provides a medium for developing a security design from security requirements. A security design describes the various factors which influence security of communications systems, and the control and organisation of those factors in order to meet security requirements. It takes the temporal evolution of those factors into account.

10.2 THE PROCESS MODEL

The process model for security development provides a definition of personnel roles and a methodological framework based on an analogy with software systems development. It thus provides guidance to those people who are responsible for security design and testing. The analogy which is drawn between security development and software development represents a new understanding of the relationships between the concepts of security requirements, threats, countermeasures and systems design.

If the development of a security system is analagous to the development of a computer system then the same development steps can be applied to both. The analogy can be used to produce a listing of the activities performed during general computer system development, and derive the corresponding activities for security development. This is summarised in Table 10.1.

If a threat successfully penetrates the security of the system, the implementation, design or requirements of the system must be reviewed and a flaw corrected or the design changed. This is analogous to a successful test which detects a defect in a system which must then be debugged. Moreover, successful threats result in loss, as do system failures due to bugs. Potential losses, or vulnerabilities, are thus analogous to bugs in a system and can be classified as such.

Table 10.1 Analagous activities in software engineering and security development.

SOFTWARE ENGINEERING	SECURITY DEVELOPMENT
Requirements analysis during which real world concepts are transformed and expressed in terms used in the computer industry.	Analysis of security requirements, the functional, financial and technical constraints to which the requirements are subject and specification of security policy.
Specification of the system to produce a formal or informal design specification of the functions which the system will provide.	Specification of a security design from the requirements, etc. identified above.
Validation of the design specification with respect to the requirements through the performance of tests which reveal defects.	Testing of the specification of the design with respect to the requirements.
Coding of the software system	Implementation of the security design which includes development of encryption algorithms, secure operating systems, physical and logical access systems etc.
Verification of the coded software system with respect to the design specification.	Verification of the implementation with respect to the specification through tests.
Installation and acceptance testing.	Installation and user acceptance testing of the security system
Operational management and maintanance.	Operational security management and improvement.

The security threats aspect of the analogy can be summarised as follows:

- Threats = Tests
- Vulnerability = Bug
- Loss = Consequence of successful test

The interaction between threats can now be treated by considering combinations of tests to the system. Future research on the process model will, in part, be directed towards the establishment of systematic methods for investigating threats and their interactions by analogy with established software testing methods. Tests may, for example, be performed first on the smallest independent part of a system. Tests would then continue on combinations of these and their interfaces. These tests would be followed by tests of system integration and then of system validation. Systematic testing follows a test plan, and systematic investigation of threats should follow a similar plan.

10.3 THE PRODUCT MODEL.

The result of designing and testing the security aspects of a communications system is called a security design. A security design should:

- respond to stated requirements for security and privacy in a communications system. The design must indicate how various factors should be organised and controlled in order to ensure that those stated requirements are satisfied

- adequately describe *all* the relevant aspects of the system influencing security. That is, it must be complete

- anticipate any changes which may occur in the communication system

- be testable in order to decide whether or not the communications system it describes meets its stated security requirements. Alternative security designs may also be compared with respect to given security requirements

- be communicable to systems designers, in order to establish the compatability of the security aspects of the communications system with other design characteristics of the system

- be communicable to managers responsible for implementing the policies and recommendations it contains

• describe the organisation and control of various factors which influence the security and privacy of a communications system.

Overview of the Product Model

The product model of communication system security is based on three features:

Elements:	the components of a security design
Topology:	the arrangement and structuring of elements
Power structure:	the relationship between elements

Elements

Each element is characterised by its:

Name:	identifies the element, and enables recognition of the element by other elements.
Data:	which is accessible only to the element itself, and data which is accessible to other elements. This characteristic data may be used when constraints are being put upon the possible actions of elements. It is also used in defining desirable states of the element, for example it may be required that a piece of the element's characteristic data remain constant over the lifetime of the element.
Functions:	define all the activities which an element can perform. Distinct functions should, as far as possible, be independent. Activities within a single function should be dependent in some sense. Functions should be of interest in themselves. If there are functions carried out by the element which are not of interest then these may be modelled as a part of the control.
Control:	defines whether and when functions are called. The control may be thought of as a constantly active function

of the element, similar to the concept of a demon in artificial intelligence terminology. The control carries out actions and calls functions in response to data received.

Message buffer: A sequence of data which has either been received or sent by the element. In general, the control part of the element may alter the message buffer. This will be used so that the element can be made to selectively remember or forget parts of his history. For example, a workstation may remember only the identity of its current user.

Class: defines the position of a particular element in relation to other elements. This information is used to abstract some of the properties of the characteristics of the element at the time for detailed modelling of an element. For example, a user who is a security manager has both the special security priviledges of the class to which he/she belongs and that of the wider class of ordinary user.

Topology

An element may send data to other elements and receive data from other elements. Permitted movement of data between elements is defined in terms of the topology of a security design. The data which moves through such a topology we call inter-element data as opposed to the data within an element. We are interested in two types of topology, link and path topology. Link topology is limited to the connections between two elements. The combination of single links form the paths which define the path topology. These paths through the graph are called data flow paths and can be classified as either physically possible or impossible and either legal or illegal. This will depend on the legality and possiblity of all intervening links. A path between two elements is physically possible if the element at the start of the path can send data along the path to the element at the end of the path without alteration of the functionality, control, or characteristic data of any element in the path. Such modifications may cause a previously impossible path to become possible. A data flow path is legal if there is at least one item of data which may be sent along the path without contravening any of the system requirements.

In a security design, **lp, ilp, lip and ilip** define the status of a path as follows:

lp   legal   possible
ilp   illegal possible

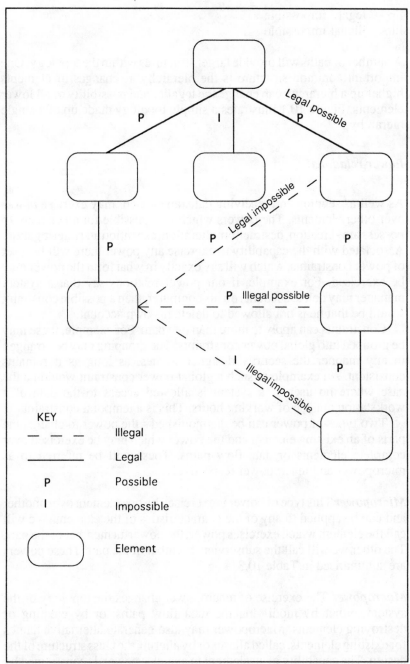

Figure 10.1 Example of a simple topology based on a single hierarchy

lip   legal   impossible
ilip   illegal   impossible

A number of paths will provide larger structures within the topology. One important common structure is the hierarchy as changes of elements higher up a hierarchy can change the legality and possibility of all lower elements. Figure 10.1 illustrates a simple topology made up of a single hierarchy .

Power relations

As well as sending and receiving data, an element may exercise *power* over other elements. The powers which it is possible for an element to possess are - creation, destruction, alteration, execution and interrogation. Associated with the capability to exercise any power there will be a set of power constraints, which will say exactly in what form the power may be exercised. For example, if our power relations say that a system manager may delete accounts on his computer, then a possible constraint would be that he is not allowed to delete his own account.

Constraints can apply to more than one path. For example, these may be grouped into global power constraints. The grouping may be arranged in any manner the security designer wishes, as long as it remains consistent. An example of such a global power constraint would be the case where no user of a system is allowed access to the data of a workstation outside of working hours. This is a temporal constraint.

Two types of power can be distinquished - the power to change the parts of an existing element and the power which may be exercised over complete elements or data flow paths. These will be referred to as micropower and macropower respectively.

Micropower This type of power is exercised by one element over another and can be applied to any of the characteristics of the element. We will call the element which exercises power, the powerful member of the pair. The other we will call the subservient member of the pair. These powers are summarised in Table 10.3.

Macropower The exercise of macropower changes the topology of the system, either by modifying the data flow paths, or by creating or destroying elements. Macropower may also generate alternative names for existing elements, called aliases or by altering the class structure of the design. The capability of an element to exercise power is constrained by the security designer. This implies that an element with the power to create new elements may create an element more powerful than itself unless the constraints explicitly prevent it from doing so.

We can further subdivide macropower into its exercise over elements (including the class structure) and its exercise over paths. If an element has macropower over elements then the possible powers are creation and deletion of elements, creation of aliases for elements and the alteration of the element class structure.

When the power of creation is exercised, the parts of the element must be specified, including its membership (if any) of a class. The additions to the path topology of the design must also be specified as must the legality of new paths. This is done in the same manner as before. Once the topology is up to date the powers which may be exercised along the new parts of the topology must also be specified.

Table 10.2 Summary of micropower applicability.

	Interrogate	Alter	Execute	Create	Destroy
Name	•	•			
MessageBuffer	•	•			
Data	•	•			
Function	•	•	•	•	•
Control	•	•			•
Class	•				

Creation of an alias for an element means giving it a new name by which other elements can recognise it. A legitimate use of this power is in the provision of alternative user identities for a computer operator, who also has a regular user account on a computer-based communications system. An unlawful application of this kind of power is the misappropriation of the operator's name by a user who is not entitled to use it.

Given that an element may lie in any position along many paths deletion needs careful consideration. For example, we would insist that any parts of the element classes, topology and power structure which refer to the deleted element must be re-specified from scratch.

Alteration of the element class structure may be regarded as a combination of creations and deletions of elements. For example, moving the element Fred from the class of System-Users, to the class of Non-System-Users can be modelled as deletion of Fred, followed by creation of a new Fred in the second class. When doing this the same procedures must be followed as if the powers of deletion and creation were exercised separately.

We feel that the presence of many elements with macropower is, in general, a bad feature of a security design. This is because such powers implicitly allow an element to influence the whole design, from which may be inferred a lack of control in the design as a whole - another bad feature. Macropowers in general are less well-defined than other parts of our product model. Conceptually they are simple to understand and even specify but the control of such wide-ranging powers to modify a design is difficult.

If an element has macropower exercised over paths, then those paths may be altered or interrogated.

The power to alter a path is the power to change the elements or the sequence of elements in the path. With each alteration a new status must be given. So we see that the power of creation/destruction is just a special case of the power of alteration. An example of a path, say (computer, modem, line, modem, computer) being altered would be a modem line being cut, which would involve alteration of the status of the (modem,line) and (line,modem) links from legal and possible to legal but impossible.

Alteration of a path means, in effect, specification of a new sequence of elements which will form the new path, along with all necessary constraints. The constraints necessary include the possibility constraints associated with link along the path and the legality constraints associated both with the links and the path as a whole.

Exercise of the power of interrogation over a path produces the sequence of elements along that path together with the legality and possibility constraints on that path.

Requirements

We divided the requirements of a system design into security requirements and functional requirements. Any requirement which impinges on security must be included in the set of security requirements. All others are in the set of functional requirements. This division is the responsibility of the security manager and is carried out in order to focus attention on the security aspects of the system. During the security design and testing process we can then regard the functional requirements as "axioms" in our design. In other words, we assume that the final system satisfies the functional requirements. Once this division has been accomplished, the design and testing process begins.

CONCLUSION

The Security Model for Communications Networks is primarily intended for use during the design and testing of security aspects of a communications system. To fulfil that aim, the model has been structured as a process model which is concerned with security design and testing methods, and a product model, which provides a means of expressing the results of that design effort. The basic relation between the components of the security model is that the process model describes the process which produces an instance of the product model.

11

Guidelines for Workstation Security

11.1 INTRODUCTION

As part of the second phase of the MARS project, the Computer Industry Research Unit (CIRU) produced a model for workstation security. This model was then further developed into a set of guidelines. These guidelines are considered to be one of the most important results of the project and has already formed the basis for further work in this area.

The approach taken is to present the system designer with a list of specific security countermeasures, determined on the basis of the requirements of the particular workstation in question. The object is to provide a reference which will allow the workstation to be secured, to whatever level is required, against all likely threats. This involves the use of both physical and logical countermeasures to protect the computer itself and, necessarily, the environment within which it is situated. An example is given, based on a banking scenario.

The Workstation Security Guidelines draw strongly upon the United States Department of Defense (US DoD) 'Trusted Computer System Evaluation Criteria' [DoD 83], popularly known as the 'Orange Book' (This is discussed in detail in Appendix B), and also in the US DoD 'Trusted Network Evaluation Criteria' [DoD 85a]. The concepts used by the DoD have been adapted in order to make them applicable to the office environment.

Other countries, mostly European, also have significant experience in IT security evaluation and have developed their own security criteria, In the UK this includes CESG Memorandum number 3, developed for government use, and proposals of the Department of Trade and Industry, the "Green Book", for commercial IT security products. In Germany, the German Information Security Agency published a first version of its own criteria in 1989, and at the same time criteria were being developed in France, the so-called "Blue-White-Red Book". France, Germany, the Netherlands and the United Kingdom decided to build on the various national initiatives, taking the best features of what had already been done and putting them in a consistent, structured perspective. The output from this was called ITSEC and was organised by the European Commission's DGXIII. As such it used many of the concepts first developed in MARS.

The workstation guidelines produced here have a wider scope than the DoD criteria in two respects. Firstly, the working environment as well as the system itself is considered in detail and, secondly, practical countermeasures are listed for achieving security at the level which is required.

Eight levels of security are defined, ranging from 0 ('No security') to 7 ('Ultra Secure'). The workstation under consideration will have a requirement for security which falls under one of the levels 0 to 7. Seven components of the workstation are defined. For each workstation component and for each level of security, a list of recommended countermeasures is given. These lists are contained in the matrices presented in Section 11.4, Step 3, below. In Appendix B, a procedure is given for testing a workstation in order to ensure that the desired level of security has been achieved.

Section 11.4, Steps 1 and 2, are concerned with the methodology for determining what level of security is required on a workstation. The basis for this process is to determine what is the *maximum level of sensitivity of activities performed on the workstation* and what is the *minimum security clearance of the least privileged user(s) of the workstation*. It is also necessary to distinguish between *'open'* and *'closed'* systems (see Section 11.4, Step 2).

11.2 DEFINITION OF A WORKSTATION AND ITS COMPONENTS

The workstation is defined as the computer, usually a PC or mini, including all physical and logical components contained within the working environment. The guidelines focus on the protection of the workstation components including the physical environment in which the workstation is kept. This includes cabling within the office but the cut-off point comes at the boundary between the workstation and the local or wide area network i.e. at the encryption box or modem.

The security of communications is not considered as the guidelines are restricted in scope to the workstation itself. Therefore, although the guidelines presented here can be applied to workstations which reside on a network, they do not cover the security of communications between these machines. This section of the report is, thus, based on the definition of a workstation illustrated in Figure 11.1.

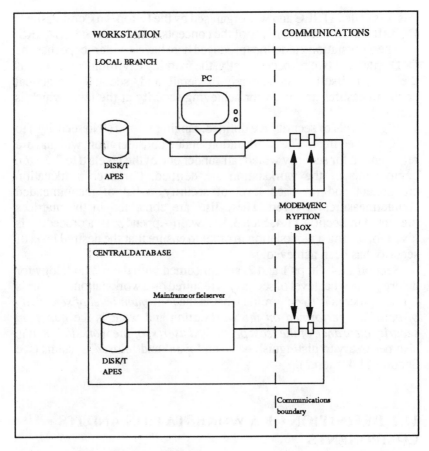

Figure 11.1 Definition of a workstation

In general, we have found that any workstation consists of the set of seven generic components defined in the following sections. It is on this set of components that we base the workstation security guidelines. The countermeasures are presented in Section 11.4, Step 3, under the component headings introduced below. The guidelines specify the type of countermeasure required. The actual implementation of these countermeasures is not covered in any detail as this is dependent on the specific configuration of the workstation under consideration.

The distinction between tangible and intangible components

The workstation components are divided into two categories - tangible components, which include the computer box, physical storage devices and cabling, and intangible components, which include memory contents, operating system, user account, and logical storage media. A tangible component is one which is physical or is vulnerable to physical attack. It is only accessible physically. An intangible component is one which is a logical entity and is not, in itself, vulnerable to physical attack. It is only accessible logically.

Tangible components are used to contain or to support intangible components. Physical protection of tangible components is necessary in addition to the logical protection of intangible components. Tangible components are more vulnerable to attack from unauthorised users since access to the environment, rather than access to the system itself, would be sufficient to allow an attack to take place. If tangible components can be secured against attack or access from unauthorised users, then, implicitly, unauthorised users cannot gain access to the system (other than from a remote device). For these reasons, a higher level of security may be required for tangible components than that required for intangible components.

The US Department of Defense 'Trusted computer system evaluation criteria', on which these guidelines are partly based, states that the lower the discrepancy between the maximum sensitivity level of data on a system and the minimum clearance of any user of the system, the lower is the level of security required (this discrepancy is referred to as the 'risk index'). The rationale behind this is that the threat of lower level users (ie users who have a lower security clearance) gaining access to highly sensitive information is more serious than any other.

This would mean that if a system contained highly sensitive data, but only high clearance users were allowed access, then the security required on the system would not be high. However, the need to restrict access to authorised users only would be extremely high. In order to account for this, the distinction between tangible components and intangible components is important.

Tangible components are vulnerable to physical attack by unauthorised users. If they can be secured, then intangible components do not face this threat. Clearly, if the minimum user clearance and maximum sensitivity level of data were both very high, then the level of security required for intangible components would be quite low, but the level of security required for tangible components would be extremely high.

Tangible Components

The three tangible components, computer box, physical storage devices and cabling are now introduced.

Computer box

We define the computer box as the actual physical components of the computer itself. This includes the computer casing and its contents - processors, memory boards, video screen etc. It does not include the physical storage devices such as disks or tapes, which are dealt with separately. Security of the computer box does not include logical protection of the data it supports. This is considered under intangible components. The primary means of protection is to prevent unauthorised persons from accessing the environment within which the computer is held. Security of the computer box may include protection against the emmittance of intelligible electro-magnetic radiation.

Physical Storage Devices

This includes any physical media for storing data, both within and peripheral to the workstation. For example, hard disks, removable hard disks, EO CD drives, diskettes, tape backup etc.

Cabling

Although communications security is outside the scope of this section, cabling between the computer box and peripheral devices such as printers, plotters, tape streamers etc. must be considered.

Intangible Components

The four intangible components - memory contents, operating system, user profile and logical storage media are now introduced.

Memory contents

Memory contents refers to the electronic storage of the operating system and all files, records, applications etc, whilst the computer is in use. This requires security separate from that given to the operating system and to the logical storage media. For example, once a protected file has been loaded into memory by one user, it may be possible for a second user to read it by interrogating memory directly.

Operating System

The operating system is an intangible component which, when in use, is stored in memory. The objective in securing the operating system is to prevent free access through this to sensitive files and applications.

User Profile or Account

The user profile or account is probably the most important component to protect because should unauthorised access be gained to the account of a high privilege user, all other protection measures become ineffective (other than post-event measures such as access logs and audit trails or special security measures such as passwords on individual files), as free access to many important files, applications and devices is then possible.

Logical Storage Media

Logical storage media refers to devices, directories and to files which hold data, applications, etc. These are intangible in that they exist only electronically or magnetically and might not be held in one single physical location. Logical storage media are protected to the extent that they are accessed through the operating system and through individual user accounts but may need additional security.

(Note: Applications programs are protected by the countermeasures which secure intangible components. Logical access is controlled through the user account and operating system and additionally through countermeasures protecting logical storage media and memory contents.)

11.3 GUIDE TO WORKSTATION SECURITY LEVELS

The security needs of the workstation can be expressed in terms of a classification of eight different 'Workstation Security Levels' developed by CIRU and related to the US DoD criteria for secure operating systems.

The eight levels are presented in Table 11.1 and are reconciled with the DoD criteria and with newer ITSEC criteria.

Table 11.1 Workstation security levels reconciled with DoD criteria

WORKSTATION SECURITY LEVEL		EUROPEAN COMMISSION'S ITSEC		DoD CRITERIA	
Level	Description	Functional class	Evaluation criteria	Class	Description
0	No Security				
1	Minimal Security	-	E0	D1	Minimal Protection
2	Basic Security	-	E0	D1	Minimal Protection
3	Discretionary Security	F-C1	E1	C1	Discretionary Access Control
4	Limited Controlled Security	-	-	C2	Weak Mandatory Access Control
5	Controlled Security	F-C2	E2	C2	Strong Mandatory Access Control
6	Highly secure	F-B1	E3	B1	Labelled Security Protection
		F-B2	E4	B2+	
7	Ultra Secure	F-B3	E5	B2+	Structured Protection with Security Domains
	Ultra Secure	F-B3	E6	A1	Plus Verified Design

In Table 11.1, there are the security levels as defined by the MARS consortium, the European' Commission's ITSEC (Information Technology Security Evaluation Criteria) as published in June 1991 and the DoD Orange Book on Trusted Computer System Evaluation Criteria (or TCSEC!) The functional loss lists the types of facilities required by the system whilst evaluation criteria defines a list of requirements that need to be met by the developers of the system.

We will concentrate on the security levels worked out by the MARS project before going on to bring the reader up-to-date with ITSEC.

As such the security levels deal more with physical security of a one-off machine which is very often the case when dealing with workstations.

A brief guide is now given to what each workstation security level is based on.

Workstation security *level 0* has the lowest possible level of security.

This lacks basic consistency checks and is unlikely to be used in the commercial world as faults are difficult to repair.

Security *level 1* would apply to a system with basic operational detection providing some integrity. This would apply to, for example, a standalone PC with DOS Version 2 or 3. Activities performed would probably include wordprocessing, small applications, spreadsheets etc. dealing with non-confidential data. More highly sensitive data may be processed if only high clearance users are allowed access.

A *level 2* system would provide the ability for simple file protection. This would probably require some extra effort as security would not be provided automatically. An example of this would be a PC with DOS Version 3.1 or higher, and with some additional utilities such as Norton Utilities and simple security packages.

Level 3 is the minimum level of security which a multi-user machine would normally require, in order to ensure a basic level of data integrity and separation of users. At this level, provision would be made for discretionary (need to know) protection. Named users and objects would be distinguished. Through the introduction of simple audit capabilities, accountability of subjects and the actions they initiate would be provided for.

Greater control must be provided at *level 4*. VMS Version 3 might, for example, be used at this level. Discretionary access control would have a higher degree of granularity. Users would be made individually accountable for their actions through more stringent login and auditing procedures.

At *level 5* the operating system would be, for example, VMS Version 4 and would have an added security shell. At this level the system automatically provides all protection rather than placing initiative on the users. A great amount of effort would be required to compromise security. [Fileservers or LANs such as Novell could fall into this category]. More monitoring facilities would be available at level 5.

An example of an operating system which may be used at *level 6* is SE-VMS (with a security shell). The trusted computing base must preserve the integrity of sensitivity labels so as not to allow the downward migration of sensitive data. Evidence must be provided to demonstrate that the reference monitor concept has been implemented.

Security at *level 7* would rarely be necessary in an office system. This type of security would be similar to that used in certain military systems and would be theoretically unbreakable. It may be demanded in exceptional circumstances for extremely confidential banking activities.

11.4 METHODOLOGY

This chapter contains a methodology for determining the level of security required for a particular system, and for applying that level to the component-countermeasure matrices in Step 3 below, which contain suggested countermeasures for the level of security required. A banking example is used but a similar approach can be applied to other types of organisation.

The methodology is divided into three distinct steps. Step 1 involves assigning a level to the maximum sensitivity of any activity on the system and to the minimum clearance of any user of the system. In Step 2, the maximum sensitivity level and minimum user clearance level assigned in Step 1 are used to determine the required 'workstation security level' for tangible and for intangible components (a further consideration for intangible components is whether the system is an 'open' or a 'closed' system). In Step 3, the workstation security level derived in Step 2 is used to determine which countermeasures should be used on the system.

Step 1 - Maximum sensitivity and minimum user clearance levels

In order to be able to determine the level of security required by the workstation, the user must first assign a maximum sensitivity level and a minimum user clearance level to the system in question.

Table 11.2 Sensitivity/user clearance levels

CLEARANCE/SENSITIVITY	DESCRIPTION
U	Unrestricted
R	Restricted
C	Confidential
S	Secret
TS	Top Secret

As explained in more detail below, the maximum sensitivity level is the sensitivity level of the particular system activity which demands the highest security, and the minimum user clearance level is the clearance level of the least privileged user.

Both the maximum sensitivity level and the minimum user clearance are expressed using the same scale as presented in Table 11.2. The meanings of the different levels are examined in the following two sections.

The assignment of a maximum sensitivity level and a minimum user clearance level is now considered in more detail, with reference to an example from the banking world.

Maximum Sensitivity Level

The maximum sensitivity level is the sensitivity level of the system activity which demands the highest security. Each of the five levels is now explained in more detail:

Unrestricted (U) applies to activities involving data which is not sensitive or classified, for example publicly releasable information within a computer system. (Such data might still require discretionary access controls to protect it from accidental destruction.)

Restricted (R) applies to activities, usually of a routine and non strategic nature, which have a definite requirement for non-disclosure and the destruction or corruption of which may cause losses, inconvenience or embarrasment to the organisation.

Confidential (C) applies to activities involving low or medium level strategic information or significant sums of money. The unauthorised disclosure of such information could reasonably be expected to cause damage to the business.

Secret (S) applies to activities involving large sums of money or high level strategic information, the unauthorised disclosure of which could reasonably be expected to cause serious damage to the business.

Top Secret (TS) applies to activities involving information which is of crucial importance to strategy or security, the unauthorised disclosure of which could reasonably be expected to cause exceptionally grave damage to the business.

In order to establish, unequivocally, the maximum sensitivity level of a workstation, a sensitivity level should be assigned to each system activity and the highest level taken as the result.

As an example of how this can be done, we have developed an example from the banking industry, modified from the work of R.W. Jones, 1985. The system illustrated in Figure 11.2 would involve the use

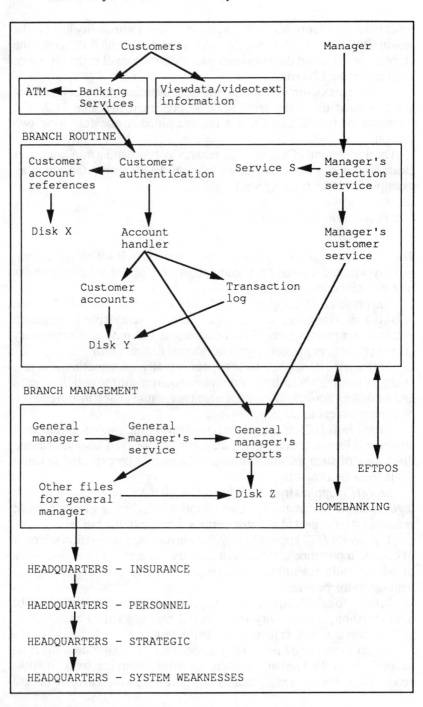

Figure 11.2 Functions of a bank

of many different workstations. Each activity in the system is assigned a sensitivity level. The maximum sensitivity level of each workstation depends on which activities are performed.

In a banking example, consideration of whether the activity involves the transfer of monetary instruments is implicit in its classification. This is particularly so at the lower levels of sensitivity. However it is not always true to say that an activity involving the transfer of money requires greater security than one that does not. For example, the processing of information involving a corporate takeover bid would be more important than the transfer of a moderate sum of money. Table 11.3 contains a checklist giving the sensitivity levels we have assigned to the banking functions introduced in Figure 11.2.

Table 11.3 Banking activity sensitivity checklist

ACTIVITY	SENSITIVITY LEVEL
Viewdata/Videotext	Unrestricted
Homebanking	Confidential
ATM	Restricted
EFTPOS	Restricted
Branch Routine	Restricted
Branch Management	Confidential
Treasury Transfer	Confidential
Head Office-Insurance	Confidential
Head Office-Personnel	Secret
Head Office-Strategic	Secret
Head Office-System Weaknesses	Top Secret

Once the maximum sensitivity level of the workstation has been determined, it must be considered in combination with the minimum user clearance in order to find the required Workstation Security Level The required level can be read from the relevant sensitivity-user clearance matrix (see Step 2 below).

Minimum User Clearance

The minimum user clearance for a workstation is simply the clearance level of the least privileged user. A workstation may support a range of activities with different levels of user clearance. The minimum user clearance level for the workstation is always defined as that of the activity which demands the lowest clearance, regardless of whether other activities require users to have a higher clearance than this. Each of the five levels is now explained in more detail:

- *Unrestricted (U)* applies to persons with no clearance or authorisation. Access would only be permitted to information for which there are no specified controls, such as openly published information. In systems which can be accessed by the general public, the minimum clearance level is always unrestricted.

- *Restricted (R)* applies to persons who are authorised access to certain sensitive information, for official use only. They must be relied upon not to disclose such information to an outside party. The information accessed would be of a routine non-strategic nature.

- *Confidential (C)* applies to persons who are allowed access to certain low or medium level strategic information or to other information, the knowledge of which might, if divulged, cause increased security threats; for example the existence or transfer of large sums of money.

- *Secret (S)* applies to persons who are allowed access to high level strategic information, on a need to know basis. The attachment of such a classification might involve some prior investigation into a persons background. This classification would normally be given only to very senior personnel.

- *Top Secret (TS)* applies to persons with the need to know information of crucial importance to either strategy or security. For example activities involving the knowledge of weaknesses in a high value monetary transfer system might only be performed by a person with such a classification.

Table 11.4 User clearance levels in a banking environment

User	Clearance Level
Public	U
Authorised Customers - 1	R
Clerk	R
Teller	R
Authorised Customers - 2	C
Branch Manager	C
Authorised Head Office Staff	C
Board and Senior Management (on a need to know basis)	S
Top Level Staff (on a need to know basis)	TS

To continue with the banking example, we have listed the probable clearance levels of different classes of banking employees and customers in Table 11.4. Authorised customers are divided into two categories. Category 1 refers to, for example, authorised users of ATM's, EFTPOS etc, whereas category 2 refers to higher privilege users, for example company treasurers using treasury transfer systems, authorised users of a large business account or a "very rich" private account. Top level staff refers to the small group of people who have knowledge of the most sensitive information, for example weaknesses in the computer systems which handle customer accounts, funds transfer etc.

Once the sensitivity and clearance levels have been determined, the user should refer to Step 2 of the methodology (see below) in order to determine the required security level for the workstation in question.

Step 2 Determination of Workstation Security Level

The required workstation security level depends on the maximum sensitivity and minimum user clearance levels assigned in Step 1 above, and on whether the system is an **open** or a **closed** one.

Open and closed systems

The classification of a system as either open or closed depends on whether it is adequately protected against the introduction of malicious logic ('virus', 'trojan horse' etc). This depends on whether applications developers have sufficient clearance or authorisation to work on a system, given the level of sensitivity of data to be processed on that system. Where clearance is insufficient, greater security is then required on the system. This would be termed an open system. Closed systems, where developers do have sufficient clearance, demand a slightly lower level of security.

An *open* system is one in which the following condition is true:

Application developers (including maintainers) do not have sufficient clearance (or authorisation) to provide an acceptable assumption that they have not introduced malicious logic. Sufficient clearance is defined as follows: where the maximum sensitivity level of data to be processed is confidential or below, developers are cleared and authorised to the same level as the most sensitive data; where the maximum sensitivity level of data to be processed is Secret or above, developers have at least a secret clearance.

A *closed* system is one in which the following condition is true:

Application developers (including maintainers) have sufficient clearance and authorisations to provide an acceptable presumption that they have not introduced malicious logic.

Given the maximum sensitivity and minimum user clearance levels assigned in Step 1 above, and the classification of the system as an open or as a closed system, the security level required for each component can be determined as follows. As explained in Section 11.2, components are divided into two categories - tangible and intangible. The method of classifying intangible components is slightly different to that of classifying tangible components and thus the user may end up with two different levels of requirement - one for tangible components and one for intangible components.

Security level for tangible components

When determining the required workstation security level for tangible components, the only consideration is the maximum sensitivity level of activities performed on the system. Potentially, any person can gain access to the tangible components of the workstation. It is the countermeasures to be used which will prevent this. Thus, the countermeasures to be used are not dependent on the clearance level of authorised users; nor are they dependent on whether the system is an open or a closed system. Figure 11.3 shows the relationship between the maximum sensitivity level and the workstation security level.

The worst scenario is that an attack would affect the most highly sensitive information. Thus, the required workstation security level rises in accordance with the highest level of sensitivity of any activity performed on the workstation.

Maximum Sensitivity Level	U	R	C	S	TS
Workstation Security Level	1	4	5	6	7

Figure 11.3 Determination of workstation security level for tangible components

Security level for intangible components

The security classification for intangible components depends on three things:

- The maximum level of sensitivity of any activity performed on the workstation (maximum sensitivity level),

- The level of security clearance of the least privileged user of the system (minimum user clearance), and

- Whether the system is open or a closed.

As in the case of tangible components, as the maximum sensitivity level rises then, *ceteris paribus*, the level of security required on the workstation rises accordingly.

The importance of minimum user clearance arises from the fact that, given that only authorised users are allowed the opportunity to access the system, the major threat to intangible components comes from the possibility of a user with a low security clearance attempting to access highly classified information. The worst scenario is that highly classified information can fall into the hands of the least privileged user. Thus the lower the classification of the least privileged user, the greater the requirement for security and so the higher the workstation security level required.

Open systems require a higher security level than closed systems because of the greater need for countermeasures such as monitoring and verification.

The relationhip between the levels introduced above and the security level required for the workstation is presented in two matrices, one for open systems and one for closed systems.

'Maximum Sensitivity - Minimum User Clearance' Matrices   The horizontal axis of the matrix relates to the maximum sensitivity level of any data on the system. The vertical axis relates to the minimum user clearance. The content of the matrix itself gives the workstation security level required, for each combination of maximum sensitivity level and minimum user clearance.

When using the matrices, the user will already have determined the sensitivity and user clearance levels of the workstation, and the classification of the system as either open or closed. If the system is an open system, the 'open systems' matrix will be used (Figure 11.8); if it is a closed system, the 'closed systems' matrix will be used (Figure 11.9). The 'workstation security level' is denoted by the number in the matrix which correspods to the maximum sensitivity level and minimum user clearance level of the system in question.

Once the required workstation security level has been determined, the next step is to define the security countermeasures necessary to fulfil that requirement.

		Maximum sensitivity level			
	U	R	C	S	TS
U	1	4	5	6	7
R	1	3	4	5	6
C	1	2	3	4	5
S	1	2	2	3	4
TS	1	2	2	2	3

Figure 11.4 Sensitivity/clearance matrix (open systems)

		Maximum sensitivity level			
	U	R	C	S	TS
U	1	3	4	5	6
R	1	2	3	4	5
C	1	2	2	3	4
S	1	2	2	2	3
TS	1	1	1	1	2

Figure 11.5 Sensitivity/clearance matrix (closed systems)

(Minimum user clearance — left axis label for both matrices)

Step 3 Component-countermeasure matrices

The countermeasures are determined by reference to the workstation component - countermeasure matrices presented in this section of the report. For each component and for each level of security required, a list of necessary countermeasures is given.

The matrices are given in the following order:

Tangible Components

Computer Box	Figure 11.6
Physical Storage Devices	Figure 11.7
Cabling	Figure 11.8

Intangible Components

Memory Contents	Figure 11.9
Operating System	Figure 11.10
User Account	Figure 11.11
Logial Storage Media	Figure 11.12

Following each matrix, a brief description of the suggested countermeasures is given. In many cases countermeasures at level n will be used also at level n+1, along with additional countermeasures. In the description the incremental countermeasures will be examined for each level.

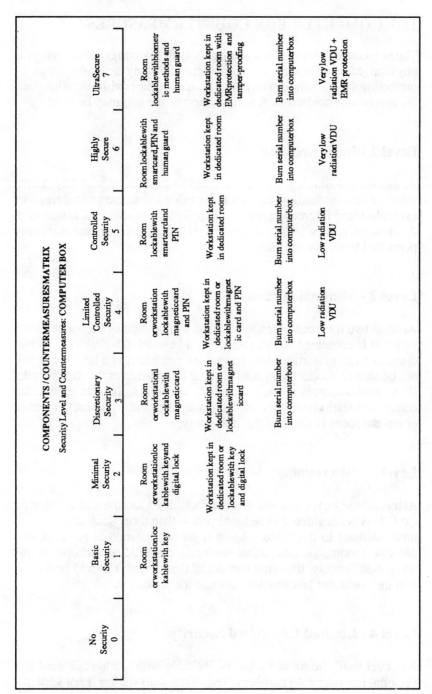

COMPONENTS / COUNTERMEASURES MATRIX

Security Level and Countermeasures: COMPUTER BOX

	No Security 0	Basic Security 1	Minimal Security 2	Discretionary Security 3	Limited Controlled Security 4	Controlled Security 5	Highly Secure 6	UltraSecure 7
		Room or workstation lockable with key	Room or workstation lockable with key and digital lock	Room or workstation lockable with magnetic card	Room or workstation lockable with magnetic card and PIN	Room lockable with smartcard and PIN	Room lockable with smartcard, PIN and human guard	Room lockable with biometric methods and human guard
			Workstation kept in dedicated room or lockable with key and digital lock	Workstation kept in dedicated room or lockable with magnetic card	Workstation kept in dedicated room or lockable with magnetic card and PIN	Workstation kept in dedicated room	Workstation kept in dedicated room	Workstation kept in dedicated room with EMR protection and tamper-proofing
				Burn serial number into computer box	Burn serial number into computer box	Burn serial number into computer box	Burn serial number into computer box	Burn serial number into computer box
					Low radiation VDU	Low radiation VDU	Very low radiation VDU	Very low radiation VDU + EMR protection

Figure 11.6 Computer box

11.5 COMPUTER BOX COUNTERMEASURES

The purpose of computer box countermeasures is to prevent access to the physical components of the computer. This may be done either by protecting the machine directly or by protecting the environment in which the machine is contained. A combination of the two may be used.

Level 1 - Basic Security

At this level a simple lock may be fitted to the computer. A key is then required in order to allow the user to begin logical access procedures. For example, many microcomputers are supplied with such a lock as standard. Alternatively, the workstation can be kept in a locked room and entry only permitted to authorised staff.

Level 2 - Minimal Security

At level two it is recommended that the workstation or the room within which it is contained is lockable using a key and a digital lock. In this circumstance an intruder who has gained possesion of a key would still not be able to access the system without knowledge of the digital code. If the workstation is not kept in a dedicated room, then, at level 2, the actual workstation should be lockable with a key and digital lock, whether or not the room is also locked in this way.

Level 3 - Discretionary Security

At level three the room or workstation should be lockable with a magnetic card. This is considered to be more secure than a key-lock as it is much more difficult to duplicate. Again if the workstation is not kept in a dedicated room, then the actual workstation should be lockable in this way. Additionally, the serial number of the computer should be burned into the computer box to allow definite identification.

Level 4 - Limited Controlled Security

At Level four, the room should be lockable with a magnetic card and personal identification number (PIN). If the workstation is not kept in a dedicated room, then it should be lockable in the same way.

Level 5 - Controlled Security

At Level five the workstation should be kept in a dedicated room. The room should be lockable with a smartcard and PIN.

Level 6 - Highly Secure

At Level six, in addition to the smartcard and PIN lock, there should be a human guard ensuring security of the room in which the workstation is contained.

Level 7 - Ultra Secure

At Level seven the smartcard and PIN should be replaced with biometric methods of identification. This could be done by, for example, retina scans, fingerprint comparisons, vein scans, voice recognition etc. The dedicated room within which the workstation is contained should be protected against the emmission of electromagnetic radiation (EMR) which may be detected from a remote location. The workstation box should be contained within a strong, tamper-proof cover, secured to the surface on which it stands.

COMPONENTS / COUNTERMEASURES MATRIX

Security Level and Countermeasures: PHYSICAL STORAGE DEVICES

	No Security 0	Basic Security 1	Minimal Security 2	Discretionary Security 3	Limited Controlled Security 4	Controlled Security 5	Highly Secure 6	Ultra Secure 7
		Read-only status possible	Read-only status possible	Read-only status possible	Read-only status possible	Read-only status possible	Read-only status possible	Read-only status possible
		Checkable	Checkable	Checkable	Checkable	Checked daily	Checked daily	Auto-check daily
								Auto repair of corrupt files
			Partitionable	Partitionable	Partitionable	Partitionable	Partitionable	Partitionable
			Backup facility	Full backup fortnightly (fireproof)	Full backup weekly (offsite)	Full backup weekly (secure offsite)	Full backup weekly (secure offsite)	Full backup weekly (secure offsite)
					Daily incremental backup	Twice daily incremental backup	Twice daily incremental backup	Twice daily incremental backup
			Tidying and file recovery	Tidying and file recovery	Tidying and file recovery	Tidying and file recovery	Tidying and file recovery	Tidying and file recovery
				No direct read	No direct read	No direct read	No direct read	No direct read
					User space quota	User space quota	User space quota	User space quota
					Remote device restrictions	Remote device restrictions	Remote device restrictions	Remote device restrictions

Figure 11.7 Physical storage devices

11.6 PHYSICAL STORAGE DEVICES

Physical storage devices include fixed disks, removable disks, tapes etc. This section deals with their security as physical entities and not with the security of their contents as logical entities i.e. files, devices, directories etc. The guidelines focus principally on fixed disks.

Note: Physical storage devices will usually be subjected to many of the computer box protection methods given above. For example, most physical storage devices are located in the same room as the computer with which they are used, so that they will be subject to any of the countermeasures relating to protection of environment. (In the case of a network the hard disks will be located within a fileserver). Tapes may be kept in the same room. Floppy disks are likely to be located in the same room as the workstation itself.

Level 1 - Basic Security

At Level one it should be possible to make a physical storage device read-only, such that changes cannot be made to its contents. The device should also be checkable, for example by running the DOS command chkdsk on a hard disk to check for disk errors, bad sectors etc.

Level 2 - Minimal Security

Additional measures to those at Level one are that fixed disks should be partitionable. If a disk is partitioned so that certain users are only allowed to address certain particular physical areas, then in effect it is as though physically distinct disks are being used and users are totally separated from the physical areas containing the files of other users or groups of users. In this case, even if a user can read a disk directly he/she can be prevented from accessing the data of another user.

A backup facility should also be possible. For example the user should be able to backup the contents of a fixed disk onto tape. The tape should then be locked in a secure location. Additionally, disk utilities should be available to allow an authorised user to recover deleted or corrupt files, tidy directories etc. This user should be someone with a high security clearance. The facility should not be available to all users as this may mitigate security.

Level 3 - Discretionary Security

Full backup should be taken at least fortnightly as a matter of security policy. An additional layer of security should be that users must be prevented from being able to read (or write to) the disk directly. For example users may only access information through files held on the disk rather than through direct access to the disk.

Level 4 - Limited Controlled Security

Full backup should be taken at least weekly. This should be kept in a fireproof environment. In addition to this, incremental backup should be made daily. Additionally, each user is given a quota on the amount of disk space used, in order to avoid proliferation of unnecessary files or data. There should also be restrictions on remote devices. For example a password may be neccessary in order to allow downloading to, or reading from, floppy disk.

Level 5 - Controlled Security

Incremental backup should be taken at least twice daily. Full weekly backup should be kept in a secure, offsite location. The device should be checked daily, for disk errors, bad sectors etc, as a matter of policy.

Level 6 - Highly Secure

At Level 6 it should be possible to make devices permanently read-only, if this is necessary. For example, CD-ROM disks could be used for storage of highly sensitive data.

Level 7 - Ultra Secure

At level seven there should be a routine to check the disk or device automatically each day. A facility should be provided for automatic repair of corrupt files found by this check. All physical storage devices should be made tamper proof, where possible. For example, fixed disks should be protected by a tamper proof cover around the workstation box.

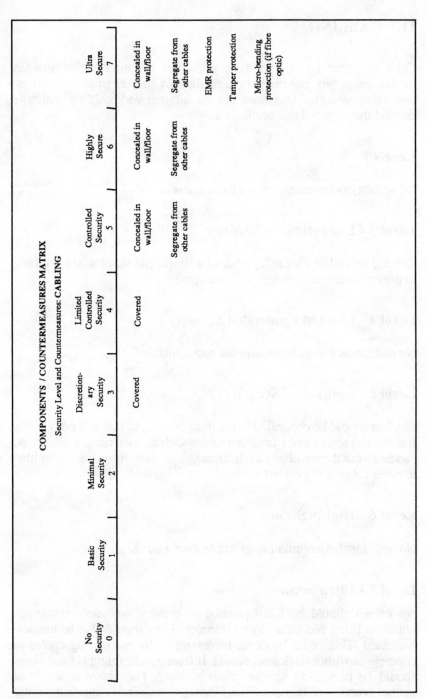

	No Security 0	Basic Security 1	Minimal Security 2	Discretion-ary Security 3	Limited Controlled Security 4	Controlled Security 5	Highly Secure 6	Ultra Secure 7
				Covered	Covered	Concealed in wall/floor	Concealed in wall/floor	Concealed in wall/floor
						Segregate from other cables	Segregate from other cables	Segregate from other cables
								EMR protection
								Tamper protection
								Micro-bending protection (if fibre optic)

COMPONENTS / COUNTERMEASURES MATRIX

Security Level and Countermeasures: CABLING

Figure 11.8 Cabling

11.7 CABLING

Cabling, within the scope of these guidelines, is limited to that between the computer box and the peripheral devices such as printers, plotters, tape streamers etc. This does not include network cabling which is beyond the scope of this section.

Levels 1 - 2

No security is necessary on the cabling itself.

Level 3 - Discretionary Security

Cabling should be covered, perhaps by simple plastic or wooden tubing to prevent them from being easily tampered with.

Level 4 - Limited Controlled Security

No additional countermeasures are recommended.

Level 5 - Controlled Security

Cabling should be concealed in the floor or wall, so that it is not visible. It should be segregated from other cables such as, for example, telephone cables, so that the possibility of electromagnetic radiation being transmitted to other cabling is avoided.

Level 6 - Highly Secure

No additional countermeasures are recommended.

Level 7 - Ultra Secure

All cables should be EMR-proofed to prevent any electromagnetic radiation being picked up by an intruder. They should also be tamper-protected. This could be done, for example, by embedding cables in concrete or within thick steel tubing. If fibre optic cabling is used, there should be protection against micro-bending. The above methods of tamper protection should suffice. Fibre optic cabling is inherently more secure as it emits no electromagnetic radiation and is almost impossible to tap other than by micro-bending methods

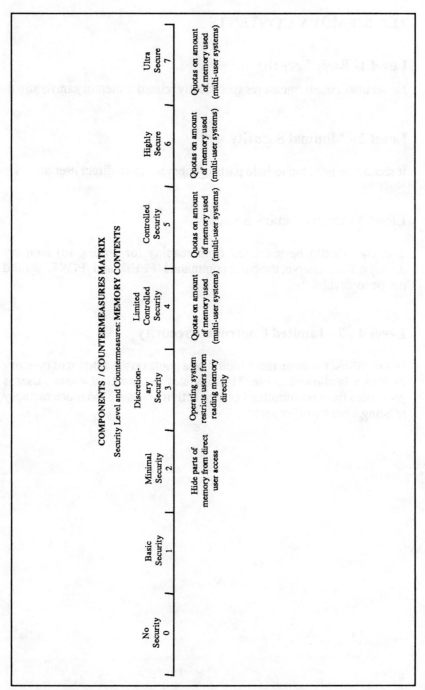

Figure 11.9 Memory contents

11.8 MEMORY CONTENTS

Level 1- Basic Security

No security countermeasures specifically related to memory are required.

Level 2 - Minimal Security

It should be possible to hide parts of memory from direct user access.

Level 3 - Discretionary Security

The user should be restricted from reading (or writing to) memory directly. For example, the basic commands 'PEEK' and 'POKE' should not be available.

Level 4 - 7 - Limited Controlled Security

In a multi-user system, there should be a quota on the amount of memory each user is allowed to use. This obviates the situation where a user is prevented from performing a system activity because too much memory is being used by other users.

COMPONENTS / COUNTERMEASURES MATRIX
Security Level and Countermeasures: OPERATING SYSTEM

	No Security 0	Basic Security 1	Minimal Security 2	Discretionary Security 3	Limited Controlled Security 4	Controlled Security 5	Highly Secure 6	Ultra Secure 7
		Disable system break-in keys	Disable system break-in keys	Disable system break-in keys	Disable system break-in keys	Disable system break-in keys	Disable system break-in keys	Disable system break-in keys
				Systems manager	Systems manager	Systems manager	Systems manager	Systems manager
				Simple system access log	Log of access to system, files, applications, prints, mounts etc.	Log of access to system, files, applications, prints, mounts etc.	Log of access to system, files, applications, prints, mounts etc.	Log of access to system, files, applications, prints, mounts etc.
					Detailed audit trail	Detailed audit trail	Detailed audit trail	Detailed audit trail
					Privilege categories	Privilege categories	Privilege categories	Privilege categories
					Interactive system monitoring	Interactive system monitoring	Interactive system monitoring	Interactive system monitoring
					Ability to write command language procedures	Ability to write command language procedures	Ability to write command language procedures	Ability to write command language procedures
						Monitoring alarm	Monitoring alarm	Monitoring alarm
							SCARF optional	SCARF optional
								Verified O/S
								Selected before and after image log

Figure 11.10 Operating system

11.9 OPERATING SYSTEM

The operating system potentially provides a means of access to all files and applications. It is, therefore, particularly important to secure the operating system.

Level 1 - Basic Security

The system break-in keys should be disabled. For example, using DOS with no security, it is possible to break out of most programs directly into the operating system by pressing the 'Ctrl' and 'Break' keys simultaneously. This type of security weakness exists in many operating systems but can be disabled quite easily.

Level 2 - Minimal Security

No additional countermeasures are necessary.

Level 3 - Discretionary Security

There should be a systems manager who can manage and monitor use of the operating system. The systems manager performs tasks such as adding or deleting users, changing file attributes, adding and configuring new applications etc. This means that the privileges of other users can be reduced to include only those which are needed and so security is tightened. There should also be a simple access log, recording who has accessed the system and at what time.

Level 4 - Limited Controlled Security

The log should be extended to include a record of what has been printed out and of which remote devices have been mounted, as well as all accesses to the system and to individual files and applications. In addition to this, a detailed audit trail should record all important transactions.

Privilege categories are introduced at this level. Different classes or levels of users should be given different privileges to perform operating system functions, depending on their need to do so and on their security clearance. This gives greater granularity than merely distinguishing between the system manager and other users. For example, users may or may not be given the privilege to mount remote devices, shutdown the system, use electronic mail etc.

At this level an interactive system monitoring should be introduced. A superuser - security manager, auditor etc - should be able to monitor system activities in real time; for example which user is using which application, which files are being accessed etc. At this level, there should exist the ability to write command language procedures should also exist. This enables greater control and security to be programmed into the operating system where necessary.

Level 5 - Controlled Security

The log should include a record of all file accesses. There should also be a monitoring alarm. Attempts at access violation should be reported to the superusers' terminal as they occur.

Level 6 - Highly Secure

The option to produce a selected after- image log is introduced. This enables a superuser to look at the entire image after processing has occured.

A System Control Audit Review File (SCARF) may also be introduced at this level. This records all items passing or failing particular tests specified in the resident code, or records a random sample of all items passing through the resident code. These tests check for the accuracy or validity of data input to, processed, or output by the computers programs.

Level 7 - Ultra Secure

A selected before and after image log can be produced. This allows comparison of the two in order to check all changes. The operating system should also be verified to ensure that no unauthorised changes have been made to it.

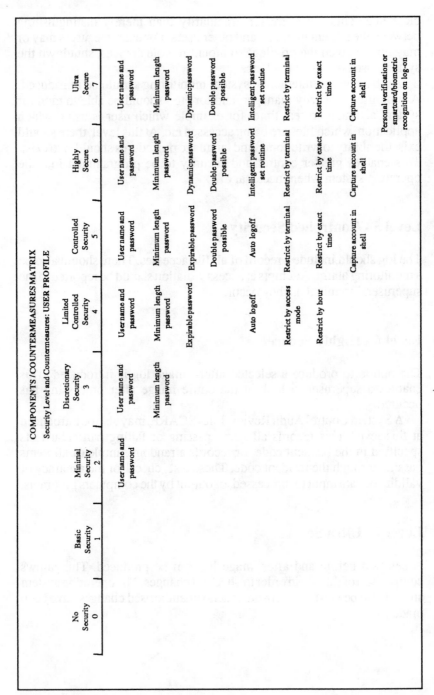

Figure 11.11 User account

11.10 USER PROFILE

The user profile pr account is, in itself, a security feature as it is a means of providing access to authorised users, and can be used as a vehicle for controlling access to certain files, applications, devices etc.

Level 1 - Basic Security

No countermeasures are required. This means that, in effect, it is not necessary to allocate accounts to separate users.

Level 2 - Minimal Security

User accounts are introduced and access is controlled by means of a username and password.

Level 3 - Discretionary Security

The password used to access a user account must be of a minimum length, for example six characters.

Level 4 - Limited Controlled Security

Passwords should be expirable. For example, users should be forced to change their passwords once a month. There should also be an auto-logoff facility i.e. if the user is logged onto the system but remains inactive for a specified period, say ten minutes, then he/she should automatically be logged off. Further countermeasures at level four are that the user should be restricted by access mode. For example it may be necessary at this stage to prevent users logging in from remote terminals. Access should also be restricted by preventing users from logging in between certain hours, perhaps 6pm to 8am and at weekends.

Level 5 - Controlled Security

Double paswords should be possible. The user has to input two passwords before access is allowed.

Access is restricted by terminal at this level. A user is only allowed to log on from a particular designated terminal or terminals. Access is restricted by exact time, giving greater control than through restricting by hour. At this level there must be no possibility that a user can penetrate the shell and arrive in the operating system. Thus if the shell crashes, the account of the user must be frozen and not returned to the operating system.

Level 6 - Highly Secure

Passwords must be dynamic. They should change each time the user logs onto the system. In this way a lost password is only a risk if the intruder acts upon it before the authorised user re-enters the system. There should also be an intelligent password-set routine. This would control the length and content of the password. It would, for example, prevent the use of obvious passwords such as the name of the user and would probably require a mixture of digits and letters.

Level 7 - Ultra Secure

Verification of a persons identity includes the use of smart cards or biometric techniques, or requests for unique knowledge personal to the user i.e. random questions are asked from a database of the users' personal details.

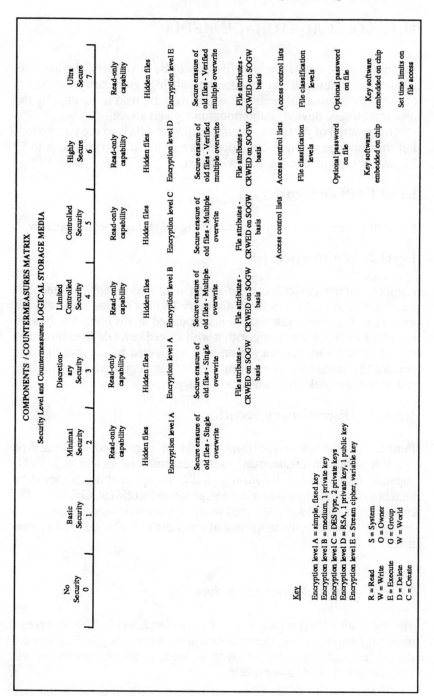

COMPONENTS / COUNTERMEASURES MATRIX

Security Level and Countermeasures: LOGICAL STORAGE MEDIA

No Security 0	Basic Security 1	Minimal Security 2	Discretionary Security 3	Limited Controlled Security 4	Controlled Security 5	Highly Secure 6	Ultra Secure 7
		Read-only capability	Read-only capability	Read-only capability	Read-only capability	Read-only capability	Read-only capability
		Hidden files	Hidden files	Hidden files	Hidden files	Hidden files	Hidden files
		Encryption level A	Encryption level A	Encryption level B	Encryption level C	Encryption level D	Encryption level E
		Secure erasure of old files - Single overwrite	Secure erasure of old files - Single overwrite	Secure erasure of old files - Multiple overwrite	Secure erasure of old files - Multiple overwrite	Secure erasure of old files - Verified multiple overwrite	Secure erasure of old files - Verified multiple overwrite
			File attributes - CRWED on SOGW basis	File attributes - CRWED on SOGW basis	File attributes - CRWED on SOGW basis	File attributes - CRWED on SOGW basis	File attributes - CRWED on SOGW basis
					Access control lists	Access control lists	Access control lists
						File classification levels	File classification levels
						Optional password on file	Optional password on file
						Key software embedded on chip	Key software embedded on chip
							Set time limits on file access

Key

Encryption level A = simple, fixed key
Encryption level B = medium, 1 private key
Encryption level C = DES type, 2 private keys
Encryption level D = RSA, 1 private key, 1 public key
Encryption level E = Stream cipher, variable key

R = Read S = System
W = Write O = Owner
E = Execute G = Group
D = Delete W = World
C = Create

Figure 11.12 Logical storage media

11.11 LOGICAL STORAGE MEDIA

Logical storage media include files, records, directories, devices etc. Logical access must be controlled, often with high granularity. Protection of the physical storage media on which they are held is covered by the physical storage device countermeasures given above.

One method of protecting logical storage media is to use encryption. For this purpose we have developed five levels of encryption, A to E. These are explained in the following text.

Level 1 - Basic Security

No countermeasures are introduced for logical storage media at this level.

Level 2- Minimal Security

Logical storage devices can be given read-only capability and , if necessary, can be hidden from directory listings so that users are not aware that they exist. Encryption is introduced at this level. Encryption Level A involves a simple algorithm with a fixed key. Old files should be erased securely so that they cannot be recovered by an unauthorised person. This would involve writing over the segments containing the file, rather than just deleting its directory entry.

Level 3 - Discretionary Security

Further file attribute capabilities should be introduced. It should be possible to attach create, read, write, execute and delete (CRWED) capabilities, in any combination, to a file. These capabilities should be attached on a system manager, owner, group and world (SOGW) basis i.e. certain capabilities are conferred to the system manager, others to the owner of each file, some to a group of users and a smaller set to all system users.

Level 4 - Limited Controlled Security

The encryption level is increased to Encryption Level B. This involves a more sophisticated key, perhaps with a minimum length. File erasure should be made more secure, with multiple overwrites replacing the single overwrites of lower levels.

Level 5 - Controlled Security

Access control lists should be used. These list the access rights to each file (or directory, record etc). This allows 'artificial' groups to be used. Instead of being a member of only one group, a user can be a member of several groups, each with access rights relevant to the activity it performs. Encryption Level C should be used. This involves use of a DES type algorithm with two private keys.

Level 6 - Highly Secure

File classification levels should be used. Each file is given a certain security level and only users with a particular clearance level are allowed access. Overwritten files should be verified to ensure that overwriting has been performed thoroughly. There should be an option to protect any individual file by controlling access to it, by means of a password. This means that an intruder who has surpassed all the other access control stages is still unable to use the file without knowing its password. Key software, such as that controlling access, audit trail, or logs should be embedded onto a chip so that it cannot be deleted easily. Encryption level D should be in operation.

Level 7 - Ultra Secure

Encryption level E should be used. Level E involves a stream cipher with a variable length key. Time limits may also be set on file access. For example access may be permitted only between certain times and on certain days. This may extend, if necessary, to allowing different users access at different times, and if appropriate, to limiting the length of time for which the file may be accessed.

Note: At level 3, file attributes are introduced. These control which operations a user is allowed to perform on a file. Users are granted access to files, either as the owner (O), the system manager (S), as part of a particular group (G) or as part of the group of all users, known as world (W). Depending on which of the above access categories the user is in, and on the requirements for security of the file in question, access is controlled on the basis of whether the user is allowed to read (R), write to (W), delete (D), create (C), or execute (E) the file. If access is denied completely, none of these privileges will be granted. Otherwise, one or more will be allowed.

12.5 CONCLUSION

Unfortunately, the ITSEC harmonised pan-European criteria, albeit provisional have somewhat replaced the security levels first 'aired' in MARS. The guidelines present a method for determining the security requirements of a workstation, which is, as far as possible, technology independent. The methodology is based on work by the US Department of Defense, but has been considerably adapted and added to, in order to make it applicable to an office environment.

The guidelines provide a very practical approach to the implementation of security, as the actual types of countermeasures necessary for each of security to be achieved, are listed in Section 11.4, in the component-countermeasures matrices. Thus, it is possible for a security designer to implement the measures necessary to attain a desired level. It is also possible for a system to be tested to see which level of security is in place.

The security countermeasures should be implemented as part of an overall security policy. This includes the fostering of good employee relations as the most common security breach has been shown in previous work to originate from disgruntled employees. Working conditions and salaries should be satisfactory. Annual holidays should be compulsory in order to decrease the possibility of detection of ongoing frauds.

Documentation should be thorough, whatever the level of security, in order to allow the system to be used and, if necessary, altered correctly. All software and changes to software should be precisely documented. User manuals should be accurate and readable and all hardware and configurations should be thoroughly recorded.

Each user should be completely aware of what level of clearance he or she has and of the sensitivity of files which are being accessed. This should be done by notifying the user, on access to the system, of their level of security and, on access to files, of the sensitivity level of the files being used. It not necessary and may be undesirable for users to know of the existence of files which have a higher level of sensitivity than they have rights to access.

The testing procedure will involve a rigorous analysis of the workstation environment. This will include a standard questionnaire to check which security measures are in place. The effectiveness of these measures will then be tested by a set of standard benchmark tests to reveal:

1   Whether or not they work as stated
2   How comprehensive they are
3   How effective they are.

Additional ad-hoc testing may be held where required if the standard tests do not provide a satisfactory answer.

12

Guidelines for Auditability

12.1 INTRODUCTION

Although auditability is an essential precondition to an audit, it is a subject which has generally received less attention than it warrants. This chapter first describes the foundations of auditability. Two important aspects of auditability - the competence of audit personnel and the time period for performance of audit are then discussed.

We then look at auditability requirements specific to the banking environment, before examining two important concepts - events based auditing and the migration concept of auditability. Following this, guidelines are presented. Firstly, for highly secure office systems, and then for workstations specifically linked to multi-user systems in general, networked workstations, and workstations linked to mainframe systems. Finally, existing auditing standards are examined. In Appendix C, all the guidelines presented in this chapter are summarised.

12.2 FOUNDATIONS OF AUDITABILITY

Traditionally, the most important foundation of auditability is the *audit trail*. An *accounting audit trail* records events and operations upon data items within a database system. An *operations audit trail* records events in relation to application procedures and system maintenance. Basically, an audit trail is a method of logging. The items of information to be logged are determined by the design of the audit trail. The design of the audit trail itself is influenced by auditability requirements.

In addition to the logged information, which is generated and maintained by the system itself, a large amount of external information is also needed. *Documentation* has to be complete, clear , transparent, topical and auditable.

Observation of specific items is a permanent function of auditing, which the system has to fulfil or to support. The need for observation of a system, especially checking and testing as subfunctions of observation, have to be accomplished by adequate auditability criteria. *Checking* and *testing* are subfunctions of observation. Both are specific control techniques for auditing. They are suitable to support permanent and detailed observation of the system. Testing can be conducted as compliance tests, weakness tests, or substantive tests (Chambers, 1981). Compliance tests check adherence to procedures and requirements, weakness tests aim to identify vulnerabilities and substantive tests examine the transaction audit trail to establish correspondence with actual transactions.

Testing must be promoted by the system, whenever it is necessary that it is conducted. In a system with distributed intelligence, test facilities or test aids must be implemented in all entities that process data independently.

Checking is performed primarily using checklists or automated check functions incorporated in the system. The basic objective of checking is to evaluate compliance of the system to any regulations imposed on it.. For an external EDP audit, complete sets of checklists for all parts of the system have been published. Using these checklists, an orderly audit can be performed. Such checklists are used to analyse the formal regularity of DP accounting, the transparency of documentation, the controllability of applications and the functional security of processing.

The *Internal Control System* (ICS) is also a component of the auditing function. The implementation of an adequate set of controls in a system aims at ensuring predetermined objectives and requirements imposed on the system from outside. The ICS, in general, consists of two different types of controls - application independent controls and application dependent controls.

Application independent controls are mostly related to and carried out in the DP centre, for example, procedures for file management and the securing of data. Application-dependent controls include procedures for source document preparation, source document input and specific control procedures for individual applications etc.

Checking the ICS helps to detect weaknesses and indicates areas for auditing. An auditor's first action is always to check internal controls. Correct functioning of controls has to be established. Self-controlling systems contain in-built controls. These automated controls have to be audited in order to be trustworthy.

Rules or regulations for auditing are components of the auditing function and also determine the requirements for auditability. Any organisation having an EDP system needs control of the system in the widest sense. Control needs are imposed on the system from within the organisation and from outside. External control needs result from more or less legally binding rules and regulations. Compliance of organisations with these regulations is checked by the external auditors. In this instance, auditability requirements are formulated as laws or guidelines.

A *computer assisted systems audit* can be defined as the auditing of complete procedures, and analysis of the functionality of system components, using client owned or auditor owned automated tools. The techniques applied in a systems audit verify system controls and not data. In contrast to the systems audit, the analysis of data is maintained by the *verification approach to auditing*. Systems audits and verification audits can be combined.

Specific auditing techniques require the existence of certain physical or logical facilities. If an individual technique is the only way to audit a system, the installation of the facilities necessary to perfrom that technique is an auditability requirement.

In order to be auditable, a system has to have specific features and certain incorporated functions. For EDP accounting systems these features and functions are prescribed by legal regulations and guidelines. Formal criteria for auditability comprise requirements for:

- the review of single transactions from their source document to the final records

- the review of the application programs, such that a competent third party should be able to evaluate the effectiveness and efficiency of the control system in adequate time

- proving that the application procedures have been used according to the versions described in the documentation.

The review of a single transaction requires an explanation of the transaction itself, the amount or quantity involved, the time of transaction confirmation by an authorised person. Correctness and authorisation has to be proved by documentation.

The review of applications and proving the use of correct procedures for all transactions requires evidence, which can be collected automatically by the system. Logging facilities have to record the time of input, the input device and the identity of the user assigned to the device at the time of use.

A review of all activities in a system must be possible . In distributed systems, this requirement is particularly urgent. Here, auditability is a distributed function.

12.3 COMPETENCE OF AUDIT PERSONNEL

According to the definition of auditability, competent persons are required to perform the audit. The level of ability required increases as the complexity of the information systems grows. Therefore, auditor competence can be regarded as a general auditability requirement. Compliance with auditability requirements by the system alone does not guarantee that it can be audited. Aditionally, the auditor has to comply with the requirement of competence. Therefore, criteria for the qualification of internal and external auditors have to be set up.

For the qualification of internal auditors, Chambers states that:"All internal auditors shall be computer auditors." [CHAM81]. This statement is supported by the growing use of computers in all types of organisation. In the banking sector, business operations without computer use are almost impossible. Furthermore, the objectives of an internal audit are not only to check compliance of the EDP system with respective regulations, but to evaluate and enhance the efficiency of data processing. An auditor needs considerable expertise to be able to fulfil this task.

The widening scope of internal audit has meant that it increasingly comprises non-accounting activities such as operational auditing. This causes a change in the type of expert knowledge required to perform an internal audit. Internal auditors today are, in many cases, computer specialists rather than accountants. The internal audit department should consist of general auditors, capable of using audit software, and of computer specialists, who are able to select and develop computer audit tools. Only the interaction of these types of specialists can achieve the necessary audit competence.

Where an operational audit of the computer centre, of system development and of general controls is performed, the knowledge of a computer specialist is needed. In contrast to this, a general internal auditor should be able to review controls in computer applications in the various departments.

The qualification requirements of external auditors will necessarily be different from those of internal auditors. The basic task of the external auditor is the review of the annual balance sheet. For this purpose, he audits the EDP based accounting system and basically the whole internal control system of the accounting department. His qualifying statements concentrate on the compliance of the system with respective regulations and on the corectness of the results. For this, the auditor must have sufficient EDP knowledge to carry out the following tasks (Duck, 1985):

- prove the auditability of EDP based accounting systems
- audit the organisational environment and evaluate the client's internal audit activities
- evaluate the necessity for specialised computer auditors
- supervise audit assistants occupied with the auditing object EDP system
- evaluate and convert the results of engaged systems specialists (in the process of formulating qualifications)
- assure the representation of the results of an EDP audit
- performance of a computer-asssisted verification audit.

The external auditor needs considerable advanced EDP knowledge to carry out tasks such as the development, test, selection and implementation of audit software, the performance of systems audit in complex EDP systems or when consulting on EDP matters.

Because of the problems which are likely to arise specifically in banking systems, it is more and more important to involve the auditor in the design phase. This can help to assure the establishment of all the relevant controls and may have a very positive effect on auditability

A similar scope of knowledge is needed if the auditor is concerned with the audit of EDP programs. Basically, the external auditor has to aquire a general knowledge basis, which he is able to transfer to the different system types he may be faced with in various organisations.

In recent years, national auditor organisations and international institutions such as the EC and IFAC, have formulated requirements for the professional education of auditors. The eighth Directive of the EC gives some general guidelines for the harmonisation of the accounting profession. IFAC formulates statements on the use of computer assisted audit techniques (CAATS) which also involve requirements for special knowledge on the parent of the auditor who employs them (IFAC, 1987).

12.4 TIME PERIOD FOR PERFORMANCE OF AUDIT

Auditing must be reperformable in a reasonable period of time. For external auditors, the legally fixed period for the audit of the annual balance sheet is a time constraint, since its publication has to be finalised within eight months following the balance sheet date. Auditability of the audit object includes the ability to finish the evaluation process on time. For all audits, the cost of auditing also imposes a time constraint. These limits cannot be named exactly. The professional rules for auditors in

West Germany, for example, state that the auditor has to act independently and determine the intensity and duration of an audit on his own.

Certain properties of the auditing object can help the auditor to overcome these time constraints. Auditing tools which are already inbuilt in the auditing object can shorten the time needed for auditing. Additionally, criteria for the quality of hardware and software products ease the audit and support auditability.

12.5 AUDITABILITY REQUIREMENTS IN BANKING

Banking systems are constructed according to specific architectures, which are then able to run banking functions and applications. The systems have to be suitable for internal and external communication. Furthermore, the internal and external systems can be connected to wide area banking networks such as SWIFT.

Auditability depends on the type of office system in use. The requirements increase in line with the integration and complexity of automation. Different organisational structures, for example, centralised, distributed or mixed, pose different problems in auditability. The more distributed the intelligence of the system, the more difficult is the realisation of auditability. An audit trail must cover all the distributed intelligence devices and the links between them. Again, the requirement for a reasonable auditing time must be emphasised.

Auditing and auditability are very tightly linked with security. The realisation of auditability requirements and auditing are properties which help to make a system secure. Security can be enhanced if a system contains security functions, such as authentication procedures, authorisation assignment and control, logging and monitoring. The adjustment and enforcement of security functions is the basis for ensuring auditability.

For internal applications, auditability requirements in banks are basically the same as in other industries.However, the involvement of money and a large amount of very sensitive client data in transactions emphasise the need for data security. Furthermore, some fundamental differences exist between banking and other types of organisations.

The large number of transactions involved in banking are, superficially analogous to the monitoring of manufacturing and the production of goods in non-banking organisations. However, in a manufacturing environment, production has to be recorded by documenting the goods and then transferring this documentation to electronic storage media, whereas in a banking environment the transfer of money is the actual production process, which is automatically recorded in a computerised form. The difference between manufacturing, retailing and banking is that in most banking systems every single piece of production is already automated, or has to be automated to be actually processed.

This fundamental difference underlines the importance of automation for business operations in banks and highlights the need for secure and orderly functioning of the information system in use.

12.6 EVENTS BASED SYSTEMS AUDITING

The term event originates in the development of innovative financial accounting systems. In contrast to traditional value accounting systems, an events accounting system stores and processes events, instead of aggregate values.

Initially, events are defined as business transactions and all the necessary evidence pertaining to those transactions (Sorter, 1969 [SORT69]). The basic impact of an events accounting system on auditing is that audit evidence is available only in a raw form, which needs further aggregation steps. A business transaction stored as an event cannot at once be identified as audit relevant, without knowing it's final result. Another problem is that the combination of two uncritical events in different processing steps can produce one critical, i.e. audit relevant, event, which cannot easily be foreseen.

In order to be able to use events as powerful evidence in an audit, it is necessary to define criteria for the selection of audit-relevant events. One possibility would be to mark events according to their degree of sensitivity and to group them into different pre-defined classes. Further aggregation of these events must automatically lead to the assignment of a new sensitivity classification for the result . This would enhance recognition of the audit relevance of a stored event.

In order to capture all events that are significant for the audit, not only all business transactions entered into the system, but also all actions that are performed involving the system, have to be recorded. Particularly important are all actions which involve security functions, especially those which allow access to or alter the state of sensitive data. These events, which are not necessarily business transactions, can be called security-relevant events.

Bearing in mind this twofold meaning of events, the following definition of events (for auditing purposes) can be formulated, events consist of all business transactions, plus the evidence pertaining to these transactions, stored in the system and all operations upon data and/or programs, which are identified as security-relevant.

The concept of auditing, which is the underlying basis for the definition of auditability requirements, is twofold. One aspect is the systems audit, which is primarily based on technical and program documentation as audit evidence for a check of program logic and identity, and partly on a verification audit of events stored in the system. Consequently, two classes of information, which provide the necessary audit evidence, have to be distinguished:

- event information, which is generated by the system itself and consists of different types of events, and

- non-event information, which can either be generated by the system itself, for example a self-documenting data dictionary, or can be prepared manually.

Auditability requires that all information needs for this twofold auditing concept are fulfilled. This chapter concentrates on the requirements which are posed by a systems audit. From our point of view, for the information which is needed in a verification audit, only general auditability requirements can be formulated. This includes the completeness of recording of transactions and respective events, and the implementation of facilities to select and evaluate them. We do not however, discuss statistical methods which have to be applied to select audit-relevant events from the available stored data.

12.7 THE MIGRATION CONCEPT OF AUDITABILITY

In EDP, the term 'migration' usually refers to the implementation of programs in sequential steps, moving from one to the next. In relation to auditing, migration is the method of performing an audit in pre-determined steps, determined by the system structure and the linking of components or even different systems. The individual steps are created by partitioning systems into entities that are auditable. The division of the auditing object into sections is done with the aim of preparing and maintaining the necessary amount of audit evidence, and making it available for the auditor, taking time constraints into consideration.

In order to be auditable, the components must fulfil certain general requirements, which have already been introduced, and special requirements which will be discussed later. All of these requirements constitute a set of preconditions for the audit of an EDP system. Since a system consists of a certain set of components, realisation and implementation has to be achieved in the components. For each component, a subset of auditability requirements can be defined. Therefore, the realisation of auditability involves some facets of the migration concept. If auditing is carried out according to the migration concept, auditability must also comply with this idea.

For networks, the workshop of the DoD-CSC revealed the need for the possibility of auditing at any location in the system (DoD 85b]. In a distributed system, auditing too must be distributed. This supports the implementation of auditability and auditing according to the migration concept.

Steps in a migration audit

Step one of the audit involves the system entity with the least complexity or that which is nearest to the user. This would usually be the workstation. The migration concept is not relevant to a standalone workstation. As an auditing object it is a single entity. However, a workstation linked to any system has to comply with basically the same requirements. Bearing this in mind, some of these requirements will be outlined here. The emphasis on individual features depends on the degree of intelligence and the relevance of functions which are carried out using the workstation.

The standalone workstation, usually a sophisticated PC, is characterised by it's own intelligence and central storage of all data. The device can be accessed very easily. The data can be modified or removed, especially if floppy disks are used. Specific protection measures have to be implemented in order to secure a standalone computer.

Security features such as authentication, the assignment and control of authorisation, forward error correction, logging and monitoring can be achieved. The most important feature for auditability is the logging of security-relevant events. These events can occur during the performance of the security functions, but also during the running of application programs. In order to be auditable, the programs used must support the logging and storage of audit data, by providing sufficient storage and processing capabilities. Physical hardware security has to prevent unauthorised access, and the modification or deletion of audit information. Furthermore the devices to be audited have to be available to the auditor, whereas the log-files have to be accessible.

Thus, as general auditability requirements for a standalone PC, the requirements for physical security, for sufficient storage capacity and for the availability and accessibility of devices have been identified.

Step two of the migration concept is needed where workstations linked to a multi-user system have to be audited. Based on the results of Step One, the links to the multi-user system and the multi-user facilities are audited.

The multi-user system as a whole is characterised by the simultaneous execution of various jobs for several users, by use of time-sharing procedures. Multiple users and peripheral devices, data transfer from central storage to peripheral devices and simultaneous access to files by several users are peculiarities which pose additional security and auditability requirements. The restriction of physical and logical access is of increased importance in multi-user applications. Auditability has to be supported by the logging of all accesses to the system.

The multi-user system is usually organised centrally , with dedicated lines connecting each device to the host. Logging is again the key issue for auditability. Recording of information is a precondition for evaluation of system performance and especially for the correct functioning of the security facilities. The hardware has to allow extensive logging without significantly affecting processing speed. The activities of the host and the critical actions of connected devices need to be logged. Physical security, and the availability and accessibility of all system components are necessary auditability requirements.

Step three in the migration concept is relevant where workstations are linked to a LAN and further gateways. This stage is also based on the results of Steps One and Two. Auditing activities are concentrated on the LAN and gateways.

Additional requirements arise in a LAN, because the linked devices can communicate with each other and the network can be opened for links with external communicators. Adjustment and the enforcement of security functions and the logging of audit evidence is again the basis for ensuring auditability. Hardware facilities, which accomplish auditability, have to be resident in the network control unit and in all communicating devices.

Communication between the linked devices must also be auditable. Suitable logging facilities have to be physically provided. As for gateways, auditability requires the ability to check changes in all connections within the network or with exterior devices, which change the initial configuration.

Step four of migration is relevant where the systems described above are additionally linked to a central mainframe. Having audited all the other components in earlier steps, the central mainframe is now subject to auditing.

The audit of a central mainframe is the most difficult and complex task facing the auditor. This system requires specific techniques for correct control. General auditability requirements for a central mainframe are physical security, availability, the accessibility of the device, sufficient storage capacities for logging, extensive logging of audit evidence and efficient evaluation aids for audit data.

We exclude wide area networks, because they are not part of the system, which is an auditing object restricted to one organisation. The WAN to which the audited system is connected is, in itself, an auditing object. By definition, a WAN is either a connection of several networks or of distantly located devices of any kind. It does not pose different auditability requirements than the networks or devices it consists of. These requirements are covered in this chapter.

Variations of the migration concept

The migration concept is a unique idea for the performance of a systems audit. However, EDP systems can be organised in many different ways. Therefore, the migration concept has to be adjusted to the individual structure and organisation of the auditing object.

Migration steps can be distinguished according to *functions*, instead of entities of the system. For example, in a centralised system, migration steps can be distinguished for functions which apply to the whole system, or alternatively for single components. For the audit of the internal control system, a mixture of both approaches can be used. The application-independent controls can be audited in one step for the whole system. Application-dependent controls can be audited during the steps where components related to these applications are checked.

A migrating audit trail

The concept of a comprehensive audit trail can be adjusted to the migration approach. The migration steps, which are created in accordance with the structure of the auditing object, divide the audit trail into sections.If in Step One of a migrating audit a workstation is reviewed, then that part of the audit trail which collects information relating to this component and it's controls, is active. Thus, the auditor is enabled to select the parts of the audit trail which he needs for the audit. These necessary parts are determined by the application of the migration concept to the auditing object. The system is then structured into auditable entities, for which the respective parts of the audit trail can be selected.

12.8 SPECIAL AUDITABILITY REQUIREMENTS FOR HIGHLY SECURE OFFICE SYSTEMS

At present, no comprehensive auditing standards for workstations exist. Specific guidelines need to be set up in this area. As stated earlier, the overall objective and scope of an audit does not change in an EDP environment. But some impact of a workstation on auditing is inevitable. The processing and storage of information affects the nature of adequate internal controls. The features of auditable workstations, described later in this chapter, can be regarded as a guideline proposal, to summarise and define the particular areas which have to be examined in an audit.

Audit Scope for Workstations

For the auditing object , the "workstation", it is recognisable that audit information is required in three areas, for hardware, software and the surrounding organisation. Corresponding to these three areas, special auditability requirements can be attached to the workstation. If it is not possible to obtain the required information in a reasonable amount of time, no audit can take place, or the system is not auditable. The audit information is used to describe audit events, which have to be first identified.

Audit information must be carefully selected. It must be relevant and comprehensive. The selection criteria must guarantee that the functions of auditability (reperformance, observation, checking and testing) are fulfilled. Furthermore the selected events must provide proof that every possible transaction is performed in an orderly and correct way. The audit information required is therefore classified as:

- organisational information
- hardware information
- software information

Organisational Information

Firstly, unauthorised persons should not have access to the computer. A set of organisational countermeasures are useful, such as physical security on the room containing the computer. Further, it is recommended that the workstation is attached in one working location and is not placed in positions with public access. Printers should be located where the output is not visible by extraneous persons, etc.

Misappropriation of data has to be prevented. Storage media must be securely archived. Diskette usage should be subject to administrative procedures. They should be under the control of the responsible person in each department. Markings should be used to guarantee the existence of only one original diskette.

Furthermore the loss or destruction of data has to be minimised by organisational means. Back-up volumes are suitable for this. Principally they have to accomplish fast restoration after a breakdown, caused by systems failure or data inconsistency. One example for a back-up procedure is the three-generation-concept with three archived copies of the data files.

All these countermeasures are considered in an audit of the ICS. Consequently a resulting auditability requirement is a directory of organisational controls. This could be achieved by a Directory of Liability.

The directory should mention the means of organisational controls and the person responsible for the effectiveness of these controls during the audit period. Liability is assigned to the same person or declared by a supervisory person. The directory of liability should provide information about:

- what tasks are executed by the WS
- what persons are working at this place
- who is allowed to have access to the WS or to parts of the WS, such as printers, diskettes, etc.

Most of the measures and the laid down responsibilities belong to the inventory of an organisational handbook for data security. This handbook is normally part of the auditing object. The necessary auditability requirements for documentation are described later in this chapter, in the section entitled "Software Information".

The system itself can contain this documentation. The directory of liability, as a part of the complete documentation, can be supported by the system, for example by an application to produce, alter or print parts of the documentation. If documentation of organisational controls is held on the system, it has to be protected by additional security means so that, for example, the audit information is protected against unauthorised access, and not updated without that update being either authorised or documented.

The directory of organisational means should include means for protecting storage media used by the workstation. Four types of information are required with regard to the audit, and as far as removable storage media is concerned:

Source Number: a single item number that allows the unforgeable identification of the storage media.

Label: a uniform description of the kind of storage media: the label should consist of information on the physical structure of the formatted device and the contents of it. The contents of the storage media should be categorised according to a limited number of classes such as program-disk, overlay-disk, help-disk, text-disk or data- disk.

Contents: a brief description of the contents of the storage media. This allows the auditor to check that only valid versions are used. It should describe the name of the program or data used and the version or the last date in use.

Purpose: a shortened description of the use of the storage media. The application has to be described in terms of additional properties. Distinction between originals, back-ups and archive-storage media are recommended.

The directory of liability should be available for the auditor to collect auditing evidence. Therefore, the directory has to be readable, i.e. clearly structured. If it is stored in the computer files, it must be capable of being printed in a reasonable amount of time. For a workstation, a reasonable amount of time means at once, if there are no exceptional circumstances. The directory should also be used as an audit trail of responsibilities. This is necessary in order to have an addressee for the audit. If there is a lack of responsibility, for example, the owner of a program-diskette cannot be identified, further audit of the right use of the program is impossible. A clear definition of responsibilities is necessary for the segregation of duties, too. Segregation of duties includes both the separation of the responsibility for the custody of assets from the records, which account for them, and the separation of functions related to control in data processing areas. (Jenkins/Perry/Cooke, 1986 [Jenk86]).

The audit of the directory of liability should follow international standards for the audit of documentation. These standards are laid down by law and by international guidelines for auditing (IFAC 1987, IDW 1986, FAMA 1/1987). These cover the use of documentation, CAATs or clients' microcomputers for the audit of documentation.

Hardware Information

Secure hardware is necessary to support the data properly. The correct functioning of every component is a hardware requirement. The auditor's task is the evaluation of the reliability of the hardware. A possible result of hardware failure is the loss or destruction of data.

Auditability requirements for hardware can be regarded in two ways. Firstly, auditability of hardware requires a method to measure hardware reliability in an easy way. The hardware itself is evaluated with its features, i.e. disturbance-tolerance, supervision of the correct voltage reference, different and independent timers and independent turn offs (Holscher/Rader 1984).

This evaluation is a verification approach to verify the absence of failures. Failures should be detected. They could have different meanings, for instance:

- frauds: undesired properties, which can lead to a failure but which must not lead to a failure, defects. Undesired properties, which are recognised as a failure, because the property is a requirement,
- errors: a deviation of a calculated value (or condition) from the correct value (or condition),
- mistakes. failures produced by human beings, which could lead to undesired results.

Consequently, the auditor needs an instrument to evaluate the reliability of hardware components. Otherwise he/she is not able to make any statements on the absence of failures.

Secondly, the auditability of hardware consists of a list with all hardware means, which support the auditor's statement that the used hardware is secure against computer fraud. As an example, additional devices are used against unauthorised access, duplication, or interception.

Hardware is also employed to prevent data theft. Locking the storage medium, for example, the disk drive, by mechanical locks is an appropriate countermeasure. Security containers, which lock the whole WS, shall prevent access of extraneous persons. Legitimation is also supported by hardware devices for performance of authentication, for example chip-cards with intelligent tokens.

Chip-cards can be used in a banking environment to help prevent invention of fictitious contractors and transactions as well as the manipulation of messages. But they cannot prevent an authorised user (possessor of the chip-card) from modifying valid transactions. Another hardware component for workstation security is the use of secure connections between components. The connection lines from the workstation to other devices such as printers should be secured. A full consideration of hardware countermeasures is made in Chapter 12.

A resulting auditability requirement is a directory of hardware controls. This could be achieved by a Configuration Directory. The configuration directory consists of an inventory of all components of the workstation. The directory is used by the auditor to identify auditing objects.

Tests of physical controls in the ICS normally consist of observation, enquiries into the procedures in force, together with a review of the documentation. In relation to the physical security of the workstation, the auditor needs to see that appropriate areas and components are built in. He will also need to visit respective areas and check the components to observe that the security means outlined are being maintained (Jenkins/ Perry/Cooke 1986).

When relying on observation as a check, the auditor should bear in mind the possibility that the checked configuration with its controls may be altered during the relevant period. To reperform any changes in the hardware, it is necessary to produce a history of configuration alterations. With respect to the average lifetime of computers, it is estimated that a workstation has a lifetime ranging from 2 - 4 years. During this period, a history of configuration changes will not grow to any large extent. But with respect to practicality, the requirement produces additional work. In contrast to workstations which are bound into a network, configuration management with logging and observation of changes in hardware components, cannot be found in today's single workstation.

The proposed audit instrument is a complete history of all configuration conditions. The configuration directory has to collect audit evidence. It is recommended that the following items are contained in such a directory.

Explanation: a short comment on the configuration changes, or on the delivered hardware.

Component: the description of the existing hardware component, with its type, product number, serial number, etc.,

Date: the date of the first use in the configuration, and, if possible, additional data such as the date of delivery (for warranty reasons),

Authorisation: a confirmation of the alterations in the configuration, made by the responsible person.

In relation to the execution of accurate work with its new components, supplementary security features are appropriate and should be available. A resulting requirement for security is the unforgeable identification of every component. To support this requirement, the embedding of a device address or identifier via hardware or software mechanisms in computer system components, is necessary. The existence of secure identification facilitates auditability because otherwise the auditor must check the existence of other controls, which attest the use of only original hardware components. Finally, the configuration directory must be an auditable instrument, and it should follow the general criteria of auditability of documentation.

Software Information

The auditability requirements for software can be regarded in two ways. Firstly, the auditability of software requires a method of assessing software, in an easy way. The software itself is evaluated by its structure, program steps and commands.

Secondly, the auditability of software requires a method of assessing the adequacy of functioning of all of the software in the system, without undue difficulties. This is a systems approach which includes the verification of single programs, but also includes the detection of any computer abuse (misfunctioning of software and computer frauds) by software means. An auditor should be able to detect all failures in a system and to determine the type of failure detected.

Consequently, the auditor needs such an instrument to evaluate the reliability of the software program, since - with respect to the enormous complexity and structure of software - without a computerised tool, the auditor is not able to make any statements on the absence of failures.

In relation to this view of auditability, auditability could be achieved by a procedure, which provides the auditor with a sufficient degree of information, so that he can form his opinion on the reliability of the programs used. The procedure could also result in a recommendation on whether the software is auditable or not. The quality of the software has to be measured with a catalogue of quality criteria, such as user-friendliness, the absence of failures, easy audit of correct functioning, easy testing, easy maintenance, easy altering, and proper documentation.

The following requirements are very important for the auditability of software.(Holscher/Rader 1984):

• The software should be divided into modules, which must be small and surveyable,

- The software modules should be easily constructed,

- There should be only one connection between separate modules.

The requirements could be achieved for example by structured programming, which is a way of refining a task step-by-step until the tasks have reached a surveyable size (Jackson 1979 [JACK79]). These requirements however only support one view of auditability, they do not extend to readability and self-descriptability.

A general view of systems auditability with regard to the verification approach has been proposed by Ahlers *et al.* 1982 [AHLE82]. At the first level of refinement, auditability is described according to the following criteria:

- availability
- understandability
- risk-assessment

Availability is the physical precondition for every audit. It is guaranteed by the access rights of the auditor and his right to get information. A possible measurement of availability is the amount of time which is needed to obtain available information.

Understandability relates to the intellectual assessment of the software system. Intellectual assessment depends on the complexity of the system and on the characteristics of the system which ease access to it for example, readable documentation.

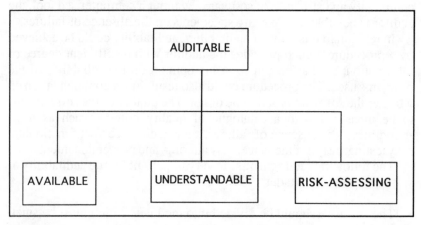

Figure 12.1 Auditability requirements for verification of systems

Risk-assessment relates to the auditing objective for evaluating potential damage to assets. It should be possible to recognise very easily the risks in the audited system, by an assessment of the construction of the software-system and its characteristics. The dependencies between these auditability criteria are listed in Figure 12.1.

Refined auditability requirements for verification of programs

The specific auditability requirements for verification of programs are listed in a more refined way in Figure 12.2 and described in the following text, following Ahlers *et al.*, 1982.

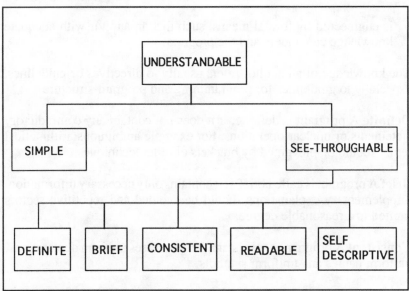

Figure 12.2 Refined auditability requirements for verification of programs

Auditable A program is auditable if the criteria of availability, understandability and risk-assessment are fulfilled.

Available A program is available, if a source code exists and this source code can be accessed by the auditor in an adequate amount of time.

Risk-assessment A program allows risk-assessment, if the impact of the program risks, for example, on the assets of the enterprise, can be easily recognised by the auditor.

Simple The term simple is used in contrast to complex. It refers to the logical structure of a program. For the measurement of programs according to simplicity, a scale of complexity measures exist. Complexity is characterised by the number of tasks carried out by a program, the amount and size of the modules and the degree of integration of these tasks. Furthermore the proportion of source and object code and the time expansion of storage without printouts of program lines indicates complexity. A program is simple, if certain limits are not exceeded.

See-throughable A program is see-throughable, if it:

• contains sufficient information for the understanding of the program,

• is engineered by formal means, such that an auditor with adequate knowledge can understand the program.

The knowledge of an auditor refers usually to directives or guidelines, especially to guidelines for programming and program-structure.

Definite A program is definite, if it does not contain any contradictory statements or unclear operations. For example ambiguous arithmetical terms should be prevented by brackets or other techniques.

Brief A program is called brief if it contains only necessary information. Supplementary explanations should be avoided and repetitive sectors limited to a reasonable degree.

Consistent A program is consistent, if it possesses uniform declarations, uniform names and uniform symbols.

Readable A program is readable, if the statements in the program can be recognised with little effort. The readability will be influenced by the layout of the program, for instance a clear structure and few commands in a row will enhance readability of programs.

Self-descriptive A program is self-descriptive, if the understanding of the program is possible within the program code. This presumes properties of a program such as self-descriptive variable names, self-descriptive datafile names, sufficient comment lines, etc.

Refined auditability requirements for verification of system documentation

The criteria have also been proposed by Ahller *et al.* for the system documentation. Figure 12.3 outlines the criteria for auditable documentation.

Documentation is necessary in order to identify which events have to be captured as audit evidence at what points in the system. The auditor's first step in a system's audit is the analysis of system documentation, in order to evaluate the orderly performance of program sequences and the adequacy of internal controls. Inadequacies in these areas determine the selection of events for further audit steps. Therefore, documentation has to fulfil the following auditability requirements.

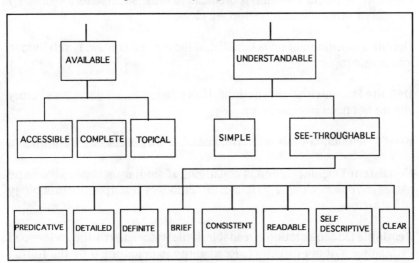

Figure 12.3 Refined auditability requirements for verification of system documentation

Available Documentation is available, if it allows the availability of all necessary information in an appropriate amount of time.

Accessible Documentation is accessible, if the material is maintained in an orderly collection and stored at a central location.

Complete Completeness is given, if all the information needs of the auditor can be satisfied.

Topical The documentation should show the latest state of software.

Understandable Documentation is understandable, if the intentions of the documented programs are obvious.

Simple The term simple is used in contrast to complex. This means that the structure, for example, table of contents and references, should be simple rather than complex.

See-throughable Documentation is see-throughable, if it:

* contains sufficient information for an understanding of the software,
* is formally designed in a way, that the auditor can understand it with his knowledge.

Predicative Documentation is predicative if the statements intended by the author of the documentation are clear.

Detailed Documentation is detailed, if the overall context is subdivided into single topics.

Definite Documentation is definite, if its statements are not contradictory and do not need interpretation.

Brief Documentation is brief, if it contains only necessary information.

Consistent Documentation is consistent, if similar facts have the same names and descriptions. This relates to methods of description, terminology and structure.

Readable Documentation is readable, if the statements can be understood by reading without difficulty. Readability is determined by the formal structure.

Self-descriptive Documentation is self-descriptive if it contains sufficient information for its understanding. This presumes properties such as self-evident headings and extensive tables of contents and glossaries.

Clear Documentation is clear if, the structure of the documentation and the description of single items is designed in a way, which allows the reader to obtain an overview as quickly as possible.

These criteria have been implemented at the University of Saarbrucken in the auditor's tool EPSOS-D, which is still a prototype. This approach to determine auditability is used to verify single data items of programs. It is not a systems auditability view, because it measures single criteria.

The most respected classification aid for verification of a system with its software is the study of the National Computer Security Center, NCSC [DoD 83].

12.9 AUDITING IMPLICATIONS OF WORKSTATIONS LINKED TO MULTI-USER, NETWORKED AND MAINFRAME SYSTEMS

Auditability Requirements for Workstations Linked to a Multi-user System

The major difference between a centralised multi-user system and a workstation appears in the role of an operator and the organisational functions he is needed for, i.e. the segregation of duties, the multi-user system requires supervision. Supervision is executed by an operator. In contrast to the concept of segregation of duties the single-user workstation user performs some security-relevant functions on his own. The user can start up/shut down a WS directly without operator intervention, connect/disconnect devices which are supported by configuration management, and perform any kind of operator function for the purposes of office automation. Furthermore he can back up his own files on removable storage media, for example, on diskettes, hard disks or tapes.

Some of the functions of a superuser, such as access to security functions, and operating and configuring the final workstation operating system are performed by the workstation user, whereas a multi-user system has a trusted system programmer/operator. (Gligor et al. 1986 [GLIG86a]).

The auditor of a secure multi-user system should determine the selectivity of the system audit functions on a per user, per process or per workstation basis. An exemplary audit mechanism for a multi-user system is proposed by the Secure Xenix WS approach, designed by IBM Corporation. This approach is described by Gligor et al., 1986 and is regarded as useful for multi-user auditability [GLIG86a].

The audit mechanism of Secure Xenix creates an auditor view of the recorded data that allows high-level reduction tools to create audit reports constituting the system's view of the audit. The necessary audit information consists of events, recorded at a low level, by the kernel. The events can be grouped in two major classes:

- System initialisation and entry events
- System/user process events.

System initialisation and entry events include actions performed by a so-called "system security administrator" who is responsible for the set-up of security parameters, i.e. the change of security labels for important data, the definition of the security level map, the performance of trusted upgrading and downgrading, the definition of the site identifier and logos, etc.

System user process events are violations of security through an unauthorised introduction of objects within a process address space, the unauthorised creation and deletion of subjects and objects, the denied access to objects, the denied interprocess signals. All security-relevant actions are observed, including actions performed by the security administrator, access privilege distribution and revocation and the use of known covert channels.

Each event of Secure Xenix has the following format:

<event sequence number, time stamp, event class and specific event, outcoming action, subject information, object information, additional details>

The *event sequence number* is an original identifier for the events-tuple, which puts events into order with regard to later audit reports. The *time stamp* logs the date and time of the event. *Events classes* are built according to the auditor's view, in the system's view of the auditor all kernel- call events and trusted process events are logged. The *outcoming action* is the action which is generated by the event. *Subject information* is information known by the subject, such as clearance, process, group and user identifiers. *Object information* is detailed information on the object, i.e. security level and object identifiers. Additionally, details may consist of kernel-call arguments and return values.

Summarised auditability requirements recommended for highly secure workstations are based on these events. For an auditor who migrates a system from a workstation via a multi-user system this is necessary audit information which he has to evaluate.

Auditability Requirements for Workstations Linked to a LAN and/or Gateway

For the workstation linked to a local area network, audit information concerning organisation, hardware and software is regarded as necessary. The job of the network is to convey information between named entities. If a workstation is connected to a network in a banking environment, external office automation procedures are invoked. Additional security requirements occur in a network. This is due to the fact that users or devices cannot be securely identified and the transmission lines cannot always be fully protected.

In a useful identification scheme, each party must be protected against all the other parties: dishonest provers cannot misrepresent themselves to verifiers that follow the protocol; dishonest verifiers cannot use their interaction with provers to misrepresent themselves later. Furthermore even coalitions of dishonest provers and verifiers cannot create or modify identities (Fiat/Shamir 1987 [FIAT87]).

The resulting security requirements can be characterised by two terms:

• Encryption, all data transmitted over the network must be encrypted,

• Authorisation, hosts may exchange data over the network if authorised to do so.

A workstation connected to a network belongs to an unspecified number of user hosts and an arbitrary number of hosts, which consist of key distribution centres (KDC) and access controllers (AC). The KDC distributes encryption keys for hosts who request to communicate. The AC supervises control by sending authorisation messages when a user host wants to communicate with another user host (Wing/Nixon 1986).

Both types of hosts are regarded as secure, if they use audited software. An auditor has to evaluate the trustworthiness of the KDC and AC, because they maintain the integrity of the system. Checking the correct functioning (as a function of absence of failures) of KDC and AC, can be achieved by means of program verification and system documentation. Another aspect in the evaluation of the trustworthiness of the network is the temporal logic of the system, which is primarily used to prevent frauds through user hosts, since every user may be a potential hacker.

Audit is used to record all security relevant events, especially events that change the security state of the system. But it is still unclear at what level auditing should take place, i.e. where should auditing be done and what should be audited (Brand/Arsenault 1985 [BRAN85]).

Suggestions for the place of auditing (such as each node in the network, one workstation, the file servers, etc.) resulting from this study indicate that auditing of the hosts is not sufficient. Components of a network, such as packet switches and access control centres, also have to be audited such that an auditor can migrate from a workstation to the host via the network. According to this suggestion it is clarified that all locations have to provide the auditor with the necessary audit information. The carrier of audit information could be a small number of centrally located network audit centres, or the information could be stored locally at each node. (Arsenault, 1985 [ARSE85]).

Concerning the question of what has to be audited in a network (for example establishment of a connection, security level of the connections, routing path of messages, every packet recorded, etc), a particular view is necessary. We have to consider that the actions to be audited are vastly different.

In a computer network, there are several different actions which a user can perform, for example, sending electronic mail, logging in at a remote host, or file transfer. Therefore, it has already been suggested that the users' actions are included in the audit trail. However, the action actually performed by a network user can be audited in the network node, not in the interworking between systems.

The recording of any security violations in the network concerning the WS and multiuser systems, (i.e. organisational events, hardware failures, failures in application programs and deficiencies in systems documentation verification, system initialisation and entry events, and the system/user process events) is an auditability requirement. Again, this is part of the auditability requirements for the network node, not the interworking between systems.

Any security violations in the network concerning the established connection should be audited. These are physical and logical connections and disconnections to hosts, or other networks to the audited network, as well as any other event that causes a change in the network configuration. This is an auditability requirement, formulated as a draft standard for a trusted network base (TNB), by the U S Department of Defense Computer Security Center (see below). Any security violations in the network concerning intrusions into a computer via an unsecure network should be audited. Intrusions are detected by the auditing mechanism of the host.

Of course it is important to audit all security-relevant events which occur in the network, for the purpose of detecting a security violation. The audit trail must be protected from tampering by unauthorised users, too.

The DoD added audit requirements for TNB to the Orange Book criteria of secure systems (see Appendix B). According to these audit principles of a TNB, the following auditability requirements have been proposed for a network [DoD 85]:

Class C1 "The TNB shall create, maintain, and protect from modification, unauthorised access, or destruction an audit trail of accesses to the resources that it protects. The audit data shall be protected by the TNB so that read access to it is limited to those who are authorised for audit data. The TNB shall be able to record the following types of events: use of host identification and authentication mechanisms, attempts to open a connection, attempts to close a connection, and changes in logical or physical connection of the network (e.g. connection or disconnection of a host, a packet switch crashing, etc.) For each recorded event, the audit shall identify: date and time of event, user, type of event, and success or failure of events. For identification/authentication events, the origin of request (e.g. host or terminal ID) shall be included in the audit record. For connection events, the audit trail shall include the host (or terminal) ID at both ends of connection. For resource access events, the audit trail shall include the resource name and location. The ADP system administrator shall be able to selectively audit the action of any one or more hosts based on host identity."

In the next class, C2, the necessary audit information has to ensure individual accountability, which is not provided at the C1 level.

Class C2 "The TNB shall be able to record any user access/use of network resources, or use of user identification and authentication mechanisms. The ADP system administrator shall be able to selectively audit the actions of any one or more users based on individual identity."

The division B relates to systems which support mandatory controls. There are three classes: B1, B2, B3 . In B1 security levels of subjects and objects are recorded. In B2 events which could cause the use of covert channels and that are a major source of compromise are additionally recorded. The requirements for B3 include supervision of data to ensure absence of compromise. Security alarms are caused at the earliest possible detection of an impending security violation, if users try to access data they are not cleared for.

Class B1 "For connection events, the audit trail shall include the host IDs and the security classification of the connection. For resource access events, the audit trail shall include the resource name, location, and security classification of the resource. The ADP system administrator shall be able to selectively audit the actions of any one or more users (hosts) based on individual (host) identity and/or the security classification of connections or resources."

Class B2 "The TNB shall also be able to audit the identified events that may be used in the exploitation of covert storage channels."

Class B3 "The TNB shall contain a mechanism that is able to monitor the occurrence or accumulation of security auditable events that may indicate an imminent violation of security policy. This mechanism shall be able to immediately notify the security administrator when thresholds are exceeded."

We regard the auditability requirements of class C1 as necessary audit information for every installed banking computer system, which aims at compliance with orderliness of data processing. The existence of more security features in the banking network depends on the assets which have to be secured. If the network is a unique system for the whole bank, auditability requirements should be extended to the higher classes.

Auditability Requirements for Workstations Linked to a Large Mainframe

Large mainframes usually have a large number of users. As with networks, identification is one of the important security functions of a mainframe. Users have to be identified. Any attempt to perpetrate the system should be recognised. In contrast to networks, mainframes have the capability to log every event via mass storage files using high computing power.

A further potential danger of a large mainframe is the dependency of the linked devices. A system break-down has to be prevented by means of organisational security functions which assure high availability, for example, with a back-up computing center.

We regard auditing as an active function, because it accomplishes part of the security policy of a mainframe. The required audit information consists of the requirements for highly secure office systems as defined in Section 12.8, with organisational information, hardware information and software information being necessary.

Organisational Information

Organisational information is provided by a directory of liability. The directory should contain all organisational security means and the identity of the persons resposible for them. According to the migration concept, only parts of the specific requirements for the mainframe have to be examined.

The mainframe is usually located in a more complex organisation.

Due to this fact, the size of the documentation of the organisation is much bigger. Nevertheless the documentation has to follow the criteria of auditability, for example, it shall be understandable. As an additional security requirement for large mainframes, the auditor must especially consider events, that can disturb availability.

Hardware Information

Hardware information is required as discussed in Section 11.9. In spite of the high complexity and the high number of users of a large mainframe, there are no additional requirements. Assistance for the auditor to conclude on reliability of the hardware is provided, since expensive hardware is checked more carefully and is much better documented by the vendor than smaller and cheaper devices.

Software Information

The whole range of software information described in Section 11.9 is required by the auditor. The main events that can occur on a large mainframe additionally to the events reported in earlier sections, are damages caused by intrusions. An auditor should be able to conclude on the absence of any intrusions.

12.10 STANDARDS

Standards of auditability are mainly set up on two different levels. National professional organisations and institutions of internal and external auditors work out guidelines for EDP-auditing. These guidelines are to be obeyed by the members of these organisations.

In Germany the IDW has a subcommittee, called FAMA, which recently published a new draft document on principles of orderly accounting with computer-based methods and their audit (FAMA 1/ 1987, IDW 1987).

These guidelines are structured in a way that first describes requirements and conditions for EDP-accounting systems, which have to be fulfilled by the system in order to comply with the principles of orderly accounting. Secondly, the guidelines outline the auditing methods, which are suitable to allow statements on the degree of compliance of the EDP-system with the forementioned principles. Auditability is formulated as formal criterion for orderliness of a system. Auditability has to realise reperformance of single transactions and reperformance of the accounting procedure as a whole.

The work of national committees is supplemented and coordinated by international organisations. In particular, the IFAC formulates guidelines for accounting, which are binding for all member organisations. Therefore the national member organisations have to comply with these guidelines, when they set up their national directives, if their work is to be internationally acknowledged.

The professional organisations of many countries, especially in Europe and the USA, are members of the IFAC and influence the process of setting up so-called "International Auditing Guidelines". In June 1985, the IFAC issued a guideline on *"The Effects Of An EDP Environment On The Study And Evaluation Of The Accounting System And Related Internal Controls"*. This statement defines characteristics of an EDP-environment, its organisational structure, the nature of processing and design and procedural aspects.

Internal controls have to be adjusted to these characteristics and to support the need to evaluate these controls. Therefore general EDP controls and EDP application controls have to be auditable. However, the international guidelines do not mention how auditability can be achieved. It is assumed that the auditability is realised and only the controls and the methods for evaluation are described.

In March 1987 the IFAC drafted a supplement to the forementioned guidelines, on *"EDP Environments - Standalone Microcomputers"*. These statements describe the features of microcomputer systems and their configuration and characteristics. They propose appropriate internal controls and outline the effect of microcomputers on the accounting system, on related internal controls and on audit procedures. The guideline gives advice on how an audit should be performed in a microcomputer environment but not on how auditability can be achieved. This leads to the conclusion that although standards for auditing have been developed, auditability as a precondition for auditing is not standardised.

12.11 CONCLUSION

The concept of a migrating audit trail has been presented in this report. Furthermore, general and special auditability requirements have been defined for highly secure office information systems in a banking environment.

The migrating audit trail is an instrument to be used by the auditor to perform an EDP-audit of a complex EDP system. The trail fulfils certain auditability requirements. For example, the audit trail allows reperformance of the procedures which are used in the processing of transactions. Checking of the documentation of the respective programs is also required. This gives rise to the requirement of auditable documentation. The audit trail consequently provides a list of criteria for this. The auditor will use this list as a checklist to control the orderliness of the documentation and to form an opinion on the accounting procedures by reperforming them with the obtained documentation.

In this context, testing is also necessary to verify the operation of the application programs. Therefore, there is a requirement for software-supported test aids. The audit trail lists the information items which the auditor has to obtain from the system in order to be able to perform testing.

Summarised, the migrating audit trail is an instrument which helps fulfil auditability requirements. It collects and presents the necessary audit information in an adequate manner and gives access to this evidence. The evaluation of this audit evidence allows conclusions to be drawn on the degree of fulfilment of the auditability requirements. If auditability is realised, the auditor can form his opinions according to his specific control objectives.

The formulation of opinions and statements belongs to the process of auditing. The objectives and methods of the audit have always to be kept in mind. They determine which information must be provided for the audit trail and where this information has to be located according to the migration concept.

The migrating audit trail is an instrument, which accomplishes auditability objectives and functions. The implementation of an audit trail in an EDP-system realises auditability.

To date, a wide range of the defined auditability requirements can be fulfilled by modern EDP-systems. Basically, the technical solutions are available. However, standards for the realisation of auditability have not yet been developed. In contrast to this, EDP-auditing itself is in a constant process of standardisation in national and international auditing committees. So the determining parameters for auditability are available with considerable reliability.

We consider it dangerous that the auditing profession does not spend enough efforts on the standardisation of auditability requirements, which are the preconditions for auditing. The auditor tends to presume that auditability is realised and relies on the audit information which is available, without considering if this evidence sufficiently fulfils auditability requirements. Therefore, it could be stated that an EDP-audit cannot always deliver qualified statements with necessary reliability on the system operation.

This underlines the necessity to design a proper instrument, which automatically obliges the auditor to check auditability and assists him/her in obtaining the adequate and necessary audit evidence. The migrating audit trail can be designed to function as such an instrument.

Furthermore it has to be considered that the design of the migrating audit trail must be a very careful compromise between audit information needs, cost effectiveness and efficiency. The audit trail must not overload the system and slow down processing speed or occupy too much storage capacity; ergonomic aspects must also be covered.

13

Introduction to the Treasury Management System

13.1 INTRODUCTION

In the final phase of the MARS project, the main effort was directed towards the application of the results of the earlier phases to the provision of security in an existing application. The application chosen for this task comprised a range of procedures carried out on a small computer system which together provided a sophisticated *treasury management system* (TMS) for a large company.

Although the security measures and architecture described here were developed specifically for the operation of the TMS using microcomputers, they are equally applicable to many advanced business and trading systems. The security measures conceived in the MARS project, and described here, cover all aspects of system security, including the assurance of the security of all operational procedures, the definition of staff duties, the physical security of computer equipment and the logical security of information during processing, storage and transmission over a network.

The approach taken by the MARS project for the provision of security in the TMS has been to specify equipment which must be used solely for the TMS operations. With economy in mind the equipment has, whenever possible, consisted of readily available general purpose hardware supplied with some operating software by the manufacturer. Many of the security measures described here can, therefore, be incorporated into existing microcomputer-based systems with minimal alterations to either the hardware or the software supplied by the manufacturer.

13.2 THE TREASURY MANAGEMENT SYSTEM

A TMS, usually operated by a large company in conjunction with its banks, provides a variety of sophisticated cash management facilities enabling the company's trained treasury staff to access and process information regarding the company's assets which are held by the company's banks. For the company, the advantages of operating such a system are the ease of management of its assets and the increased speed and flexibility provided by the system when handling all types of financial transaction. The main benefit for the banks is that an increased level of service can be offered to their clients.

Although there is a wide diversity of treasury management activities, a small core of activities has been identified which comprises banking, borrowing, investment, foreign exchange and working capital control. Providing these few core procedures in an automated TMS is sufficient to furnish a company with a flexible and efficient means of controlling its liquid assets.

With the automated TMS, the company treasurer can raise transaction orders for cash transfer and is able to ensure that any required funds are made available at an appropriate time in the correct currency. The main advantages of using the TMS for cash transfer are that the transaction is effected speedily and the company's treasurer can monitor and retain complete control over the entire operation.

As well as enabling efficient cash transfers, the TMS also provides a range of functions to assist in financial planning, allowing the treasurer to make a detailed analysis of the company's use of its assets. Financial planning functions include the provision of a summary of the company's most recent use of its assets and enable the forecasting and prediction of future financial requirements based on an historical analysis of previous trends. These functions are provided to aid the company in the efficient planning of its use of assets.

13.3 THE TMS ENVIRONMENT

One of the requirements of the TMS is that all operations may be performed by a company's treasurer, on the company's own premises. A company making use of the TMS will maintain a single computer to be used for all the company's automated TMS operations. The computer will provide all the facilities necessary for generating transaction orders and monitoring and forecasting the company's use of its assets. Although these functions can be performed in isolation by the company's treasurer using the TMS computer, they operate on information which is normally held by the company's banks. A secure and efficient means of transferring information between a company and its banks is therefore necessary for the effective employment of the TMS.

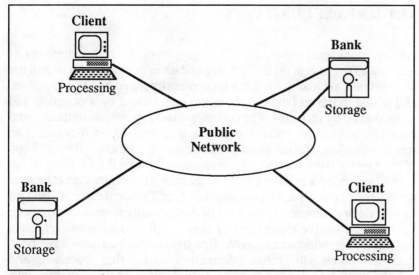

Figure 13.1 The banks and their clients communicate via an insecure public network.

In the MARS project, the TMS network was devised to provide the means of transferring information between the companies who use the TMS and their banks. Figure 13.1 is a diagrammatic representation of the TMS network which is used by a number of companies each of which may be the client of several separate banks. The companies use the network in order to transfer information to and from storage at the bank to enable local processing.

Thus from a company's point of view, the banks' TMS facilities allow data storage and retrieval, whilst all processing is controlled by the company's staff using the company's own workstation. The companies' TMS computers therefore contain all the hardware facilities and software utilities necessary to provide both the TMS cash management facilities and the communications with the bank's equipment.

For convenience and economy, all communications carried by the TMS network may take place over an existing public network, such as the telephone network. Each company may link a single TMS computer to the TMS network, enabling communications with any number of banks of which it is the client. To allow the banks to respond to requests generated by the companies' computers, each bank may connect several end systems to the TMS network. This allows simultaneous communications between a single bank and many of its clients. The TMS does not require either communications between individual companies or between banks, although the network may be used by the banks and the companies to provide for this if necessary.

13.4 DATA SECURITY

An important aspect of the MARS project involved the development of
techniques to provide for the security of data in the TMS both within the
end systems, such as in the TMS computers operated by the companies,
and whilst in transit between the computers owned by a company and
those owned by its banks. The computers used are microcomputers and
communications are carried over the insecure public network. The
measures required for the assurance of data security include the provision
of the mechanisms necessary to ensure security and the adoption of the
correct procedures to ensure that the security mechanisms are effective.

Wherever possible, the components of the TMS make use of standard
or proprietary equipment. Because of this, security measures have been
devised which can be applied to equipment which itself provides inadequate
facilities to provide secure, error free operation. Measures have been
designed which will protect information both during processing and
storage in a computer and during transmission over a communications
network.

Although it is infeasible to provide a security system which can ensure
comprehensive security with absolute certainty, it is possible to provide
security measures and operational procedures which can together eliminate
the vast majority of unintentional errors and make a determined malicious
attack both difficult and prohibitively expensive. To this end, a detailed
risk analysis was commissioned, which was used to identify the
vulnerabilities arising from the use of a TMS. This enabled the construction
of a set of guidelines for workstation security, which were evaluated with
reference to a case study of the use of a TMS in a large commercial
organisation.

Using the guidelines for workstation security, together with the results
of the case study, it has been possible to devise a system architecture
which will provide the necessary security facilities whilst taking into
account the operational procedures of the TMS. Other influences on the
final architecture include practical aspects of economy and the nature of
the system components whilst the development has been influenced by
the work of the international standards organisations. In particular, the
security framework produced by ECMA for the application layer of open
systems, although covering a broader scope than necessary has proved to
be the most appropriate for the MARS project.

The physical components of the companies' computer systems include,
for reasons of economy and convenience, an industry standard personal
micro computer. The security architecture requires that additional software
and hardware elements be incorporated with the standard equipment. In

the MARS project the microcomputer, together with all the additional hardware and software security features and any additional peripheral devices is known as the *TMS workstation*.

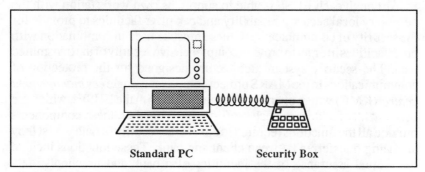

Figure 13.2 A standard personal computer is used together with a security box

The security architecture devised for the protection of information during processing and storage in each of the TMS workstations places all the necessary security functions in a single logical component which is known as the *end user security facility* (EUSF). Much of the software which comprises the EUSF remains resident in the computer during the operation of the TMS, along with the TMS application software. Some additional software is contained in a separate hardware component, known as the security box, which is permanently connected to the computer (see Figure 13.2).

The computer is provided with a direct data connection to the security box which supports the security functions carried out by the EUSF. Some of the hardware components contained in the security box are concerned with; aspects of cryptography, some are provided to control other hardware devices in a secure manner, and some provide general hardware support such as the combined clock and calendar. All of these functions are available, via the data connection, to the software running on the computer.

In addition to the security architecture designed in the MARS project for the protection of information within a workstation, a complimentary security architecture was developed in parallel with this to provide for the protection of information which must be transmitted between two workstations during the operation of the TMS. As already described, all information transmitted between workstations is carried over the existing public communications network, which provides little or no protection against a determined attack. The design of the EUSF incorporates those facilities which are necessary to ensure the security of data in transit between two workstations over the existing public network. In addition to the inherent insecurity of the transmission medium, the architecture also takes into account its maximum capacity and the cost of communications where appropriate.

Although each EUSF is able to supply its own workstation with the necessary local security capability and can offer facilities to provide for the security of communications, these must be used in combination with other facilities in order to provide comprehensive security of the transmitted data. The security system architecture designed for the protection of communications in the MARS project comprises a single *key management centre* (KMC) which operates in conjunction with the EUSFs, which are permanently resident in each workstation. Together, these components provide all the functions required to ensure the security of data whilst they are being transferred between client and bank. These functions include the mutual assurance of the identities of a bank and its clients, data integrity and data confidentiality.

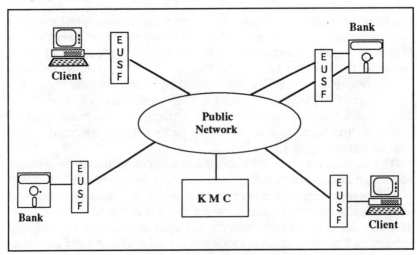

Figure 13.3 The TMS with communications security facilities

Each end system, such as a client's workstation, is ensured the security of its transmissions by its EUSF. The identity of the other communicating party and the integrity of received information is checked by the EUSF, using information which has been previously obtained from the KMC. Security of data whilst held by a client for processing or in storage is facilitated by the adoption of suitable operational procedures, together with the use of the security functions which are provided by the EUSF.

14

Operation of the Treasury Management System

14.1 INTRODUCTION

Operation of the TMS involves the execution of a range of tasks, the overall aim of which is to ensure the efficient and secure execution of the treasury functions which are performed by a company's normal treasury staff. The tasks performed on the automated system can be classified and are broadly divided into two groups: those which are carried out in order to perform the normal treasury functions and those which are concerned with the system's management. All system users are similarly classified according to their duties, the classification reflecting the aforementioned broad division of tasks, but with additional refinements according to more specific requirements of the users' tasks.

This chapter firstly describes the TMS in terms of the functions it provides to a company's treasurers. This is followed by a description of the full classification of system users and the operations performed by the users. Treasury related functions and system management functions are addressed separately, reflecting the division described above. The emphasis of the description is from the view of the company using the TMS, although points relevant to the banks and the TMS key management centre are also mentioned.

14.2 TREASURY FUNCTIONS

From the company treasurer's point of view, the TMS is an internal management system which can be used for a variety of cash management activities including reporting, planning and preparing transactions. All of the TMS operations are performed by a number of procedures which remain resident in the workstation, although some of these procedures operate on data which must either be transferred from the company's banks before processing or to one of the company's banks after preparation. From the bank's point of view, the TMS is providing an electronic banking service for its clients. The main difference between the TMS and

241

traditional electronic banking is that the clients' banking services are all provided by their own workstations. Thus the banks' workstations will perform a different rôle to those maintained by the companies. In particular, the banks' workstations will be used mainly to examine the requests from the banks' clients and to forward these requests to the banks' own internal systems whenever appropriate.

The operations performed on a company's workstation can be divided into three groups: monitoring and forecasting, transaction orders and data transfer. The data transfer functions are provided to support the other functions. An entirely different set of operations are performed on the banks' workstations, namely obtaining their clients' account data from the bank's main computers and transferring the incoming transaction orders for internal processing.

Monitoring and forecasting

The monitoring and forecasting functions are performed locally, using the functions provided within a company's TMS workstation which operate on the account data provided by the company's banks. Data may be transferred by the company's treasurer from each bank at which the company holds an account, to be merged and analysed to provide a comprehensive review of the company's present use of its resources and a forecast of its future requirements. These functions require the use of the network only for the receipt of data since during their operation there is no requirement for the transfer of data to a bank from the workstation.

Daily account statements generated by the TMS provide a clear and up to date record of the company's ledger balances. Although these statements are not used by the cash management facilities of the TMS, the records must be maintained by the company for bookkeeping purposes.

Other functions made available by the TMS allow a treasurer to monitor and forecast turnover by analysing more general account statements which are provided by the system. These statements, unlike the simple daily statements, include both items which have already been booked to the accounts and pre-booked items for which contracts exist although the item has not yet been booked.

As an aid to the cash manager, value dated balances are provided which give a forecast of cash availability based on the transactions which have been recorded. Both booked and pre-booked items are used in the generation of these balances, which show the actual and predicted cash flow and the funds available at any given time.

Transaction Orders

Two types of transaction order may be prepared on a TMS workstation, namely domestic bank transfers and direct debits. Similar procedures are involved in the preparation of either type of order. All relevant information will be manually entered by the company's personnel with authorisation to do so, after which it may be checked a number of times by more senior personnel during the various stages of preparation.

The preparation of all transaction orders will be performed locally, using only the procedures and data that are provided by the company's TMS workstation. Once a transaction order has been prepared, it can be stored along with other orders in the workstation for further processing, checking or for future transmission to the bank. If a previously prepared transaction order is found to be incorrect, or is no longer required, it may be amended or deleted as appropriate before transmission to the bank.

Data transfer

Data transfer to and from a bank is required at some stage by the monitoring and forecasting functions and after the preparation of transaction orders. A connection must be set up with the necessary banks only for the duration of the data transfer. In the case of transaction orders, this will be after preparation. For monitoring and forecasting, data transfer may be required at pre-defined intervals to ensure that the information held on the workstation is kept up to date.

Under some circumstances, data may also need to be transferred to or from storage in computers other than those used for the TMS operations. TMS workstations will accept transaction orders which have been prepared on other equipment. At a bank, the company's account data may be transferred to and from the bank's other computer equipment where transaction processing is performed.

Obtaining account information

Having received a request for account information from a client, the TMS application in the bank's workstation will first check the validity of the request before issuing a request to the bank's own computers. The format of the request issued by the workstation will be tailored to the requirements of the bank's existing system. The information supplied by the bank's system will be suitably formatted by the workstation before transmission of the response to the client.

Transfer of transaction orders

In addition to handling requests for account information, the banks' workstations will receive transaction orders from the clients which will be checked by the TMS application before being passed to the banks' internal system. Once a transaction order has been accepted and stored internally by the bank, an acknowledgment of receipt will be prepared on the workstation and transmitted to the originator of the order. On completion of the instructions by the banks' internal system, the TMS application running on the workstation will be informed. A receipt will then be generated on the workstation for transmission to the originator.

14.3 CLASSIFICATION OF USERS

For the normal operation of the TMS, three main classes of TMS users have been identified. These classes cover the various types of operation which are performed on the client's workstation, at the bank, and at the KMC. Both the client and the bank must provide personnel from their staff to perform the duties of each of the user classes which are appropriate to their use of the TMS. The classes which have been defined correspond to the segregation of duties often found in many organisations.

The three main classes are defined as: the TMS user who performs the normal TMS operations; the security officer who is responsible for the secure running of the system, and the auditor who must check the security of the system when required. The users who perform the normal TMS operations can be further divided into sub-groups, according to the specific duties which they perform. Four such TMS user sub groups have been defined corresponding to four classes of TMS operation which require different levels of responsibility to be placed on the users. Although these additional classes and the broad categories of operation have been defined in the MARS project, the specific duties and operational privileges which divide users into the different groups are decided by the security officer who is in charge of security policy and its application to the workstation.

With the four classes of TMS user, the auditor and the security officer, a total of six workstation user groups have been defined, although not all groups are appropriate for all workstations. This classification includes only those users who are involved in the normal day to day running of the TMS workstation and does not include other personnel such as the maintenance staff who are required for installation and maintenance of the hardware and software components. Staff duties relevant for each group are briefly described below.

Group 1

During the operation of the TMS, the client may require the local processing and intermediate storage of data either for preparation prior to transmission or for analysis after reception. These operations can be carried out using the workstation's local processing capability entirely off-line, as there is no requirement for communications with the bank's workstation. Since the users who are solely involved in the local processing, storage and retrieval of data need never use any of the facilities associated with network communications, they can be provided with a minimum subset of the available TMS functions. Users who only ever require functions from this restricted subset are classed together as group 1 users. Since the local processing of data is performed neither on the banks' nor on the KMC's workstations, the Group 1 classification of users is appropriate only to the clients' TMS users.

The security facilities of the EUSF are required by Group 1 users to maintain the confidentiality and integrity of locally prepared data, using the cryptographic capability of the security box. As communications are not required, the only cryptographic keys which need to be obtained by these users are those symmetric keys which are used for the protection of locally stored data. The EUSF ensures that Group 1 users are unable to access any other functions, such as those regarding communications and does not provide the user with any asymmetric keys.

Group 2

A second group of users is defined with similar local processing capabilities as those users belonging to Group 1. In addition to these local operations, the Group 2 users are able to access TMS functions allowing them to transmit some types of locally prepared data and to retrieve data held remotely, using the network for communications. The data transfer activities which are performed by this group of users may form a limited subset of all such activities, as defined by the security officer. For example, the security officer may specify that Group 2 users can perform operations such as account enquiries, but cash transfer operations are restricted to more privileged users.

Again, these operations are performed only by the users of the clients' workstations, so are therefore not appropriate for the staff at either the bank or at the KMC.

Only a subset of the communication facilities will be available to Group 2 users which are sufficient for the types of operations performed but will not allow any of the more privileged operations. To enable secure communications, Group 2 users must be furnished with the asymmetric key encipherment keys and certificates used for key distribution. Symmetric data encipherment keys will be made available to ensure the confidentiality and integrity of both locally stored data and data in transit between the two parties.

Group 3

In addition to the limited data entry and retrieval functions performed by the Group 2 users, the clients' Group 3 users are able to input data for cash transfers. An example of the type of operation performed is initiating a direct debit or domestic cash transfer. Additional security is needed for these operations, in the form of a digital signature for proof of delivery and proof of receipt of the instructions.

At the bank, Group 3 users are authorised to sign messages acknowledging receipt of their clients' instructions and to sign final receipts confirming that the instructions have been carried out. The signed acknowledgments and receipts will be stored on the bank's workstation for transmission to the client on request.

The users classed in Group 3 can take part in a pre-signature or double signature process. It must be ensured that the EUSF of both the client's and bank's TMS workstation contain information on the authorised signatories and the correct order of signatures.

Group 4

Group 4 users have the same privileges as Group 3 users, but in addition can perform other more specialised operations. The exact nature of these operations is defined by the security officer responsible for the particular workstation. Generally, Group 4 operations will be those which either need to be performed infrequently or are of a such a nature that the security officer wishes to limit them to a small subset of users.

An example of Group 4 operations is the transfer of files between a TMS workstation and other computers over a local area network. For a client, this operation would be performed only when data has been prepared on, or requires processing by computers other than the TMS workstation. Since the TMS workstations contain all the necessary facilities for the preparation and processing of TMS data, the file transfer operation would be unusual, and could be subject to abuse if it were accessible by a large number of users. At a bank, the transfer of files to and from the bank's other computers may be more common, for example in order to process the clients' instructions, but due to the sensitive nature of the information should still be restricted to a small group of users.

At the bank, the entry and alteration of data on a TMS workstation, other than the usual acknowledgments or receipts, will be an unusual operation which is to be performed only in exceptional circumstances, whilst for the client data entry would be performed more frequently. The execution of this type of operation would therefore ideally be restricted to the privileged users from Group 4 at the bank, but could also be performed by users in Groups 1, 2 and 3 for the client.

There are no Group 4 users present at the KMC, since no TMS operations are performed on the KMC workstation, which is primarily concerned with the provision of a security service for the other workstations.

Group 5

Group 5 users perform the auditing functions which are necessary to ensure the correct operation of the workstations, and are called the auditors. The auditor's duties do not include any of the normal TMS operations performed by users in Groups 1 to 4. The auditor is able to access all files for reading, and possesses a data key which allows access to the audit log and non-repudiation files. By examining these files, the auditor can trace the history of operations performed at the TMS workstation.

The auditing functions performed by the auditor include
- checking on the internal security controls and operating procedures
- checking the effectiveness of access controls
- checking that transactions are complete, accurate and correctly authorised
- checking that data, updating and processing are complete and accurate
- checking all aspects of business and organisational efficiency.

Using auditing facilities which are not available to any other class of user, the auditor can determine which users accessed the system at a given time and which operations were performed by them. If the auditor is called upon as a result of a security incident, the auditor will be able to determine the status of the system when the incident occurred and the problems involved.

Audit log files are generated and maintained automatically by the system to enable the auditor to perform the analysis of its operation. The audit log files which are to be stored in an archive must be transferred from the TMS workstation to the archive by the security officer, in the presence of the auditor, who ensures that the operation is carried out properly. The auditor is then responsible for the safe keeping of the archived information.

Group 6

Users belonging to Group 6 are the security officers, who are responsible for all the security related administrative operations for their workstation. There is only one security officer with the responsibility for a given workstation who, like the auditor, does not perform any of the usual TMS operations carried out by the users belonging to Groups 1 to 4.

The responsibilities of the security officer include the following:

- Initialisation of the workstation, using the key transport chip card;
- Enrolling and expelling users belonging to Groups 1 to 5;
- Management of user profiles;
- Local key management;
- Certificate management;
- File maintenance and back up.

The security officer will maintain a written log of users who have been enrolled, disenrolled, black listed or have had their keys or certificates revoked. This log will be available for examination by the auditor. A security policy which is to be applied to the TMS workstation and its operation is set and maintained by the security officer. All aspects of security management are then carried out by the security officer.

Summary of user groups

Table 14.1 gives a summary of the six user groups described above, showing the permitted operations. The users in Groups 1-4 perform the normal TMS operations, whilst the other two user groups are concerned with administrative tasks. The TMS operations of the users from Groups 2-4 are described in terms of the operations performed by the users in the preceding groups, with the additional operations indicated. The normal TMS users thus form a hierarchy, with the minimum number of functions being performed by users in Group 1 and the maximum number accessible to the Group 4 users. Group 5 and 6 users are not able to perform any of the TMS operations carried out by the other users.

All workstations require the presence of a security officer and auditor, but there are differing requirements for the presence of the TMS users. Clients may require users belonging to each of the user groups described above, although for those clients with a limited staff a Group 4 user could also perform the operations of the Group 1-3 users.

At the bank, the operations are concerned mainly with servicing the clients' requests, with no requirement for the entry of the requests themselves. The bank's operations are mainly concerned with signing receipts and handling the clients' account data. Due to the nature of these operations and the sensitivity of the data, the banks' TMS users belong only to Groups 3 and 4.

Table 14.1 Summary of user options

Group	Permitted operations by client's staff	Permitted operations by bank's staff	Permitted operations by KMC staff
1	Only local data preparation	Not applicable	Not applicable
2	Group 1 + Operations	Not applicable	Not applicable
3	Group 2 Pre-signature of cash transfers	Signature of receipts	Not applicable
4	Group 3 + Local file transfers	Group 3 + Local file transfers	Not applicable
5	Only auditing	Only auditing	Only auditing
6	Only security administration	Only security administration	Only security administration

Since the rôle of the KMC is primarily to provide a security service for the users of the TMS, it supports none of the normal TMS functions and has no TMS staff from user Groups 1- 4. The users present at the KMC are concerned only with administrative and security matters and will be only the security officer, auditor and general maintenance staff.

14.4 USER OPERATIONS

Users belonging to the six groups described above are each involved in different aspects of the running of the TMS. A complete TMS session on the client's workstation requires that users acting for the client sign onto the workstation for the local preparation, signing and transmission of data. Signing on only allows those operations which may be carried out without any communications between the local workstation and other workstations. To enable communications with a bank's workstation for data transfer, after signing onto the client's workstation, a user must then log onto the bank's workstation. Data may either be transferred from the bank to enable analysis of the account information, or to the bank for automated cash transfers.

The operations described below refer only to the normal day to day running of the TMS application procedures, performed by users belonging to Groups 1- 4. Management and security related activities which are performed by the auditor and the security officer are described in a later section.

Power up

A switch on the security box controls the power to the entire workstation, including the security box itself and the computer. The advantage of placing the power switch on the security box is that the security box can then ensure that the entire workstation is powered up in a secure manner. With the power supplied via the security box, one of the functions of the security box will be to control the start up procedure by determining when power is to be supplied to the rest of the workstation.

For security purposes, the parts of the workstation which are not contained within the security box will be supplied with power only after the user has been satisfactorily identified and authenticated. Once power has been supplied to the computer, software comprising the operating system, EUSF and TMS application will be loaded from the workstation's hard disc. An application in the security box can check that the EUSF software has been successfully loaded and is running on the computer.

Sign on

All users must sign onto a TMS workstation before performing any of the TMS operations and must sign off when finished. The purpose of the signing on procedure is to authenticate the identities of the user, chip card and the EUSF. Only after a user has signed on will power be supplied to the computer and the application software be loaded, allowing the user to perform local TMS tasks such as the preparation of data. The action of signing on by itself does not allow any communication with other TMS workstations.

To sign on to a TMS workstation, after switching on the power, a user must insert a chip card into the card reader on the security box and enter a PIN using the key pad provided on the security box. Authentication of the user's identity is provided solely by the entry of a correct PIN, a copy of which is stored on the chip card and is compared with the value entered by the user on the key pad The card and EUSF are able to authenticate each others' identity by means of a shared hash function which is used to compute a hash value for items of data exchanged between the card and the EUSF. The EUSF will also check the card contents of the validity field stored on the card. Finally, the security box will check the user black list, maintained by the EUSF, before supplying power to the computer.

If after the maximum allowed number of attempts authentication is unsuccessful, the chip card will be invalidated by the EUSF, which will alter the information contained in the card's validity field. At the same time, the ID of the security box and the time of day will also be written to the card. Whether the authentication has been successful or unsuccessful, the attempt to sign on will be recorded in the audit log. The audit entry will include the time of day and the card ID, which also serves to identify the owner of the card. After a user has successfully signed on, the security box will supply power to the computer, enabling the EUSF software and TMS application software to be loaded.

Data preparation

The preparation of data is performed by a company's employees locally using the company's workstation, prior to transmission over the network to the relevant banks. No access to any of the communication software is needed during this local preparation of data. Specific modules of the TMS application software will be provided to allow all the necessary data preparation steps, including input, editing, printing and deletion of data, although the full range of facilities may not be available for certain groups of users. If necessary, the cryptographic facilities of the security box may be invoked by the application software to ensure the confidentiality or integrity of the prepared data whilst in storage within the workstation. Depending on the security policy set by the security officer, these additional facilities may be invoked on request by the user for particular files, or may be invoked automatically for all files.

Whenever the cryptographic facilities are required for the protection of locally stored data, a symmetric data encipherment key must be generated in the security box, to be used for either the generation of a MAC to verify data integrity, or for encipherment of data to ensure confidentiality. The cryptographic key will then be stored in the security box to enable the MAC to be checked or the data to be deciphered when required by the user. An entry will be made in the audit log indicating the generation of a key for that user. Since the data may not need to be accessed until a later session, the encipherment key must remain in storage between TMS sessions, when the workstation's power will be turned off.

For logical access control and to enable any data generated by a user to be accessed after its protection by cryptography, the user's identifier and the identifiers of any files to which the key applies will be stored by the EUSF. This will ensure that the appropriate keys can be used each time the files are accessed. When all the files which have been protected by a particular key have served their purpose and have been removed from the system, the key which was used for their protection can then be deleted from the security box. As part of the security policy, the security officer may wish to restrict some users to the processing of data stored in only one file at a given time, so that an individual user will only ever need one data encipherment key to be stored in the security box.

Although the data encipherment keys stored in the security box are normally not transferrable between users, the security officer will be aware of all such keys from the entries in the audit log. In exceptional circumstances, such as when a user is black listed, data from any file can be recovered by the auditor who has access to every data encipherment key that is held in the security box and thus may access any of the TMS data files. Once the data have been recovered, they can be stored in new files, protected with new keys. The old files and their associated keys can then be deleted.

Data processing

An important function of the the TMS workstation allows the processing of financial data to provide a company with an overview of its use of resources and to predict future trends based on past records. Once the data is available at a workstation, all further processing may be carried out locally on that workstation. Most of these functions could be made available to the widest range of employees (for exmple all user groups), although it may be preferable for some functions such as printing to be restricted to a smaller sub-set.

Signing data

Once data has been prepared, it may be signed by a user acting for the client, belonging to one of the Groups 2, 3 or 4. The signing process requires the use of the digital signature service provided by the security box, based on the use of public key cryptography. If the data has already been prepared by an entry clerk and temporarily stored by a user other than the assigned signatory, then any key which may have been used to protect the data must be available to the signatory to allow access to the data.

Thus when data which has been prepared by the data entry clerk and is ready for signing but require protection in storage before signing can take place, the TMS software enables the data entry clerk to identify the assigned signatory. The security box will then be instructed to generate a symmetric key for use by the entry clerk only in order to protect the data during storage and for use by the named signatory for retrieval of the data. When signed, the data may then be stored again if necessary, protected by another key, generated by the signatory, ready for further signing or transmission.

Some operations may require two signatures from appointed signatories in user Groups 3 or 4. Operations which require double signatures are specified by the security officer and signatories are appointed by the security officer. Likely choices of operation requiring double signatures are domestic transfers and direct debits. The first signatory, from user Groups 3 or 4 will sign the information using the signature function of the security box and, if file protection is necessary, will specify the second signatory, also from user Groups 3 or 4, to the TMS software. A symmetric key will be obtained from the security box which will be used by the first signatory to protect the data, but which can be used by the second signatory to access the data.

Log on

When prepared and signed data is ready to be transmitted from a company's workstation to its bank, or when account data is required from the bank, a user acting for the company must first log on to the bank's workstation, establishing a secure communication channel before any data can be transmitted. The purpose of the log on procedure is for the mutual authentication of users and to establish a secure channel between the TMS application modules resident in each of the client's and bank's workstations.

Mutual authentication of a client's and bank's users is provided by the exchange of information previously obtained by each party from the KMC. The information is contained in a pair of off-line certificates, generated by the KMC in response to requests from the client and the bank. A separate certificate is provided to each client and bank which serves to bind a public key to a particular user name. This ensures that a successful decipherment of received information with the public key is sufficient to convince the recipient of the validity of the claimed identity of the sender. A more detailed account of the operation of this scheme is given in a later section.

With the pair of certificates exchanged, and the identities of the two parties authenticated, the next stage is for the client's security box to generate a symmetric encipherment key to be transmitted to the bank's workstation. This new key may then be used by either party for the protection of any further data transmitted between the two workstations.

Although several exchanges of information are made, logging onto a bank's workstation is a simple operation for the user, as only the name of the bank need be specified. The other information is either already held in the security box or is generated by the security box, under the control of the TMS application software, with the minimum of user intervention.

Users belonging to Groups 2,3 and 4 are able to log onto a bank's workstation for the normal TMS activities. The exact operations which may be performed by particular users vary according to the privileges assigned by the security officer. The security officer may also log onto a bank's workstation, but for administrative duties only. A record of the entire logging-on operation is entered in each of the audit logs maintained by the client and the bank.

Service request

After logging onto the bank's workstation, the user who is acting on the behalf of the client may select one of the TMS operations, such as raising a transaction order or obtaining account information. The types of operation which may be performed by a particular user depend on the privileges which have been assigned to that user by the security officer. If the data to be transferred has already been prepared or has been pre-signed, the appropriate files must first be retrieved from local storage and deciphered if necessary. After retrieval and transmission, any encipherment keys which have been used solely for protection of the data during local storage can be destroyed as necessary. With transaction data ready for transmission, the TMS application software will allow a digital signature to be appended if required. Other controls may additionally be applied to ensure the integrity and confidentiality of the data during their transit between the two workstations. Any of these three security measures providing confidentiality, integrity or digital signature may be independently selected as required by the user. Since the digital signature mechanism also provides integrity, however, this mechanism will probably not be used in conjunction with the separate integrity mechanism.

Print files

Any of the information held in a TMS workstation may be printed on a local printer which must be connected to the workstation. Because much of the information relating to the TMS operations which is held on a workstation is of a sensitive nature concerning the company's financial matters, access to any of the printers which are connected to the workstation is restricted according to the security policy set by the security officer. Restrictions apply both to physical access to the printers and to logical access to the printing procedures which form part of the TMS software. The restrictions apply for the printing of both to the files stored locally on a client's workstation and to those obtained via the network from a bank.

Locally stored TMS data files, containing the financial information, may be printed by users in Groups 3 and 4 only if they hold the appropriate cryptographic key or have otherwise been granted access to the files. The auditor will have access to enable the reading and printing of all locally stored TMS data files as well as the audit related information. No other users may print any information concerning the TMS transactions, although users in Groups 1 and 2 may be able to access some of the files for reading or updating.

The auditor, who has access to every file held within the workstation, will also be able to print the contents of the audit file, a directory of contents and a status report from the EUSF. The security officer will not be able to print any of the TMS data files, but will be permitted to view and print selected portions of the audit log, a directory of contents and a status report generated by the EUSF.

Pending Receipts

When a signed request for a direct debit or domestic transfer is received by a bank, it will be stored on the bank's workstation for further attention. The instructions will be examined by one of the bank's employees who will generate a signed message for the client, acknowledging that the instructions have been received and understood. The bank will then act on the client's instructions and provide a final receipt when the transaction is eventually completed, possibly several days later. The initial transaction request and acknowledgment are illustrated in Figure 14.1(a) where the acknowledgement is shown as an indication that a transaction receipt is pending.

Once the signed acknowledgement has been received by the client, the TMS application software will create an entry in a file at the client's workstation in which the acknowledgement will be stored, indicating that a receipt from the bank required after the execution of the instructions. For future reference by the TMS software, the stored information will consist of a unique transaction identifier, the identities of the sender and receiver, the type and details of the transaction and the signature of the bank's user.

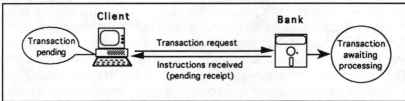

Figure 14.1 (a) A transaction is requested by the client for which the bank provides a signed receipt

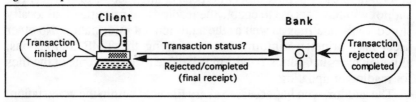

Figure 14.1 (b) A final receipt is provided only after the instructions have been acted upon

Since there may be a lengthy delay between the bank's acknowledgment of the request and the instructions being carried out, the entry in the pending receipt file will be retained in the workstation and reviewed regularly by the client's TMS users. Every time the file is reviewed, a request for a receipt will be generated using the information stored in the file and will be transmitted to the bank, as illustrated in Diagram 14.2(b). The reply from the bank to this request may be to indicate that the transaction has not yet been processed, or that the request has been rejected, or that the request has been accepted and the instructions carried out. If the reply indicates that the transaction has not been processed, the entry will remain in the pending receipt file to be reviewed again later.

When the bank supplies a final signed receipt in reply to the request, the receipt will be stored in the client's workstation and the appropriate entry in the pending receipt file will be deleted. The audit logs of both client and bank will be updated at each stage of the transaction to include a description of the request, the receipt and the nature of the transaction response.

Local file transfers

Most of the TMS functions available to the user of a client's workstation operate on data which has either been obtained from or must be passed to another workstation located at a bank. Normally, data to be transmitted will be manually entered into the workstation by the clients' employees and data to be processed will be processed by the workstation, where it will also be stored. In some companies, however, it may be more convenient to enter, store or process the data using other computer equipment. In this case, data must be transferred to the TMS workstation before transmission to the bank and from the workstation to the other computers after reception of account information from the bank.

Although it is assumed that local data transfers will rarely be required to and from the clients' workstations, they will be frequently carried out to and from the banks' TMS workstations, since the main storage for the customer account information will usually be provided by a separate computer system. At a given bank, therefore, the transaction orders will need to be passed on from the TMS workstations where they arrive to the bank's main computer where transaction processing is carried out. Other operations, such as the TMS users' account enquiries require that some of the account information stored on the banks' main computers will need to be transferred to the TMS workstation before it can be transmitted to the client.

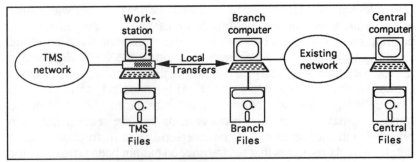

Figure 14.2 Example file transfers at a bank

All TMS workstations contain the components necessary to enable the transfer of files to and from other nearby computers using a local area network. In some cases, such as at one of the branches of a bank, the data files may normally be held on a remote computer, for example a central computer at the bank's head office. Since the local area network can not be used to transfer information from the remote site, any remotely held files that are needed must first be transferred from the central computer to the branch computer before they can be transferred to the workstation. The bank will use its existing communications procedures to transfer files from the central computer to the branch computer. This example of file transfer procedures is illustrated in Figure 14.3.

The transfer of files between the TMS workstation and other computers as described above will frequently be required during the normal TMS operations performed by the banks. Operation of the TMS by a company, however, requires that data originate mainly from manual input to the workstation or from communications with the banks using the TMS network. File transfers between a company's computers and its TMS workstation will be required only in exceptional circumstances and it may be required that this operation be restricted to a small privileged group of users. The EUSF functions will be used in the normal way to monitor and log all file transfers, and to provide cryptographic protection during the transfer if required

14.5 MANAGEMENT OPERATIONS

A number of management operations concerned with the day to day running of the system are required in order to support the normal user operations. Most of these operations necessarily involve security aspects and are carried out by the security officer. Assurance that the management operations are carried out in the correct manner and that the system is being operated properly is provided by periodic audits, undertaken by the auditor. System components are provided to facilitate both the security officer's and the auditor's functions.

Enrolling users

The enrolment of users in Groups 1-5 is carried out by the security officer, who must first be satisfied of the identity of the candidate, for example by examining a pass card. The security officer must then go to the KMC to be identified and to request a new chip card for the user to be registered. This card, which will contain the names of the user and their company or bank, will be handed directly to the security officer to be passed on to the user. The PIN associated with the card will be sent directly to the user by the KMC supervisor. If the user to be registered is employed by a client but requires access to data held by a bank, the security officer must first negotiate the appropriate access rights with the bank. Similarly, if the user is to act as a signatory for cash transfers, the staff at the bank must be informed.

Once a user has possession of both a chip card and the corresponding PIN, the security officer will sign onto the workstation in order to register the user locally with the EUSF. The user's identity and operational privileges will be supplied to the EUSF by the security officer, after which time the user may also sign onto the workstation.

If the user is to be granted access to a bank's workstation via the TMS network, this will require the creation of a pair of asymmetric key encipherment keys and a certificate. The key encipherment keys will be generated in the EUSF at the client's workstation, whilst the certificate will be generated at the KMC and transmitted over the network to the EUSF, protected by a digital signature. Both the key encipherment keys and the certificate can only be generated in response to commands from the security officer, in the presence of the user whilst both are simultaneously signed on at the workstation.

If the user to be enrolled is an auditor, neither a key encipherment key nor a certificate will be generated, but a symmetric key must be generated by the auditor to be stored in the security box for the protection of the audit files. The action of enrolling an auditor will itself be recorded in the audit log.

In order to register a user as a security officer, a separate enrolment procedure is followed. Before enrolment as a security officer, the candidate must be presented to the KMC for identification by the staff at the KMC, using an agreed proof of identity such as a pass card. After identification, two chip cards will be provided by the KMC: one of which is a key transport chip card, containing the keys for the initialisation of the security box; the other is a personal chip card containing keys and authentication information to be used by the security officer allowing access to the TMS workstation. The security officer will be registered with the EUSF when the security box is initialised using the key transport chip card. After the initialisation of the security box, the security officer will use the personal chip card for future access to the workstation.

Initialisation procedure

The security officer is initially identified to the EUSF using the key transport chip card, obtained from the KMC after a visual identification by the staff at the KMC. Like the users' chip cards, the key transport chip card contains a PIN which is checked against the value entered at the keyboard in order to authenticate the identity of the security officer to the EUSF. The master keys will then be loaded into the security box from the card which will be erased to remove all records contained within it of both the keys and the authentication information. The key transport chip card cannot be re-used and must be returned by the security officer to the KMC after the initialisation of the TMS workstation.

When the keys have been loaded into the security box, the security officer will enrol an auditor, who will request that the security box creates an encipherment key to be used to protect the audit log. With the auditor and security officer enrolled and the master keys loaded, the initialisation procedure is complete.

Certificate generation

Although the certificates are used to mutually authenticate users in Groups 2, 3 and 4, they are initially generated by the KMC only in response to a request by the security officer, for example when the user is enrolled. When a request for a certificate is made, the security officer's security box will generate a pair of asymmetrical keys, the public part of which is to be contained in the certificate and the private part will be held securely only in the security box.

Each certificate has a period of validity associated with it, which is regularly checked by the EUSF. When the life of the certificate runs out, the EUSF may automatically request that the KMC generate a new certificate. In this case, the old keys held in the security box will be replaced with the new ones. All these steps are recorded in the audit log.

Black lists and key revocation

Any of the users and keys which fall within the jurisdiction of a security officer may be placed on a black list by that security officer. The user profile, stored in the EUSF, will be updated to indicate that the user or key has been placed on the black list, and the EUSF will alert the KMC and other EUSFs by broadcasting a message on the network.

A key may be black listed due either to its loss, for example through system failure, or its compromise. Users may be black listed at any time prior to their disenrolment on the discretion of the security officer. In certain circumstances, black listing may also be initiated automatically, without any action from the security officer. For example, when a new security officer or auditor is appointed, the EUSF will automatically update the relevant files to indicate that the previous post-holder.is on the black list.

If the user is black listed, signing on to the TMS workstation is disabled and all the user's keys are automatically revoked. If it is only the user's key which is black listed, the user can still sign on to the workstation, but can not communicate using the network, or append a signature to any of the prepared data. To allow the user to perform these operations once more, the user must first be disenrolled and then enrolled again by the security officer.

When a user's keys are black listed, the key encipherment keys are deleted, but the data encipherment keys remain, to allow access to locally stored files. If the user is black listed and all keys are revoked, the EUSF will still allow access by the security officer to all local files which have been enciphered using the data key. Once these files have been deciphered, the data encipherment keys are deleted.

Audit functions

The purpose of auditing the TMS is to convince a third party, the auditor, that the system is being run in a proper manner and that the security policy is both appropriate and enforced effectively. To assist the auditor, the EUSF software will provide a log of certain events, detailing the initiator the time of day, the type of event and some other information relevant to the particular event. Other software will enable the auditor to analyse this log.

During the normal operation of the system, all noteworthy events such as transaction requests, users signing on and file accesses will be entered in an audit log. By analysing the audit log, using the tools available at the workstation, the auditor will be able to trace the operation of the system at a given time. Information obtained from the audit log will help to establish the correct state of the system, for example which files should be stored at the workstation, and any discrepancies with the actual state will become apparent. This and other information obtained from the audit log may help to find the cause of system inconsistencies and may help to locate potential security breaches

When system auditing is required, all auditing operations will be carried out by an independent auditor who has been previously appointed and registered with the EUSF by the security officer. The auditor will be able to examine all files and records which have been maintained regarding the operation of the particular TMS workstation. An audit function available at the workstation will enable the auditor to efficiently locate, extract, view and print all relevant information, for example from the audit log.

Since the audit log will be large and will be regularly archived by the security officer, one of the functions of the auditing facility will allow archived material to be loaded, searched and merged. Information in the archived files will then be accessible for auditing in the same way as the locally stored information.

Maintenance Procedures

To ensure the correct and efficient day to day operation of the system, constant maintenance is necessary for the detection and correction of faults or for enhancements to the system. All maintenance procedures will be simplified if a number of procedures are defined when the system is designed. Wherever possible, procedures should be defined both for normal operations, such as the installation of additional software, updated software or additional hardware, and emergency operations such as the removal or repair of faulty equipment.

The security implications of all such procedures must be carefully considered. In particular, whenever any changes are made to the system whether to the hardware or software, the security officer must be present to inspect the work. All corrections or enhancements to the software must be controlled by the original software supplier whenever possible and additional software must be carefully evaluated before installation.

Similarly, all hardware repairs and additions must be carried out by a recognised supplier or maintenance contractor and carefully inspected by the security officer.

14.6 USER LIFE CYCLES

With the ability to enrol and disenrol users, a security officer has complete control over the system life cycles of all users of the TMS workstation. Figure 14.4 is an illustration of possible user life cycles. Two security officers are shown, one each for a company and a bank. These security officers are responsible for the enrolment and disenrolment of the users of their own TMS equipment. In the figure, each security officer enrols a user who signs onto their own TMS workstation in order to perform some TMS operations. The company treasurer is shown to log onto the bank's TMS workstation in order to transmit and receive information. Since data is processed locally, the transmitted data is prepared before logging on and the received data analysed after signing off. When users are no longer permitted to operate the TMS, they are disenrolled by their security officer. This is likely to be after a large number of operations such as the example given in the figure.

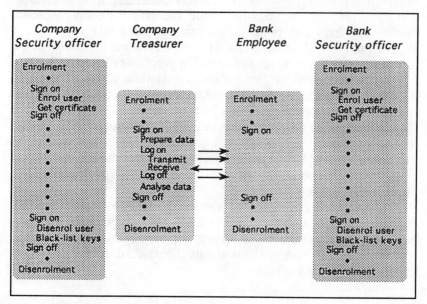

Figure 14.3 TMS User Life-cycles

15

Overview of Security Design in the Treasury Management System

15.1 INTRODUCTION

The TMS provides a company with a wide range of sophisticated facilities for cash management, allowing for the efficient control by the company of its own assets whilst they are held by its bank. A suite of functions is provided, which enables the company's treasurer to monitor and forecast the use of the company's assets and to be able to raise transaction orders when required. Although the majority of the processing, such as that required for forecasting, can be performed using the company's own computer equipment, for effective operation many of the functions of the TMS require access on demand to the most up-to-date information held by the bank. This information must then be transferred from the bank's storage to the company's workstation for processing. Additionally, all transaction information which is generated by the company must be transferred from the company's equipment to the bank's. For this reason, the TMS provides facilities for secure and efficient communications between the bank and its clients, the company treasurers.

For purposes of cost and ease of implementation, the design of the TMS has been based on readily available proprietary equipment. Thus, computers such as those forming the workstations consist of standard personal microcomputers, whilst communications between them make use of the existing public network. Because these existing systems alone do not incorporate the measures necessary for the provision of the high degree of data security which has been identified in risk analysis as necessary for the TMS, a number of additional functions and operational requirements have been defined which, together, will provide the required level of data security.

This section is not concerned with the detailed operation of the cash management functions of the TMS itself, but only with the measures necessary to provide for the security of data both in transit during communications between a bank and its clients and during processing or in storage within a workstation.

264

15.2 RISK ANALYSIS

A detailed risk analysis of the TMS was commissioned during the early stages of the MARS project in order to form a sound basis upon which to base decisions regarding the employment of security measures. The process of risk analysis, described in detail in Chapter 2, comprises the four steps of threat evaluation, assessment of the system components, analysis of the consequences of a successful attack and an evaluation of the vulnerability of the system.

Table 15.1 Classification of threats

| | Deliberate | | Accidental | |
	Passive	Active	Passive	Active
External Physical	The threat is from outsiders who may require copies of equipment for a furtther active or passive attack. The result is that the equipment such as a key or a communication interface is copied allowing unauthorised access	The threats arise from the actions of people, often known as intruders, who have no authority for the use of teh equipment. An attack may result in the damage to, modification of or the theft of equipment.	Not Applicable	Threats in this category arise from outsiders and from nature. Some examples are fire, flood, operator error and chemical spillage. The consequences may be the loss of, destruction of, or damage to equipment.
External Logical	Threats in this category come from intruders who are able to monitor operations such as the transmission of data. Such monitoring may also be aided by the actions of authorised users. The consequence of this type of attack is the disclosure of data.	These threats arise from the direct actions of intruders, or from the actions of unauthorised software such as viruses or logic bombs. The results of an attck may be the modification, loss of or delay to operations and transmitted data.	The unintentional actions of outsiders, for example by eavesdropping.	These threats arise from outsiders and from nature. Some examples are operators' errors such as incorrect input or deletions and random electromagnetic noise. The modification or loss of data may result from this.
Internal Physical	The threat is from people who have the authority to access equipment. They may use illicit copies for unauthorised purposes or to pass on to outsiders.	Essential operations may be omitted or incorrectly carried out whilst other unauthorised actions could be taken by the system users or the maintenance staff. Threats may be due to strikes or illicit action., Consequences could be modification to, damage	Not applicable	The threat comes from authorised users and from the equipment itself. Examples of this are incorrect operation by the staff or the malfunction of a component such as power supply. Consequences are destruction of, loss of or damage to equipment.
Internal Logical	Personnel with the authority to use the system may also be able to make unauthorised copies of data or software. This could be passed to outsiders. The consequences are that data or details of the system's operation are disclosed.	For reasons such as strikes or illicit action by the system users or maintenance staff, the system may not be operated correctly. These actions could result in the modification or loss of data with the resulting degradation of the service.	The threat comes from authorised users who may unintentionally use software or information in such a way that it may be accessible to unauthorised users. Copying and insecure disposal are examples. Consequences are the disclosure of data or system details.	Unintentional incorrect operation of the system is the source of this threat. Examples are human error such as omission, incorrect entries or incorrect operations and the malfunction of components. This could result in the modification or loss of data.

In the first stage of the risk analysis, the perceived threats were classified, as summarised in Table 2.1 which gives a brief description of each threat and describes possible consequences. In order to produce the classification, all aspects of the system were evaluated, including the functions provided by the TMS, the data used, the working environment and the way in which the system is operated.

The next stage involved listing all system components. All system assets, including data and programs, were described in detail to enable an assessment of the cost of rectifying any damage which may result from the types of attack previously identified. The TMS functions described in Chapter 14 were specified in detail, indicating which system components must be used and the nature of the information that is required during each stage of operation. This enabled the consequences of loss, disclosure or alteration of each item of information to be assessed, and allowed the individual data records to be classified accordingly.

Each of the system components were considered in turn in order to evaluate the consequences of an attack based on the cost of returning the system to its state before the attack, or the cost incurred due to the unavailability or untimely disclosure of sensitive data. The description of the working environment, including the operating environment of the workstation, the public network and the local network with its attached equipment was used, enabling a list of the perceived threats to be drawn up. This lead to an analysis of the consequences of the realisation of each of these threats The whole process of the evaluation of the severity of a successful attack was carried out in a qualitative manner, using estimates in those cases where exact figures were unavailable for the direct or indirect costs incurred by the inopportune loss or disclosure of information or the cost of replacing lost or damaged assets.

The earlier analysis of the environment, system functions and operations was used in the final stage of the risk analysis in which an estimate of the probability of a successful attack being carried out was made for each of the identified threats. Combining these probabilities with the consequences of a successful attack, an estimate of the vulnerability of the system to each threat was reached. Table 15.2 summarises the perceived threats, with the estimated probabilities and vulnerabilities given as high, medium and low. The vulnerability is directly related to the probability in each case because the consequences bore a similar gravity. This relationship arises in the TMS because of the sensitive nature of most of its data. Thus, any attack which results in the loss or disclosure of data could prove very expensive.

Table 15.2 Perceived threats

Threat	Probability	Vulnerability
Repudiation	High	High
Message stream modification	High	High
Electromagnetic noise	High	High
Computer virus or worm	High	High
Logic bomb	High	High
Human error	High	High
Wire tapping	Medium	Medium
Denial of service attack	Medium	Medium
Spurious connection initiation	Medium	Medium
Malfunction in network component	Medium	Medium
Traffic analysis	Low	Low
Strike	Low	Low
Eavesdropping	Low	Low
Crossed connections	Low	Low

15.3 WORKSTATION SECURITY

After ensuring that the system operations are carried out in a secure manner, the next step in the provision of security for the TMS is to consider the security of the individual workstation components and their integration into the complete workstation. Most of the data used by and stored on the workstations is of a sensitive nature, requiring protection against both alteration and disclosure. The security of all workstations must be considered, whether they are used by the bank or by the client, requiring at each location the careful choice of equipment and installation together with the correct maintenance and operating procedures. Although no financial information is held by the KMC, it holds a large number of cryptographic keys upon which depends the security of all communications between clients and their banks.

There are many ways in which the data held on a computer may be corrupted, either accidentally or intentionally, each of which poses a threat to the correct operation of the system. For example, threats to the integrity of data could come from the equipment or its operators, since corruption of data could arise due to an electrical fault or as a result of an operator's mistake or deliberate alteration to data. Threats to the confidentiality of data could arise due to the poor choice of location of computer equipment or inadequate access control, since passers-by may be able to read a display screen or unauthorised personnel may have access to computer equipment which enables them to learn confidential information.

The consequences of the realisation of such threats, due to the inadequate security of a TMS workstation, could prove disastrous for an individual client. For example, incorrect transaction orders may be generated or the client may be unable to correctly manage its finances due to incorrect data or because the workstation has been rendered inoperable. At a bank branch, data is held on the behalf of a number of clients, each of which could be inconvenienced if the bank's computing facility is subject to attack. Inadequate security measures relating to the computers at the KMC could provide scope for fraud on a large scale, as all communications between banks and their clients could be at risk.

An important part of MARS, carried out during the final phases of the project, was the specification of security countermeasures which are appropriate for use with workstations such as those used in the TMS. All the security functions within the workstation together comprise the EUSF, including those necessary to provide the security of communications over an insecure transmission medium, used in the architecture described above. The parts of the EUSF which is concerned with the protection of information whilst it is being processed or is in storage within a workstation are described below.

Security of the information used in the workstation is ensured by the EUSF which is realised by components both in the security box and the computer. Protection afforded by the EUSF is both physical and logical and applies to the hardware, software and data of both the security box and the computer. Where possible, standard components have been used. In the security box, the electronic hardware comprises readily available components, providing the processor, clock, memory, encipherment, interface and controller functions. Some software, however, must be developed specifically for the security box.

Hardware components

The workstation hardware consists of an ordinary microcomputer containing an internal hard disc drive. The computer is permanently connected by a cable to a separate security box designed to meet the requirements specified in the MARS project. Interface modules are provided, allowing the connection of the workstation to the TMS network, the local network, local printers and back up storage devices. Wherever possible the hardware modules are constructed from readily available components.

To conform with the security requirements, the conventional microcomputer may require some minor modifications to its hardware. The hard disc contained in the computer, which must remain permanently attached to the workstation, must be connected in such a way that it is non-removable. To prevent internal tampering, the computer's casing must be sealed in such a way that unauthorised attempts to access its components are thwarted. The use of tamper resistant screws and secure locks may be necessary to prevent the removal of the external casing.

Once the necessary software has been installed on the internal hard disc, all other storage devices, such as floppy disc drives, and external interfaces must be rendered inaccessible. Interfaces will be retained, however, to enable the connection of the computer to the security box, the TMS network, a local printer and a local network if necessary. The power for the computer will only be supplied from a connection to the security box. Attempts to power the computer from alternative sources must be foiled, for example by replacing a removable power lead with one that is securely connected inside the computer's casing.

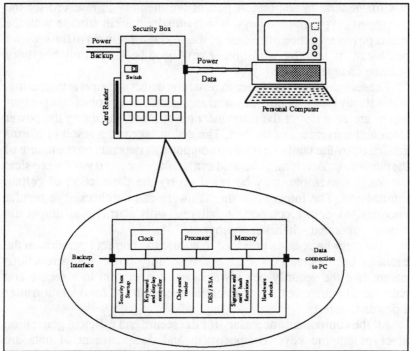

Figure 15.1 The Workstation Components

All hardware components which are supplied as integral parts of the computer are assumed to operate correctly. Thus the monitor, keyboard, processor, memory, hard disc drive and all device controllers require no modification prior to their use in the TMS. Although these hardware components will not themselves be altered, some additional software checks on their operation may still be performed as part of the normal operation of the EUSF. For example, verification that all files have been correctly stored on the hard disc may be enforced by the EUSF software before the memory contents are deleted.

Many of the security functions of the EUSF are provided by a security box which must remain permanently connected to the computer. A simple diagrammatic view of the security box attached to a personal computer is shown in Figure 15.1. Some of the main functions are labelled in the figure.

The power switch on the security box also controls the power to the computer, ensuring that the computer is operated only when the security box is switched on. When the power to the security box is switched on, a relay can ensure that power is supplied to the computer only after certain checks have been performed by the other components.

A processor, some memory and a clock are provided in the security box for general operations. A part of the memory is reserved for the storage of cryptographic keys, which must remain in storage with the mains power switched off. Some of the keys must remain in the security box for many months, whilst other keys need be stored only briefly or must be changed frequently.

The security box is designed to resist and detect attempts at tampering, with a sturdy lock to control physical access and a selection of components which are able detect the disconnection of leads, including the power leads and movement of the box. The action taken as a result of alarms generated by the tamper detection components depends on the nature of the tampering. An alarm generated as a result of repeated violent physical shocks, for example, may be acted on by the destruction of certain information. The integrity of the hardware can be checked at regular intervals, to detect component failures, with alarms and diagnostic reports generated whenever appropriate.

A battery back-up is provided to ensure the correct operation in the event of unexpected power loss. The security box start-up functions ensure that the security box always begins operation in a secure and consistent manner, both during normal operation and for operation after a power failure.

All the components necessary for the secure and efficient generation of cryptographic keys, encipherment and decipherment of data are contained within the security box. Cryptographic keys stored in the memory of the security box will be retrieved as necessary for the cryptographic operations. Both symmetric and asymmetric cryptographic algorithms are supported by the hardware. A data connection to the computer enables the transfer of data for encipherment and decipherment between the computer and the security box, as required by the application process. Encipherment will usually be employed for the cryptographic protection of transmitted data, but may also be used to protect data files stored on the hard disc.

One use of the asymmetric cryptographic capability of the security box is in the provision of digital signatures for selected portions of information as required by the TMS application software. For this purpose, a signature hash function is provided, which can produce the digest necessary for the signature, which will then be appended to the information. A second hash function is provided to be used for the authentication of the chip card.

To enable the identification and authentication of users and to ensure the secure installation of cryptographic keys, the security box contains a chip-card reader, a simple keyboard and a display. Most chip-cards used in the TMS serve solely for the identification and authentication of users and contain information giving the user's identity, a secret PIN and an entry indicating validity of the card. In addition to this, the key transport chip-cards are used to install a set of master keys during the initialisation of the security box. All information contained in the key transport cards is deleted immediately after use and they are then returned to the KMC. The chip card reader and controller supervises these operations.

Software components

Most of the software used during the operation of the TMS will reside in the computer, with some modules permanently resident in the security box and some in the external devices such as the software which is used to control a local printer. Software which is to be executed by the computer will be stored mainly on the computer's internal hard disc, with a small ROM-based start up procedure supplied with the computer in order to control the initial loading and execution of the main software components. In the security box and the peripheral devices, the software will normally reside in permanent memory, to be executed when the devices are initially switched on.

The software comes from a variety of sources including the equipment manufacturer, third party software suppliers and the suppliers of the TMS application and EUSF software. It is assumed that the software supplied with the computer equipment and any software utilities which have been obtained from reputable suppliers operate with a high degree of reliability and contain no malicious code. For security purposes the software can be divided into four categories as follows:

- the computer's operating system;
- the computer's system utilities;
- the EUSF software;
- the TMS application software.

The computer's operating system and system utilities will be supplied with the computer and will be executed exclusively on the computer. The TMS application software will contain all the modules necessary to perform the TMS functions and will also run exclusively on the computer. The EUSF software will contain the security functions necessary to ensure the secure operation of the system and will be executed both by the computer and the security box. Both the TMS application software and the EUSF software will be developed specifically for the TMS in a controlled manner, paying particular attention to the interaction between the various components.

Direct interaction between the users of the system and the computer's operating system or the system utilities is considered undesirable for the secure operation of the workstation. For this reason, the only software directly accessible to users is that comprising the TMS application software and the EUSF software. The TMS application software, which runs on the personal computer, requires constant user interaction in order to perform most of the TMS functions. The EUSF software, which is executed both by the computer and the security box, requires direct user interaction in order to perform such security functions as authenticating a user's identity. Any system functions that may be required by a user can be accessed indirectly by issuing commands to the EUSF software or the TMS application software.

To ensure that the users are able to interact directly only with the TMS application software, it must be ensured that when power is supplied to the computer, the start up procedure will always load an appropriate portion of the application software. Once the TMS software is loaded, it must not be possible for a user to interrupt its normal execution in such a way that the operating system commands or system utilities may be used directly. Thus, keys which are normally used for the termination or suspension of active programs must have these operations disabled. All exceptional circumstances which may result in the interruption of the normal execution of the TMS software must leave the system in a known state. For example, a sudden loss of power, followed by power recovery must result in the activation of the memory-resident start up procedure to restore the application software.

TMS Data

In addition to the treasury data processed by clients, the TMS workstations must hold a large amount of data concerned with the running of the system. When the workstation is initially installed, some permanent files will be installed on the computer's hard disc such as software, including the system software, the EUSF software, the TMS application software and information concerning the operation of the EUSF including details of the user's privileges, blacklists of users and compromised or revoked keys, active keys and certificates and the audit and non-repudiation logs. Files containing the EUSF information will be enciphered with a secret data encipherment key to prevent unauthorised access, although they will be deciphered by the EUSF when accessed correctly. Access to the software will be restricted, and checks to detect unauthorised changes will be provided by the EUSF.

The location of the information held in storage depends on its sensitivity and where it is to be used. For example, the EUSF software to be executed in the security box will be stored in the security box, as will the encipherment keys which are considered sensitive and are used in the encipherment modules of the security box. Table 15.3 gives a summary of the data and its location when stored within the workstation.

At the client's site of TMS operation, the treasury data will normally be held entirely within the TMS workstation. It is of prime importance that the correctness of this data is ensured at all stages of the TMS operation. The first steps toward the assurance of correctness begin with data entry, where the TMS software will be carefully designed to minimise the amount of undetected incorrect input and data corruption during processing. Where possible, checks will be made on the validity and consistency of input, with careful attention being given to the design of the user interface. Other treasury data, supplied by the bank will be protected during transmission, to be checked by the receiving workstation before being accepted. All treasury data will be enciphered for storage within the workstation.

At the bank's site of operation, treasury data will either be stored on the bank's main computers or will be received from a client in the form of instructions. There will be little need to store treasury data on the workstation for any length of time as the only records which must be kept are those regarding incomplete transactions and a log of the transactions which have been completed. However, the system data, EUSF data, software and report files must still be maintained in the banks' workstations with the same high degree of security as is maintained in the clients' workstations.

Table 15.3 The location of data

Data Stored on the Computer's Hard Disk		
TMSFiles	**SystemFiles**	**EUSF Files**
TMS Executable Files	System Exectuable Code	EUSF Executable Code
TMS Data	Systemparameters	Non-Repudiation Log
Management Report Files	NetworkAddresses	Audit Log
Pending Receipt Files		User Profiles
		User Black List
		Key Black List
		File Access Rights
		Certificates
Data Stored in the EUSF Hardware		
Security Box	**Normal Chip card**	**Key Transport Chip Card**
All Encipherment Keys	CardValidity	Public Key of the KMC
EUSF Exectuable Codes	Replacement Card Flag	Security Officer's Keys
Hash Functions	Hash Function	Hash Functions
Security Box ID	User's ID, PIN & Group	Security Oficer's ID & PIN

15.4 COMMUNICATIONS SECURITY

Security of communications is of prime importance in the TMS due to the sensitive nature of the information which must be transferred by the system on behalf of the principals who act for the banks and their clients. For example, in some circumstances, incorrectly transmitted information could cause an erroneous or duplicate transaction order to be raised and in other circumstances could cause a company's treasurer to produce a wildly inaccurate forecast of the company's financial needs. Some of the transmitted information regarding the financial affairs of a company may prove detrimental to that company if disclosed to unauthorised persons and so must remain confidential. If it is possible for a client to raise a transaction order and later successfully claim that no such order was raised, the TMS could provide the opportunity for fraud. There is also the possibility of fraud if it is possible for an outsider to successfully imitate a client's transmissions to its bank.

Whether the source of potential corruption of information is from faulty or error-prone equipment or from a determined intentional attack, the consequences of unauthorised changes or irregularities are potentially serious for the operations performed by TMS. The risk of corruption has been identified in a risk analysis as great enough to require specific countermeasures for certain threats. The system devised for the security of communications and described below is that required to protect against the most significant threats identified in the risk analysis, whilst allowing the required level of service.

There are four primary aims of communications security in the TMS. These are to provide assurance to the communicating parties of the identity of each other; ensure that the information received has been recently transmitted by the other party without unauthorised alteration in transit; ensure that sensitive information has not been learned by a third party who may also have been receiving the transmission and to provide a means by which either communicating party can indisputably prove the content of any transactions. These aims can be summed up as the four security requirements of party to party authentication, data integrity, data confidentiality and the non-repudiation of information interchange respectively. As part of the risk analysis, the degree of importance which must be attached to each of these requirements in the various TMS operations has been determined and security countermeasures have been defined accordingly.

When performing the risk analysis, it was necessary to take into account the nature of the transmission medium itself - the cables, switching equipment and associated software. In the TMS, this consists of the existing public network, which must be considered to be both insecure and error prone. Because it is not feasible to alter the components of the existing public network, the enhanced security must be provided solely by mechanisms which operate from within the banks' and their clients own equipment. Any additional transmissions which may be necessary for security purposes must be possible within the constraints of the existing network.

The above requirements, together with the operational requirements of the TMS itself, have been the major influences in the design of the communications security architecture. Facilities provided by the TMS communications equipment operate to enhance the security of the existing public network service to form the secure TMS network.

Party to party authentication

In TMS operations, the bank must ensure that its information is passed only to the appropriate clients, and that any transaction orders are raised only by authorised personnel. It is also in a client's interest to ensure that the information he/she receives was indeed supplied by the bank, and that transaction orders are passed to the correct bank. These requirements are met by the TMS security modules, which can assure each communicating party of the identity of the other before any information can be exchanged.

For one party to be assured of the identity of a second party, it is required that the second party supplies some information which convinces the first of its identity. The types of information which can be used to authenticate an identity in this way have been categorised into the following three groups:

something known,	such as a password;
something possessed,	such as a token;
something intrinsic,	such as a person's fingerprint.

All the information that needs to be transferred in order to establish a claimed identity of a party is collectively known as the credentials of that party. The credentials can contain a number of separate pieces of information from any combination of the above categories.

Techniques from the first category have been identified as the most appropriate for application in the TMS for use in communications, as they can provide the necessary level of assurance of identity using existing technology. Additionally, the transmission overheads associated with these techniques can be kept small. Note, however, that for this scheme to prove effective, it must not be possible for an intruder to alter any credentials indetectably, nor should an intruder be able to copy or forge credentials to allow masquerading. Thus, the party to party authentication mechanism must make use of data integrity and data origin authentication mechanisms, which are described later.

One possible way of using something known to provide the assurance of an identity would be for each communicating party to share some secret information with the other. Exchanging this information would provide mutual assurance of identity, if it can be assumed with a high degree of confidence that the information is not known by another party. The main drawback to this simple scheme is that the administration of the shared information can become unwieldy.

The solution applied to the TMS involves the use of a third party, the KMC, which holds secret information allowing it to verify the identity of each of the communicating parties. The two parties can obtain from the

KMC a 'certificate' which has the property that it can guarantee the authenticity of its holder. The nature of the certificate and the manner of its use ensure that an outsider cannot forge a certificate or use an intercepted certificate to impersonate its legitimate holder. The contents of the certificate and details of its use are described in a later section.

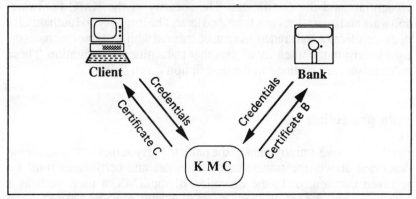

Figure 15.2 The communicating parties obtain a certificate of authenticity from a third party.

Operation of this method is summarised in Figures 15.2 and 15.3. To provide proof of identity, a client or bank must first present its credentials to the KMC. The credentials are checked by the KMC to assure it that the claimed identity is genuine. The KMC will then supply a certificate of authenticity which can be used by its holder as proof of identity to another party in any further communications. Once the certificates have been obtained, any two parties may verify each others identity and communicate securely without any further interaction with the KMC. Certificates used in this manner are sometimes referred to as off-line certificates.

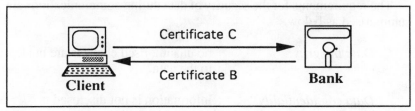

Figure 15.3 The two certificates can be used to provide the mutual assurance of identities

There are a number of additional security requirements which must be fulfilled if this scheme is to be effective: the communicating parties must regard the KMC as being competent and trustworthy, so that they are assured that the identity of the other party has been corroborated and so they are assured that false certificates would not be issued; and the certificates themselves must contain proof that they were issued to the holder by the KMC and have not since been altered.

The requirements can be summarised as the assurance of the integrity of the KMC and the assurance of the integrity and authenticity of both the credentials and the certificates. The security of the KMC hardware, software and operations are described later. The integrity and authenticity of the certificates and credentials can be ensured with the same mechanisms used to ensure the integrity of the other transmitted information. These mechanisms are outlined in the description given below.

Data protection

For the effective employment of the party to party authentication scheme described above, the transmitted credentials and certificates must be received unchanged. In the operation of the TMS, a user, such as a company treasurer acting as the client of a bank, must be assured of the accuracy of all information received from the bank in order to effectively manage the company's assets. It is also of great importance that all transaction orders raised by a treasurer must be received by the bank unaltered, and that the bank is sure of the source of the instructions. The information used in the TMS regarding the user's finances will often be of such a nature that the user requires assurance that it is not disclosed to unauthorised parties. In addition to these requirements, to resolve possible disputes between bank and client it may be necessary for a bank to provide proof to another party acting as a judge that it has acted on genuine instructions issued by its client, or for the client to provide proof that instructions were issued to the bank.

The requirements for the security of data during communications are summarised as below:

Data integrity:	no unauthorised changes are made to the data
Data confidentiality:	information is not disclosed to unauthorised parties
Data origin authentication:	it can be confirmed that information was generated by the claimed party
Non-repudiation of Information Exchange	the sender cannot falsely deny having sent data and the receiver cannot falsely deny having received data.

The most common method of checking the integrity of transmitted data involves the computation of a summary of the original data using a mathematical function. This summary is then transmitted along with the data to the recipient who can check the value of the summary against the value obtained by applying the same function to the original data. A discrepancy indicates that the data has been changed since the first summary was computed. In some methods, the summary can supply enough additional information to enable the reconstruction of the original data from a corrupted copy. Much research has been undertaken on the design of efficient algorithms which produce the smallest summary capable of the highest degree of error detection or correction.

Many computer communication systems use these summaries, termed error detecting or error correcting codes, to guard against random errors to data, such as those which may be caused by the effects of electromagnetic interference on standard data transmission cables. Although these methods generally work well for the random unintentional changes to data, it would be possible for a determined intruder to intercept a transmission, alter the data, use the mathematical function to calculate a new summary which is correct for the altered data, and then transmit these new data to the originally intended recipient. It is for this reason that the integrity mechanisms chosen for use with the TMS involves the use of cryptographic techniques.

Using cryptography to provide the assurance of data integrity has the added advantage that with the appropriate choice of encipherment scheme, a single mechanism can simultaneously fulfil the other security requirements of data confidentiality, data origin authentication and non-repudiation of information interchange. Note, however, that the use of cryptography together with error detecting codes cannot alone ensure integrity, it can only verify the integrity of an arbitrary portion data. To provide integral data communications, the detection mechanism must be combined with a separate mechanism for the recovery from loss of integrity, such as retransmission.

An asymmetrical encipherment scheme is used in the TMS to produce a digital signature which can be used both to check the integrity of transmitted data and verify the source of the data to their recipient. Asymmetrical encipherment schemes have the property that for each encipherment key there is a single complimentary decipherment key. Thus if data is encrypted with an encipherment key, it can be decrypted only by using the complimentary decipherment key. Conversely, if any known data are successfully decrypted with a decipherment key, then it can be deduced that it must have been encrypted with the complimentary encipherment key.

This property is used in the digital signature mechanism, which is realised as an extension of the error detecting mechanism mentioned above. A mathematical function is first used to produce a summary of the data to be transmitted. This summary is then encrypted using a secret encipherment key known only to the sender. The data is then secure from undetected deliberate alteration because an outsider cannot produce a valid summary without knowledge of the encipherment key. If an asymmetrical encipherment system is used, the recipient can decrypt the summary using the complimentary key to that used for the encipherment. If the decipherment is successful, the summary will match that produced by applying the mathematical function to the received data. If the identity of the holder of the secret encipherment key is known with a high degree of certainty, this provides the proof of the identity of the originator of the data. Note that the scheme requires that the receiver be certain that it holds the decipherment key corresponding to the sender's secret encipherment key, but there is no requirement that the decipherment key be kept secret.

No additional functions are required to provide for the assurance of non repudiation of transmission if a third party acting as a judge can be convinced that the decipherment key corresponds to the sender's secret encipherment key. It can then be demonstrated by the recipient to the third party that the summary can be successfully decrypted with the widely available public key, so must have been encrypted by the sender, who is the only holder of the secret encipherment key. To ensure the non repudiation of receipt, the receiver of the data must provide the originator with a digital signature which can then be used to prove that the data have been received.

Another property of the asymmetrical encipherment algorithms is that data which is encrypted with either of the complimentary keys can be decrypted with the other. For this reason, the keys are often referred to as secret and public keys. If a public key is used for encipherment, then only the corresponding secret key can be used for successful decipherment. To ensure data confidentiality, the entire transmission can be encrypted using the intended recipient's public key. Since only the recipient is in possession of the decipherment key, no one else will be able to read the information contained in the transmission. To provide confidentiality of the majority of the data transmitted in the TMS, however, a symmetric encipherment algorithm is provided.

Protocols for communications security

Before any exchange of data can take place, it must be possible for the KMC to verify the claimed identities of the clients and the banks. To enable this, pairs of asymmetric encipherment keys are generated at the KMC, a separate pair for each client and each bank. Each pair of keys is then copied onto its own chip card which is manually transported in a secure manner to a known client or bank, where a security officer is responsible for its safety. Only the public part of each key pair is stored at the KMC, indexed by the identity of the client or bank to whom it was sent. Because it is known at the KMC that each secret key is unique and the holder of each secret key is known, proof of the use of a secret key verifies its user's identity to the KMC.

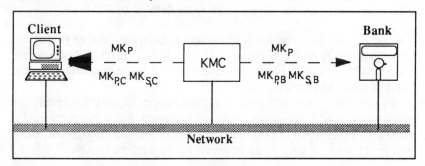

Figure 15.4 (i) Initial manual key distribution

The manual distribution of these asymmetric keys is illustrated in Figure 15.4 (i) which uses the following notation:

$MK_{SC:}$ the secret key for client C, obtained from the KMC.
$MK_{PC:}$ the public key corresponding to C's secret key.
$MK_{P:}$ the public key of the KMC.

The notation used here gives the prefix 'M' to all encipherment keys that are generated by the KMC.

For the mutual verification of identities, the KMC holds its own pair of asymmetric encipherment keys. The secret key is known only to the KMC and is never disclosed, but a copy of the corresponding public key is held on each of the distributed chip cards. The use of the secret key in communications with a holder of one of the chip cards is sufficient to verify the identity of the KMC because the holder of the card trusts that the public key on the card is genuinely the public key of the KMC.

Mutual authentication with the KMC is performed at the same time as a request for a certificate. The certificate request is generated by the holder of a chip card, who can then use the secret key stored in the card to produce a digital signature for the request. The data transmitted in the certificate request include the identity of the sender and the public portion of an asymmetric encipherment key pair which has been generated by the requester.

The certificate request is illustrated in Figure 15.4 (ii), in which the following notation is used:

KK_{PC}	A public key generated by client "C".
C	The identity of the client, in this case, "C".
B	The identity of the bank, in this case, "B".
$MK_{SC}\{H\}$	The message summary, H, encrypted using the secret key belonging to C, generated by the KMC.

The prefix 'K' is given to all asymmetric encipherment keys that are generated by the EUSF of either client and bank. The curly brackets are used to represent encipherment of the data inside the brackets using the encipherment key outside the brackets.

In the figure, the top arrows represent the request for certificate generation, whilst the bottom arrows represent the subsequent reply. Although requests from both bank and client are shown together, there will probably be a long delay between the two interactions.

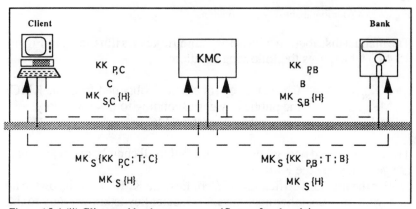

Figure 15.4 (ii) Client and bank request a certificate of authenticity

There is no requirement to conceal the contents of the request since security of communications relies neither on the secrecy of the requester's identity nor the secrecy of the public keys. It is necessary, however, to ensure the integrity of the request. On receipt of the request, the KMC can use the identity contained within the message to locate the appropriate decipherment key with which to check the digital signature. If the signature is genuine, the identity of the sender is verified to the KMC and the contents of the message are accepted as authentic. Thus both data integrity and data origin authentication are ensured with the use of the digital signature mechanism.

On receipt of an authentic certificate request, the KMC generates a certificate which contains the identity and the private key which were obtained from the request. An additional component of the certificate gives the period of time during which the certificate is valid. The certificate is encrypted with the KMC's secret key and transmitted to the requester along with a separate digital signature which is used to verify the integrity of additional header and trailer information.

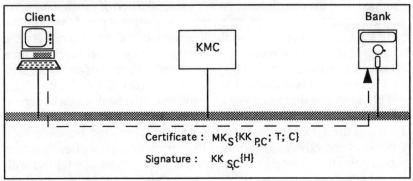

Figure 15.4 (iii) Authentication of client to bank

The certificate reply is illustrated in Figure 15.4 (iii), in which the encrypted certificate is represented by:

$MK_s\{KK_{pc} ; T ; C\}$ where:

MK_s: is the secret key of the TMC, used to encrypt the certificate to provide the signature;

KK_{pc}: is a public key, generated by an EUSF, and sent in the request;

T: is the time of validity, decided at the KMC;

C: is the identity of the requester, obtained from the request.

The signature, $MK_s\{H\}$, protects the integrity of header and trailer information not shown in the figure.

When the certificate is encrypted using the KMC's secret key, a party with knowledge of some of its contents can then be assured that it was indeed generated by the KMC and that its contents are genuine when the known information is revealed on decipherment with the KMC's public key. The certificate is, in effect, a statement signed by the KMC that the named user is the holder of the secret key that corresponds to the public key given in the certificate. It is said that the certificate *binds* an identity to a public key. This binding is used by the holder of a certificate to convince another party of its identity in the following manner.

For client C to convince bank B of its identity, C sends the certificate to B along with some other information which includes C's identity and the time of transmission. The message containing the certificate is signed, using C's own secret key to encrypt a summary. On receipt, B will decrypt the certificate using the public key of the KMC, revealing the name in which it was issued and the public key bound to that name. The binding assures B that the public key came from C. Since the entire message has been signed by C, B can check its integrity and origin using the public key obtained from the certificate to enable authentication of the signature. As only C knows the secret key, an authentic signature is proof that both the certificate is genuine (because the key it contained was correct for the name given) and that it was sent by C. Additionally, B can check the time of transmission to ensure that the message is not a copy of an earlier one.

The operation is illustrated in Figure 15.4 (iii). Similarly, the client can be assured of the identity of the bank when the bank sends its signed certificate, as shown in Figure 15.4 (iv).

When these exchanges have taken place, client and bank are each assured of the others identity and they possess copies of each others public keys, the client then generates an encipherment key for use with a symmetric encipherment scheme and sends this, encrypted with the bank's public key, to the bank. The message is signed with the client's secret key. The new encipherment key can be used by both parties to ensure the confidentiality of all further information transmitted between client and bank.

The exchange is illustrated in Figure 15.4(v) where:

DKCB: is the new symmetric data encipherment key ;
KK_{PB}:   is the bank's public key, used to encrypt the new key;
KK_{SC}:   is the client's secret key, used to provide the signature.

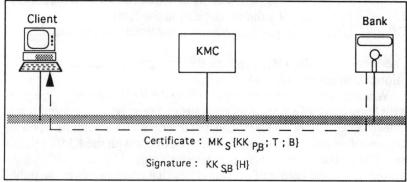

Figure 15.4 (iv) Authentication of bank to client

The data encipherment key, DKCB, can also be used to ensure the integrity of data by encrypting a message summary in a similar manner to that used with the asymmetric encipherment algorithms. A summary encrypted with a symmetric algorithm is often termed a *message authentication code* (MAC). Note that a symmetric algorithm can not provide proof of data origin to a third party because either party can use the key to generate the MAC.

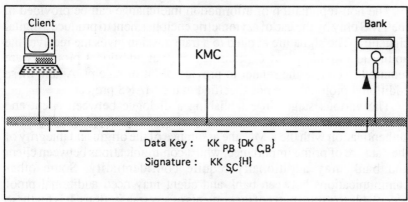

Figure 15.4 (v) Transmission of a data encipherment key

The use of encipherment

Although the requirements for the protection of data are different during each stage of the establishment of a dialogue between client and bank, encipherment can be used to provide the necessary protection. The basic uses of encipherment are to provide confidentiality and to verify the integrity and origin of transmitted or stored data.

Confidentiality is required simply to prevent unauthorised disclosure of information and can be provided by applying encipherment to all the data to be protected, using either symmetric or asymmetric encipherment schemes.

Integrity is required to ensure that the information content of data is not altered during transmission, storage or processing. This can be expressed as three goals: to ensure that data has not been altered, to ensure that the order of data is preserved and to ensure that a number of pieces of information are bound together. Although encipherment cannot prevent changes to data, it can be used in conjunction with other mechanisms to meet all of the above requirements. Unauthorised changes to data can be detected by the use of an enciphered message summary using either symmetric or asymmetric cryptographic algorithms.If care is taken when choosing the algorithm used to produce the summary, most violations of integrity can be detected.   Schemes which enable the detection of integrity violations are most useful when used together with mechanisms for the recovery of uncorrupted data, for example in communications protocols which provide retransmission facilities. The correct ordering of data units also requires additional communications protocols. This level of protocol is not defined in the MARS project.

The non-repudiation of information interchange can be provided in the TMS only by the use of asymmetric encipherment to produce a digital signature. The signature applied to a transmission gives the receiver the ability to provide proof of transmission, but additional protocols are required to enable the sender to provide proof of receipt. Again, these additional protocols are not specified in the MARS project.

The various stages in establishing a dialogue between client and server require different services provided by cryptography. For authentication with the KMC, the assurance of the origin and integrity of the data are of prime importance, whilst communications between client and bank may additionally require confidentiality. Some other communications between bank and client may need additional proof acceptable to a third party of the contents of any transactions. It is for these reasons that several separate types of cryptographic keys are described for use with the TMS which can be grouped according to their function, giving four groups of keys, summarised in Table 15.7.

The master key pair, MK_s and MK_p is used to ensure the authenticity of the certificates generated by the KMC. The only copy of the secret part of the key, MK_s is stored securely at the KMC, whilst the public part, MK_p, is stored securely on each key transport chip card which forms part of an EUSF. Although the secrecy of the public part of this key is not important, it is important that each EUSF contains an accurate copy as its use provides the only means of verifying the authenticity of the KMC. This key has a long lifetime because of the difficulty of manually distributing a new key to all TMS participants.

Also generated by the KMC and stored on the key transport chip cards are the master keys used by the clients and banks to provide proof of their identities to the KMC. Again, these are for use in an asymmetric encipherment algorithm, and are represented above by $MK_{s,X}$ and $MK_{p,X}$, where X is the identity of the client or bank which is the designated holder of the secret part. A copy of the public part of each of these keys is held at the KMC. The key transport chip card holds the only copy of the secret part and a copy of the public part. These keys are used to authenticate the identity of a client or bank to the KMC and to ensure the integrity of communications between the KMC and client or bank by means of a digital signature. These keys can be changed more frequently, since only one new card needs to be issued for each change of key.

Table 15.4(a) Cryptographic keys used in exchanges involving either the KMC directly, or data generated by the KMC

Key	Function	Lifetime	Generated by	Stored at
MKs	Integrity of Certificates	Long	KMC	MKs: KMC
MKp	Authentication			MKp: EUSF
MKsx	Integrity of data to KMC	The lifetime of the chip card	KMC	MKsx: EUSF
MKpx	Authentication			MKpx: KMC

Table 15.4(b) Cryptographic keys used only in communications between clients and banks involving information originating from either party

Key	Function	Lifetime	Generated by	Stored at
KKsx	Authentication Confidentiality;	Short	The Security Officer	The Security box of the EUSF
MKp	Integrity; non-repudiation			
DK	Confidentiality and Integrity	One session	The User	The Security box of the EUSF

Asymmetric encipherment keys generated at the EUSF for a bank or client identified as 'X' are given the notation KK_{sx} and KK_{px} for the secret and public parts respectively. The only copy of the private part of one of these keys is stored in the security box of the EUSF where it was generated. The public part is distributed in a certificate, its integrity protected by the master key, MK_s. A new KK key pair is generated each time a client or bank requests a certificate from the KMC, thus the lifetime of these keys is much shorter than the lifetime of the keys stored on the chip card. The certificate request and generation of these keys is the responsibility of a security officer assigned by each client and bank.

The KK encipherment keys can be used for the mutual authentication of the identities of the communicating parties, since the certificate assures the parties that they hold an authentic copy of the others' public key. Data confidentiality can also be ensured by the use of the public key for encipherment. The assurance of the integrity of the transmitted data can be provided by the use of a digital signature which also ensures the non-repudiation of information interchange since the certificates unambiguously associate an encipherment key with each party. Note that whereas the MK_{sx}/MK_{px} key pairs are used in communications only with the KMC, the KK_{sx}/KK_{px} key pairs are only used in communications between clients and banks.

Chapter 16

ITSEC and Standards

16.1 OVERVIEW

In its first phase, the MARS project performed a thorough state-of-the-art study of threats, risk analysis, user requirements and countermeasures. In Phase 2, a model for communications security, and models and Guidelines for the security of workstations were developed. The results of this research were applied, in Phase 3, to design security for a theoretical treasury management system.

In beginning with a thorough state-of-the-art study, covered by Part 1 of this book, the Consortium was able to build a considerable up-to-date knowledge base from which to produce guidelines for security. Computer security is an issue which needs to be considered in its entirety, and with a view to integrated solutions. The three axis model of threats, countermeasures and components illustrates this very well. All components must be guarded against all threats, in each case using the appropriate countermeasures. If a threat or component is considered in isolation, then security can be partially implemented, but vulnerabilities might remain due to other threats which haven't been considered, or to components which haven't been secured.

Chapter 1 provided an overview of the threats facing computer installations and the consequences should they be realised. In classifying threats, three broad distinctions were made between deliberate and accidental threats, active and passive threats, and logical and physical threats. A thorough knowledge of the threats being faced is an essential starting point to securing a system.

Risk management builds upon the study of threats facing the system. This was the subject of Chapter 2. Threats must be translated into risks and this involves some quantification of the loss which would be incurred should a threat materialise, along with the likelihood of that happening. On this basis decisions can be made on the cost-effectiveness of implementing countermeasures. This is a complex task and can be approached in various ways. Methods of qualitative and quantitative risk analysis have been discussed along with an examination of automated tools for risk analysis.

In Chapter 3, the subject of user requirements was studied. A thorough analysis of user requirements is necessary in order to know what we are trying to achieve in defining security measures. The user in this case is the organisation rather than the individual. The approach taken, in making a generic analysis of user requirements, was to study existing literature on the subject, send questionnaires to organisations and perform case studies at a number of organisations. The findings showed that surprisingly few organisations have given sufficient consideration to the security risks facing computer systems. Present security levels are often inadequate when confronted with the threats posed by the converging technologies of office systems, telecommunications and data processing. Even today this remains true.

Chapters 4 to 9 continued with a state-of-the-art study of techniques used in systems security. In Chapter 4, the subject of access control was examined. This included restriction of access to the environment in which computing equipment is contained as well as the procedures and mechanisms used to restrict entry to the computer itself, or to software or data within the computer.

We found that the usefulness of physical access restrictions is often understated. For standalone workstations, or for systems whose components are contained within close locality to each other, physical access controls can reduce many of the problems which are usually addressed by logical access controls. Although almost always necessary, the importance of logical access control is much greater in multi-user systems, where the logical separation of users and resources is required, and in systems which can be accessed remotely.

In Chapter 5, we looked at user identification and authentication. User identification refers to the action of the user claiming his/her identity when communicating with a device. Authentication is the process of proving that the claimed identity is genuine. The many techniques used in identification and authentication tend to fall into three categories:

- those which rely on something the user knows (for example password)

- those which rely on something the user owns (for example token),

- those which rely on some physical characteristic of the user (for example fingerprint).

The advancement of technology is leading to increasing emphasis being placed on the second and third of these, although the first is still predominant.

In Chapter 6, terminal identification and authentication was addressed. This procedure is usually used in conjunction with user identification and authentication and is designed to verify the location of users attempting to access a system, and thereby establish whether or not they possess authorisation.

Terminal identification and authentication offers a useful and necessary supplement to user identification and authentication. Because of the distributed nature of many computer systems and their ability to be accessed from remote locations, it is important to verify whether an access point is authorised or not. Without terminal identification and authentication, it would be very difficult to isolate hackers. However, since it is always possible to duplicate hardware components, terminal identification and authentication should be considered as only one strand in a security system.

Chapter 7 looked at secure data communications. This is of fundamental and increasing importance to many organisations, especially where electronic funds transfer is involved. This affects an ever increasing number of organisations and individuals as services such as electronic retail payment and home banking become more widespread. But the requirement for secure communications is not limited to the field of financial transactions. Other flows of sensitive information need to be protected. The three major aspects studied in Chapter 7 were 'objectives in communications security', 'techniques' and 'protocols'.

In Chapter 8, we looked at techniques for auditing computer systems. The difference between auditing a computer-based system and auditing a manual one is greater than is often realised. Although the overall objectives of auditing in an EDP environment are the same as in a non-automated organisation, by necessity the techniques used differ considerably.

Auditing can take place 'around' or 'through' the computer. We have concluded that only a computer assisted systems audit is able to produce reliable evaluations of the performance of computerised information, given the restricted time schedules imposed. An efficient audit can no longer be achieved with an audit around the computer using traditional auditing methods.

In Chapter 9, the subject of security modelling was discussed and a state-of-the-art study was made of existing security models. Security modelling provides a means of designing, testing and implementing security as an integral part of the system and provides a simplified overview of the system as a whole. It also provides a tried and tested basis for implementing security, a means of verifying that security has been achieved when the system is put into practice, and a means of demonstrating to a third party that the system is secure.

There exist three basic approaches to security modelling: access matrix models, high-water-mark models, and information-flow models. Access matrix models, which define a set of subjects which can manipulate objects, appear to have the greatest theoretical value and provide the basis for much important work in the security area. In fact many of the major operating systems which have high US Department of Defense security certifications have their security based on the access matrix principal.

However, it was found that most existing models could not easily be applied to the modern workstation since they tend to have been designed for the purposes of military security, and are thus highly stringent and less flexible than might be desirable. Furthermore many of the important models are fairly dated and tend to be restricted to operating system security. For these reasons, it was important for the Consortium to concentrate some effort on the area of security modelling during the second phase of the Project.

In Phase 2 of the Project, covered by Part 2 of this book, models were designed by the Consortium for communications security and for workstation security. Guidelines were also developed in these areas and in the area of auditability. Chapter 10 describes the communications security model, MoSel (MOdel for Security devELopment). The model provides both a systematic approach to security design and testing and a medium for expressing the results of that activity.

The MoSel model is primarily intended for use during the design and testing of security aspects of a communications system. To fulfil that aim, the model has been structured as a process model, which is concerned with security design and testing methods, and a product model, which provides a means of expressing the results of that design effort. The basic relation between the components of the model is that the process model describes the process which produces an instance of the product model.

A model for workstation security was designed by the Computer Industry Research Unit during the second phase of the Project. This was further developed into the 'Guidelines for Workstation Security' which were presented in Chapter 11. These guidelines are an important result of the MARS Project and are considered further below.

The guidelines are intended to give their user a complete overview of the issue of securing a system. A generic set of components is considered along with details of countermeasures to guard those components. A methodology for determining the level of security required is also included. This methodology is technology independent. The overall object is to provide a reference which will allow the workstation to be secured, to whatever level is required, against all likely threats.

In Chapter 12, the 'Guidelines for Auditability', developed by the University of Cologne, were described. Auditing is an important, but often understated, area of computer security. Much work was performed, during the course of the Project, in the area of auditability of computer systems and it has been found that although systems auditing is a well developed field, with established guidelines and standards, the issue of auditability has not previously received sufficient attention. In order for an auditor to be able to express an opinion on the proper design and functioning of a system and its internal controls, a thorough audit must take place. The efficiency and extent of this audit is dependent on the degree to which the design of the system assists or hinders the auditors role. These guidelines are therefore an important contribution and we consider it important that work continues in this area in the future.

In the final phase of the Project, covered by Part 3 of this book, the main effort was directed towards the application of the results of earlier phases to the provision of security in an existing application. The application chosen for this task comprised a range of procedures carried out on a small computer system, which together provided a sophisticated treasury management system (TMS) for a large company.

The treasury management system and the security designed for it were described in Chapters 13 to 15. Although the security measures and architectures described were developed specifically for the operation of the TMS using microcomputers, they are equally applicable to many advanced business and trading systems. The security measures described cover all aspects of system security, including the assurance of the security of all operational procedures, the definition of staff duties, the physical security of computer equipment and the logical security of information during processing, storage and transmission over a network.

16.2 FUTURE DIRECTIONS

The results of the MARS Project are being forwarded as input to further research efforts and it is hoped that they will make a significant contribution to future European guidelines and standardisation work. At present, some important initiatives are taking place within the Community, with a view towards security standardisation. Before examining these, we will introduce the context within which these are taking place and give an indication of their urgency.

Concern has been expressed by many European computer system manufacturers over the lack of a European framework for dealing with security in a business environment. In the USA the Department of Defence (DoD) has produced the 'Orange Book' criteria for the security of military systems [DoD 85] (see Appendix B) and has provided a corresponding conformance test centre which can issue certificates of conformance to its criteria. Some of the DoD work is relevant to commercial information systems and many US computer manufacturers have already obtained DoD certificates for their products. European manufacturers, however, find it unattractive to obtain a DoD certificate because there are enormous administrative barriers for non-US firms, the process is very expensive and the certificate is only valid in the USA.

When considering the European market, there is still no clear single set of guidelines available to system designers, and neither is there a centre for testing systems against such guidelines. The result is that European manufacturers can not at reasonable cost demonstrate the compliance of their products to a recognised security standard. Consumers are faced with the choice of attempting to compare the security provisions of products with no single standard as a basis, or to specify products with a US certificate. This situation is limiting both the competitiveness of European computing products and the freedom of market choice for purchasers.

Another area in which concern is growing is the lack of clarity over the provisions in existing European legislation for ensuring adequate 'duty of care' when using or supplying computer services, and the effectiveness of the law when dealing with computer related crime. This subject is rarely addressed when considering the security of commercial information systems despite the importance of a good understanding of the legislation over the whole of Europe. Other aspects which are developing as of the early 1990s is the local networking and advanced metropolitan or wide area networked communications networks based on ISDN or the new ultra-fast broadband networks. Even LANs can operate at ultra-fast speeds such as Digital's FDDI LAN.

Identification and authentication systems using smart cards with sophisticated access control systems are becoming the norm. Encryption techniques using RSA-type public key algorithms with digital signature capability and MAC mainframes providing the data integrity are widely spoken of as the norm but their use in practice is only increasing very slowly. DES encryption of information and messages is more economical although the length of the key is still being discussed. DES can be broken but the cost of so doing is large. For most businesses digital signatures using RSA with MAC integrity control and DES encryption will provide for most needs.

This still leaves us with the disgruntled employee who walks away with a password, smart cards or unique key who can do damage to a business. Hence the concept of a privileged user or super user who has access to all keys, can view nearly everything in the system and can change/override most systems.

The so-called super user is both a necessity and a weakness. An administrative necessity which probably always will provide an area of weakness.

16.3 MARS GUIDELINES

There is the need in Europe for a clear set of guidelines, and a centre for testing systems against such guidelines. It is with this in mind that we consider the most important result of the Project to be the 'Guidelines for Workstation Security'.

In CIRU's draft exploitation plan for the MARS Project, it was stated that in Europe *"system builders, designers and users do not have a well developed framework for dealing with security"* and that there is *"a clear need for some level of certification within a relevant business context for Europe"*. The Guidelines are an attempt to work towards such a framework and this work is being continued beyond the end of the MARS project, with its scope extended to include a greater emphasis on networking.

In order both to clarify the legal rights and obligations of computer system suppliers, users and service providers, and to restore fair competition in the field of commercial information systems, further work on the guidelines will have the following objectives:

to develop a single comprehensive, easy-to-use set of security guidelines covering both the computer related and the legal aspects, and to assist in progressing these guidelines towards a firm European standard

to develop a method for the application of the recommendations made in the guidelines to commercial networked computer information systems

to determine ways in which networked computer information systems and products can be tested for conformance with the security guidelines, and to create a pilot conformance testing centre in order to determine the suitability of the guidelines for this purpose.

It is hoped that the new easy-to-use classification scheme will be used as the basis for a new European guideline or standard which will make the certification of commercial systems comparatively inexpensive, thereby removing an advantage enjoyed by US manufacturers. In addition, the guidelines will provide industry with a clear understanding of their legal standing and will aid insurance assessors when dealing with computer related equipment.

Two other important initiatives are also taking place in this arena. CEN/CENELEC, the European Commission standards body are performing work in the area of security for open systems; and a draft set of 'Information Technology Security Evaluation Criteria' (ITSEC) have been produced jointly by French, German, Dutch and UK agencies.

16.4 CEN/CENELEC

The regional standards bodies for Europe are Comité Européen de Normalisation (CEN), and Comité Européen de Normalisation Electrotechnic (CENELEC), which are often referred to jointly as CEN/ CENELEC. CEN/CENELEC are working to produce standards in many areas of information technology and telecommunications as part of the drive towards the single European market. One area which is receiving attention here is security in IT and telecommunications.

An *ad hoc* group on security has been established by CEN/CENELEC. The aim of this group is to give further consideration to the standardisation of security for open systems, in particular those aspects which are of specific concern to European interest and future European standardisation activity. The scope of the group is to:

- establish a taxonomy of security standardisation

- establish a statement of requirement for future standardisation work

- identify the appropriate mechanisms and channels for European activity with respect to this statement of requirement.

- make recommendations on future activities.

This taxonomy will address a broad range of issues - technical, operational, procedural, administrative etc. - concerning the standardisation of security, with particular regard to European interest. It is intended to provide a comprehensive classification of security standards, in a way that is useful as a referencing system to European standards developers, procurers of

IT, users and other interested parties. The taxonomy is therefore intended to provide a basis for future standardisation activity.

The taxonomy will be concerned with various areas of open systems security, including communications, distributed applications, databases, systems management and open distributed processing. The scope will include, as a minimum, the following categories:

- communications and networking
- IT security frameworks and models
- OSI service and protocol work applications
- IT techniques and mechanisms
- open systems management.

In addition, the broader categories of standardisation, such as administrative control and procedures, legal and regulatory issues, audit and accountability etc., will be considered. The taxonomy will take into account the difference between technical and non-technical or "quality" issues.

The INFOSEC initiative and other similar activities, argue for the need for common security specifications. The rationale for the common security specification concept would appear to be:

- encouraging the provision of products containing 'appropriate' security features.

- providing a useful vocabulary for requirement and product processes.

- easing the use of, and operation of, the evaluation process.

There are a number of themes, underlying such common security specifications. These include: security objectives, functionality and mechanisms. These provide the means of specifying security requirements in terms of specifications such as Security Sub-Profiles, Security Targets and Functionality Classes. These types of specification are used for different types of purpose e.g. product implementations and security evaluation.

Security sub-profile are a subject of standardisation normally derived from base standards (although some are derived from *de facto* industry standards), developed at a regional level, agreed between regional workshops, and standardised at the international level within ISO/IEC as ISPs (International Standardisation Profiles). These profiles, as defined essentially as a specification of functionality together with a range of realisable quality. They are closely related to the service oriented aspects of products and are associated with conformance and interoperability testing.

Security targets on the other hand are specifications that are the subject of evaluation. Targets are similar to profiles in their general scope and coverage of security objectives. However, they tend to be more specific in particular with regard to quality and are not necessarily based on standards.

Security objectives as used in the specification of targets and profiles, and are specified using a selection of security functions. In terms of ITSEC a specific selection of these functions is referred to as a 'Functionality Class'.

16.5 STANDARDS

Several European countries have developed their own IT security criteria. In the UK this includes CESG Memorandum Number 3, developed for government use, and the Department of Trade and Industry's "Green Book" proposals for commercial IT security products. In 1989 the German Information Security Agency published a first version of its own criteria and in France, the "Blue-White-Red Book" was developed.

Seeing that work was going on in this area and that much still needed to be done, France, West Germany, the Netherlands and the United Kingdom recognised that the work needed to be approached in a concerted way, and that common, harmonised IT security criteria should be put forward [ITSE91]

It was therefore decided to build on the various national initiatives, taking the best features of what had already been done and combining them in a consistent, structured way. Maximum applicability and compatibility with existing work, most notably the Orange Book, was a constant consideration in this process. Thus, the Information Technology Security Evaluation Criteria (ITSEC) were developed.

The ITSEC Guidelines make an important distinction between products and systems. An IT product is a hardware and/or software package which can be bought off-the-shelf and used in a variety of operational environments. An IT *system* is designed and built for the needs of a specific user; it has a unique operational environment. (This distinction is one which has also been made in the MARS Project and implicitly in the MARS guidelines). For a system to be secure, all components must be protected to the required level.

The distinction between products and systems affects the way in which an evaluation can be made. The system has a real world environment and is subject to real world threats. In the case of a product, only general assumptions can be made about its operating environment and it is up to the user, when incorporating the product into a real world system, to make sure that these assumptions are consistent with the environment of that system.

16.6 ITSEC

In context, IT security means, according to ITSEC definitions

*   confidentiality - prevention of the unauthorised disclosure of information;

*   integrity - prevention of the unauthorised modification of information;

*   availability - prevention of the unauthorised withholding of information or resources.

ITSEC also has a number of other definitions which are reproduced below:

An IT system or product will have its own requirements for maintenance of confidentiality, integrity and availability. In order to meet these requirements it will implement a number of technical security measures, in this document referred to as security enforcing functions, covering, for example, areas such as access control, auditing, and error recovery. Appropriate confidence in these functions will be needed: in this document this is referred to as assurance, whether it is confidence in the correctness of the security enforcing functions (both from the development and the operational points of view) or confidence in the effectiveness of those functions.

Users of systems need confidence in the security of the system they are using. They also need a yardstick to compare the security capabilities of IT products they are thinking of purchasing. Although users could rely upon the word of the manufacturers or vendors of the systems and products in question, or they could test them themselves, it is likely that many users will prefer to rely on the results of some form of impartial assessment by an independent body. Such an evaluation of a system or product requires objective and well-defined security evaluation criteria and the existence of a certification body that can confirm that the evaluation has been properly conducted. Systems security targets will be specific to the particular needs of the users of the system in question, whereas product security targets will be more general so that products that meet them can be incorporated into many systems with similar but not necessarily identical security requirements.

For a system, an evaluation of its security capabilities can be viewed as a part of a more formal procedure for accepting an IT system for use within a particular environment. Accreditation is the term often used to describe this procedure. It requires a number of factors to be considered before a system can be viewed as fit.

Functionality and Classes

The term Target of Evaluation (TOE) is used to refer to a product or system to be evaluated.

A brief description of TOE follows. This is taken from the introduction to ITSEC

In order for a TOE to meets its security objectives, it must incorporate appropriate security enforcing functions, covering, for example, areas such as access control, auditing and error recovery.

These functions must be defined in a way that is clear and understandable to both the sponsor of evaluation and the independent evaluator. They may either be individually specified, or they may be defined by reference to a pre-defined functionality class.

Example functionality class F-DC is intended for TOEs with high demands on the confidentiality of data during data communication. An example candidate for this class is a cryptographic device.

Example functionality class F-DX is intended for networks with high demands on the confidentiality and integrity of the information to be communicated. For example, this can be the case when sensitive information has to be communicated via insecure (for example: public) networks.

There is no restriction on the specific functionality which can be claimed or required as a security target. The security enforcing functions of any security target can be fully described within the available specification formats. The existence of pre-defined classes will not therefore restrict product manufacturers seeking to advance the state of the art, but will lessen the work involved in specifying products or systems which are similar to the stereotypes described, and will provide a basis for comparison of functionality offered. Product security targets may, even when claiming conformance to a pre-defined class, specify additional constraints and details of the required surrounding environment in order to assist potential users to determine if the product would be suitable for their actual real-world environment.

Assurance levels

In all cases, the sponsor of an evaluation must define the security target for the evaluation. This must define the security enforcing functions to be provided by the TOE, and will also contain other relevant information, such as the security objectives of the TOE and the envisaged threats to those objectives. Details may also be given of the particular security mechanisms that will be used to implement the security enforcing functions.

The security enforcing functions selected to satisfy the security objectives of a TOE form but one aspect of the security target of a product or system. No less important is assurance that the security objectives are achieved by the selected security enforcing functions and mechanisms.

Assurance needs to be addressed from several different points of view and, in these harmonised criteria, it has been decided to distinguish confidence in the correctness in the implementation of the security enforcing functions and mechanisms from confidence in their effectiveness.

Evaluation of effectiveness assesses whether the security functions and mechanisms that are provided in the TOE will actually satisfy the stated security objectives. The TOE is assessed for suitability of functionality, binding of functionality (whether the chosen functions work together synergistically), the consequences of known and discovered vulnerabilities (both in the construction of the TOE and the way it will be used in live operation), and ease of use.

In addition, evaluation of effectiveness assesses the ability of the security mechanisms of the TOE to withstand direct attack (strength of mechanisms). Three strength levels are defined - basic, medium and high - which represent ascending levels of confidence in the ability of the security mechanisms of the TOE to withstand direct attack.

Evaluation of correctness assesses whether the security enforcing functions and mechanisms are implemented correctly. Seven evaluation levels labelled E0 to E6 have been defined, representing ascending levels of confidence in correctness. E0 represents inadequate confidence. E1 represents an entry point below which no useful confidence can be held, and E6 represents the highest level of confidence. The remaining levels represent an interpolation in between. Correctness is addressed from the point of view of construction of the TOE, covering both the development process and the development environment, and also the point of view of operation of the TOE. See Appendix D for further information and analysis.

If a TOE fails any aspect of evaluation at a particular level, because of a lack of information or for any other reason, the deficiency must be remedied, or the TOE withdrawn from evaluation at that level. Otherwise the TOE will be assigned a result of E0.

The six successful evaluation levels E1 to E6 span a wide range of potential confidence. Not all of these levels will necessarily be needed by or appropriate for all market sectors that require independent evaluation of technical security measures. Not all combinations of functionality and confidence will necessarily be sensible or useful. For example, low confidence in the functionality required to support a military multi-level security requirement will not normally be appropriate. In addition, it is unlikely that high confidence in the correctness of a TOE will be combined with a requirement for a low strength of mechanisms.

These harmonised criteria are not a design guide for secure products or systems. It is up to the sponsor of an evaluation to determine the security objectives of his TOE and to choose security functions to satisfy them. However for each evaluation level, the assurance part of the criteria can be thought of as a compulsory 'security checklist' to be satisfied.

Assurance profiles

The criteria in this document require the sponsor to state the evaluation level as part of the security target. All of the security enforcing functions listed in the security target are then assessed to the same level of confidence, as required by the stated evaluation level.

For some TOEs, there may be a requirement to gain higher confidence in some security functions and lower confidence in others; for example, some security functions may be more important than others. In these circumstances, the sponsor may consider producing more than one security target for the TOE. The details of how this is achieved, and under what conditions, is beyond the scope of these criteria.

The TCSEC defines seven sets of evaluation criteria called classes (D, C1, C2, B1, B2, B3 and A1), grouped into four divisions (D, C, B and A). Each criteria class covers four aspects of evaluation: Security Policy, Accountability, Assurance and Documentation. The criteria for these four areas become more detailed from class to class, and form a hierarchy whereby D is the lowest and A1 the highest. Each class covers both functionality and confidence requirements.

The criteria set out in the ITSEC selection of arbitrary security functions and define seven evaluation levels representing increasing confidence in the ability of a TOE to meet its security target. Thus these criteria can be applied to cover a wider range of possible systems and products than the TCSEC. In general for identical functionality at an equivalent level of confidence, a TOE has more architectural freedom to meet the ITSEC criteria than to meet the TCSEC, but is more constrained in its permissible development practices.

A number of example functionality classes have been defined to correspond closely to the functionality requirements of the TCSEC classes C1 to A1. They are included as F-C1 to F-B3.

The functionality classes examine the following concepts:

• identification and authentication
• access control
• accountability and audit
• object reuse
• mandatory mechanism

The items which are to be considered in each are shown in Table 16.1

Ten example pre-defined classes are given below. They are:

• Example functionality classes F-C1, F-C2, F-B1, F-B2 and F-B3 are hierarchically ordered confidentiality classes which correspond closely to the functionality requirements of the US DoD classes C1 to A1.

• Example functionality class F-1N is for TOEs with high integrity requirements for data and programs. Such requirements may be necessary in database TOEs for example.

• Example functionality class F-AV sets high requirements for the availability of a complete TOE or special functions of a TOE. Such requirements are significant for TOEs that control manufacturing processes, for example.

• Example functionality class F-DI sets high requirements with regard to the safeguarding of data integrity during data communication.

The intended correspondence between these criteria and the TCSEC classes is as follows:

Table 16.1 Example Functionality Classes

US DoD	F-C1 / C1	F-C2 / C2	F-B1 / B1	F-B2 / B2	F-B3 / B3 and A1
	discretionary access control	finely grained discretionary access control making users individually accountable for their actions through identification procedures, auditing of security relevant events and resource isolation	mandatory access control over all subjects and storage objects under its control and has functions to maintain security labels over exported information	mandatory access control to all subjects and objects plus stronger authentication requirements	compared security administration and the signalling of security relevant events
Identification & Authentication	simple mechanism	uniquely and for each event	uniquely and for each event	uniquely and for each events handled by a trusted path	system can request authentication
Access control	broadly defined simple mechanism	each user & a variety of rights	full user profile & access control matrix with defined rules giving rights with security labelling	separate administration rights plus no cost channels	roles of operator, administrator and security officer are distinct
Accountability	exists	exists	exists with greater detail	exists with even greater detail	exists with even greater detail
Audit	exists	tools	tools	tools	tools & signalling
Object Base	all objects sanitised before reuse	all objects sanitised before reuse	all objects sanitised before reuse	all objects sanitised before reuse	all objects sanitised before reuse
Mandatory mechanism				foolproof mechanism always masked & small enough to be tested	

Table 16.2 Intended Correspondence between US DoD and ITSEC criteria

These Criteria		US DoD TCSEC Class
E0	◄—►	D
F-C1, E1	◄—►	C1
F-C2, E2	◄—►	C2
F-B1, E3	◄—►	B1
F-B2, E4	◄—►	B2
F-B3, E5	◄—►	B3
F-B3, E6	◄—►	A1

It should be noted that there is no functionality class F-A1 as the functionality requirements of the TCSEC class A1 are the same as for class B3. A product which has been designed with the objective of successful evaluation against both the ITSEC and TCSEC, and which has been shown to meet one of the classes or combinations in the table above, should pass evaluation against the other criteria at the equivalent class or combination. However, at C1 the TCSEC requires evidence to be provided of system developer testing. Thus an [F-C1, E1] evaluation would only be equivalent to C1 evaluation if the sponsor had chosen to satisfy the optional E1 requirement to provide test documentation as evidence of adequate testing against the security target prior to evaluation.

Throughout the TCSEC, the combination of both the security enforcing and the security relevant portions of a TOE is referred to as a Trusted Computing Base (TCB). TCSEC TOEs representative of the higher classes in division B and division A derive additional confidence from increasingly rigorous architectural and design requirements placed on the TCB by the TCSEC criteria. TCSEC classes B2 and higher require that access control is implemented by a reference validation mechanism, a mechanism which implements the concept of a reference monitor [AND]. Such a reference validation mechanism must be tamper proof, it must always be invoked, and it must be small enough to be subject to analysis and tests, the completeness of which can be assured.

The Evaluation Process

The objective of the evaluation process is to enable the evaluator to prepare an impartial report stating whether or not a TOE satisfies its security target at the level of confidence indicated by the stated evaluation level.

The evaluation process requires the close involvement of the sponsor of the evaluation. The higher the evaluation level. The greater will need to be the involvement of the sponsor. Both users and vendors can act as sponsors for evaluation. It is likely that a system evaluation will be sponsored by the intended end-users of the system or their technical representatives, and that a product evaluation will be sponsored by the product manufacturer or a vendor of the product, but this need not be so. Any party that can supply the necessary technical information may sponsor an evaluation.

First the sponsor must determine the operational requirements and the threats the TOE is to counter, In the case of a system, there is a need to examine the real world operational environment for the system, in order to determine the relevant threats that must be addressed. For a product there is a need to decide what threats to security the product should address. It is anticipated that industry organisations and international standardisation bodies will with time define standard functionality classes for use as product security targets. Product developers who have no predetermined specialist market niche or type of user in mind may find that such pre-defined functionality classes make good security targets to design their products to match.

The security objectives for the TOE can then be determined considering legal and other regulations. These form the contribution to security (confidentiality, integrity and availability) the TOE is intended to provide. Given the security objectives, the necessary security enforcing functions can then be established, possibly in an interactive way, together with the evaluation level that the TOE will have to achieve to provide the necessary level of confidence.

The results of this work - the definition of the security enforcing functions, the identified threats, the identified security objectives, any specific security mechanisms to be employed - becomes the security target for the development.

For each evaluation level, the criteria enumerate items to be delivered by the sponsor to the evaluator. The sponsor must ensure that these items are provided taking care that any requirements for content and presentation are satisfied and that the items clearly provide or support the production of, the evidence that is called for.

In order that evaluation can be performed efficiently, and at minimum cost, the evaluator must work closely with the developer and sponsor of the TOE, ideally from the beginning of development, to build up a good understanding of the security target, and to be able to pinpoint the evaluation implications of decisions as they are made. However, the evaluator must remain independent and must not suggest how to design or implement the TOE. This is analogous to the role of an external financial auditor, who must likewise build up a good working relationship with a financial department, and in many cases will, after examination, make use of their internal records and controls. However, he too must remain independent and questioning.

Security test and analysis requirements within the criteria deserve special mention; in all cases the responsibility for testing and analysis will rest with the sponsor. The evaluator will perform test and analysis work only to audit the results supplied, to supplement the evidence provided, and to investigate vulnerabilities. At evaluation level E1 it is optional as to whether testing results are provided. If not, the evaluator must in addition perform functional testing against the security target.

The Certification Process

In order for these criteria to be of practical value, they will need to be supported by practical schemes for the provision and control of independent evaluation, run by appropriately qualified and recognised national certification bodies. These bodies will award certificates to confirm the rating of the security of TOEs, as determined by properly conducted independent evaluations. They will approve procedures, as required by these criteria, for guaranteeing the authenticity of the delivered TOE. They will also be responsible for the selection and control of approved evaluators. Details of the procedures to be used by such bodies are beyond the scope of these criteria.

These criteria have been designed to minimise the subjectivity inherent in evaluation results. It will be the responsibility of national certification bodies to maintain the uniformity of certified evaluation results. How this is achieved is beyond the scope of these criteria.

In order for the results of an evaluation against these criteria to be certified by a national certification body, the evaluator will have to produce a report containing the results of evaluation in a form acceptable for consideration by the certification body. The precise format and content of such reports are beyond the scope of these criteria.

The differences between the three sets of criteria are shown again in Table 16.3

Table 16.3 Workstation security level reconciled with DoD criteria

WORKSTATION SECURITY LEVEL		EUROPEAN COMMISSION'S ITSEC		DoD CRITERIA	
Level	Description	Functional class	Evaluation level	Class	Description
0	No Security				
1	Minimal Security	-	E0	D1	Minimal Protection
2	Basic Security	-	E0	D1	Minimal Protection
3	Discretionary Security	F-C1	E1	C1	Discretionary Access Control
4	Limited Controlled Security	-	-	C2	Weak Mandatory Access Control
5	Controlled Security	F-C2	E2	C2	Strong Mandatory Access Control
6	Highly secure	F-B1	E3	B1	Labelled Security Protection
7		F-B2	E4	B2+	Structured Protection with Security Domains
	Ultra Secure	F-B3	E5	B2+	
	Ultra Secure	F-B3	E6	A1	Plus Verified Design

Both the US DoD criteria and the ITSEC criteria dwell primarily on operating system controls. The MARS workstation level controls also include alternative controls over the entire workstation including the physical areas of control (tangible areas) as well as the intangible and operating system area.

Many office-based systems are internal to a corporation's security domain and therefore rightly or wrongly are thought to have little need for high security. Hence the MARS security levels were more dense at the lower levels of security whilst then ITSEC criteria on the higher level. As such it is more relevant for military or secret service use than, we believe for business use at the workstation level.

Within the new advanced broadband telecommunication systems throughout Europe the problem may be reversed. Governments and their secret services may want to monitor confidential documents and may want access to 'secret' encrypted information. In the same way a super user may want access so too security functionality classes at too high a level may eventually prove a problem of Government security services.

The object of an evaluation is known as the 'security target'. The purpose is to establish assurance of the correctness and effectiveness of its security functions. Seven evaluation levels, labelled E0 to E6 have been defined, representing ascending levels of confidence in the correctness of security mechanisms. E0 represents inadequate confidence and E6 represents the highest level of confidence. Only if the target is successfully from the point of view of correctness, will its effectiveness be considered. Evaluation of effectiveness assesses whether the security functions and mechanisms provided in the target actually satisfy the security requirements.

The necessity of these various work efforts towards guidelines should not be underestimated. The need to establish a European mechanism for security evaluation and testing is paramount in of improving the competitive position of the community. The most important result of the MARS Project is the provision of input to this process.

Appendix A:

Countermeasures to Threats

Threats	Countermeasures
Deliberate, Active, Physical Threats	
Fire	Entry control
	Building design
	Fire-resistant materials
	Fire extinguishers
	Back-up equipment
	Spare parts
Theft	Entry control
	Alarms
	Safes
	Locks
	Back-up equipment
	Spare parts
Deliberate, Active, Logical Threats	
Logic Bombs	Access control
Computer Worms	Authorisation
Computer Virus	Identification
	Access control
	Memory protection
	Checksums
	Hash protection
	Encryption
	Call-back systems
	Auditing
Message Stream Modification	Message sequencing
Replay of Messages	Polling
Spurious Connection Initiation	Access control

Threats	Countermeasures
Audible Eavesdropping	Entry control Authorisation Identification Locks/Safes Shredding Encryption
Electronic Eavesdropping	Tempest technique Co-axial cables Fibre optics Pressurised seal cables
Traffic Analysis	Dummy traffic Encryption
Cipher Breaking	Big key space Secure algorithms Cipher block Chaining Public key systems

Accidental, Active, Physical Threats

Nature Lightning Fire Flooding Cold Heat Dust Mistakes Ommissions	Building design Alarms Building design Spare parts Backup equipment

Accidental, Active, Logical Threats

Software Errors	Code inspection Testing Auditing
Transmission Errors	Co-axial cables Fibre-optic cabling

Threats	Countermeasures
	Error detection codes
	Numbering of packets
	Re-transmission

Accidental, Passive, Physical Threats   Not Applicable

Accidental, Passive, Logical Threats

Audible Eavesdropping	Entry control
Visual Eavesdropping	Authorisation
Electronic Eavesdropping	Identification
	Locks
	Electronic safes
	Shredding
	Encryption
	Co-axial and fibre optic
	cables
	Tempest techniques

Appendix B

U.S. Department of Defence (DoD) Trusted Computer System Evaluation Criteria ("Orange Book")

In this appendix we outline the security criteria established by the US Department of Defence (DoD). In 1983, standards and recommendations for evaluation were synthesized in the "Orange Book", a set of guidelines which evolved from workshops and research activities conducted in the seventies. [DoD 83].

The purpose of the criteria is to encourage business and industry to incorporate trusted computer-based security features, the emphasis being on military application. These provide policy and model concepts applicable to secure computer systems. It is worth stating that the criteria do not require any specific architectural security measures to be present in order to accredit a given system in a particular category.

The requirements included in the criteria, with respect to secure computer systems, are related to two different areas:

- Specific security requirements
- assurance requirements

The specific security requirements are intended to cover the area of general purpose computers, and may, therefore be interpreted when regarding special application or processing environments. The DoD believes that the criteria are sufficiently general to apply to other areas in automated information systems.

BASIC REQUIREMENTS

The criteria propose some basic requirements which must be present, in one way or another, in different subsets before a successful rating can be achieved:

- Implementation of the reference Monitor model with the associated design requirements.

312

- Implementation of an internal structure which allows information at different sensitivity levels to be labelled.

- Implementation of a Mandatory Access Control (MAC) mechanism.

- Implementation of a Discretionary Access Control (DAC) mechanism.

- Implementation of permanent protection facilities, manual or otherwise.

- Implementation of individual accountability.

THE STRUCTURE OF THE EVALUATION PROCEDURE

Formal evaluation of a secure general-purpose operating system uses a classification based on eight classes and four major divisions. The divisions are called A, B, C, and D, where division A represents the most secure systems and division D the systems which fail to meet the criteria. Each division is again subdivided into intermediate classes. An increment from a lower class to the next higher class indicates reduced risk, and greater protection for sensitive information. The increments are cumulative, meaning that each higher class encompasses all the features in the previous class.

- security policy
- accountability attributes
- assurances of system behaviour
- documentation provided

Class D

This class refers to systems which have been through a formal evaluation procedure, but failed to meet any higher classification.

Class C1 Discretionary Security Protection

In this class, DAC mechanisms are available to allow users to specify and control access to sensitive information. Identification and authentication must be provided to guarantee a proper DAC mechanism. Assurances of correct control mechanism behaviour are primarily based on security testing to find out if the protection mechanisms can be by-passed.

Class C2 Controlled Access Protection

Individual accountability must be provided here, together with explicit auditing to allow a special audit trail to ensure that each individual user is responsible for his/her actions. In addition, the TCB ensures that no objects, subject to reallocation to an authorised use, include sensitive information.

Class B1 Labelled Security Protection

When entering this class, requirements for an explicit model, specifying the protection provided, are stated. In order to enforce such a policy, each subject and storage object (for example, process, file, segment) must be labelled. All security-critical components in the system must be identified in order to ensure their proper operation, particularly during the normal life-cycle, where software updates occur frequently. Distinguishing between security-critical and harmless components are essential for maintaining continuous confidence in the system.

Class B2 Structured Protection

In this class, the hardware and software must be structured in a way that facilitates the actual evaluation process. There will be distinct and identifiable storage objects. Within the central mechanism itself, there will be functionally distinct modules capable of identifying which module is providing which part of the protection. Increased trust is required in the authentication process. This is accomplished by ensuring that it is the real system which asks for passwords and not a faked process. Analysis is performed to identify each covert channel possible and to determine the maximum bandwidth of these. Life-cycle assurance is provided mainly through enhanced configuration management, including automatic tools for the generation of new versions of the TCB (Trusted Computing Base) from the source code, and tools for comparing new versions with old versions to ensure that the new versions include only the intended changes. Finally, a formal model of the security policy and a Descriptive Top-Level Specification (DTLS) must be provided.

Class B3 Security Domains

This class emphasises the third design requirement in the Reference Monitor concept, which states that the Reference Monitor must be small and simple. This is accomplished by separating those portions of the system that are security sensitive from those that may provide some necessary and common service to the users, and do not really relate to security. At this level, there is a demand for a highly-structured implementation of the design. Trusted paths must be provided between the TCB and the users. Recovery procedures must ensure that following a system failure, no compromise of sensitive data is possible.

Class A1 Verified Design

Functions provided in this class are essentially identical with those in Class B3. The main difference, however, is the increased confidence provided by automated verification tools. FTLS must be proved to correspond to the security model, and the correspondence between the actual implementation of the TCB and the FTLS informally verified. Further formal analysis techniques must be applied to identify the possible existence of covert channels.

Beyond Class A1 (Class A2) Verified Implementation

Systems belonging to this class are among the most advanced. Although this is still a developing field, the DoD has outlined some evaluation criteria:

- a fully-verified implementation, i.e. formal verification of the source code.

- an extensive verification method, related to the correct behaviour of hardware.

- a trusted design environment, operated by trusted personnel only. Consideration to be given to the suitability of the tools used in the TCB development (for example, compilers, assemblers, loaders).

- an advanced security testing process which automatically generates test cases from the formal top-level specification.

Appendix C

Summary of Auditability Guidelines

The auditability requirements analysed in Chapter 12, are here summarised and presented as a proposal for a possible guideline for auditability of Highly Secure Office Information Systems.

General auditability requirements have been defined, which have to be fulfilled by any system. They form the underlying basis for the definition of special requirements. Special requirements take the particularities of a specific auditing object into account.

General auditability requirements have to support verification of data and systems audit. General requirements relate to the auditing object system, the auditor and the time consumption for the audit process.

As general requirements for the system, the following are recommended:

- availability of the system components
- accessibility of the system components
- physical security
- physical support of logging
- implementation of security functions
- implementation of auditing functions in the software for selection and preparation of audit-relevant events
- individual accountability.

A general requirement for the auditor is:

- adequate competence.

General requirements for audit time expansion are:

- efficiency of audit process
- reliance on pre-audit system evaluation.

Special requirements have been defined for the different stages of the migration concept and for the areas of audit information, which have to be collected and presented by the audit trail, in order to provide sufficient audit evidence for the auditor.

316

The stages of migration for which special requirements have been defined relate to four (physical and logical) locations of auditing:

- a workstation (WS)
- a workstation linked to a multi-user system
- a workstation linked to a LAN and gateways
- a workstation linked to a large mainframe.

The areas of information which have to be covered by the audit trail in any step of the migration concept are:

- organisational information
- hardware information
- software information.

REQUIREMENTS FOR THE WORKSTATION

Organisational information

Survey of organisational controls with an audit trail instrument, called Directory of Liability.

The necessary audit information is based on an audit trail. For example, information relating to removeable storage media would consist of:

<source number, label, contents, purpose>.

Hardware information

Survey of hardware means to prevent failures and to protect the workstation, with an audit trail instrument, called Configuration Directory.
    The necessary audit information is based on an audit trail as a combination of:

<component, date, authorisation, comment>.

Software information

Verification view of programs with refinements of auditability, i.e. availability, understandability and risk-assessment

REQUIREMENTS FOR A WORKSTATION LINKED TO A MULTI-USER SYSTEM

Organisational information

Same as for the workstation.

Hardware information

Same as for the workstation.

Software information

Same as for the workstation, and additionally:

- logging of system initialisation and entry events
- logging of system/user process events.

The related audit trail consists of a tuple of the following items:

<event sequence number, time stamp, event class and specific event, outcoming action, subject information, object information, additional details>.

REQUIREMENTS FOR A WORKSTATION LINKED TO A LOCAL AREA NETWORK AND GATEWAYS

Organisational information

Same as for the workstation and the multi-user system

Hardware information

Same as for the workstation and the multi-user system

Software information

Same as for the workstation and the multi-user system. Additionally, logging of events of the following types: use of host identification and authentication mechanisms, attempts to open a connection, attempts to close a connection and changes in logical or physical conection of the network.

The audit trail should also include:

> <(origin of request), (node identifier), time stamp, user, type of event, success or failure of event, (resource name and location)>.

REQUIREMENTS FOR A WORKSTATION LINKED TO A LARGE MAINFRAME

Organisational information

Same as for the workstation, multi-user system, network and additionally further organisational information is required, concerning functional security of a large organisation. The audit trail may consist of a checklist, which checks agreements, security of location, functional security, personnel security and data protection.

Hardware information

Same as for the workstation, multi-user system and network

Software information

Same as for the workstation, multi-user system, network and additionally further software information is required with respect to the detection of intrusions by means of user-profiles, i.e. login and session activity, command or program execution, file access activity.

The necessary audit information is based on an audit trail as a combination of:

These sets of information have to be available for any phase of a migrating audit. The system structure determines which individual sets have to be selected and audited. Therefore, the auditor is enabled to structure an individual audit trail for the specific system, which constitutes the auditing object. The concept of the migrating audit trail provides a very flexible instrument.

Appendix D

ITSEC Evaluation of Correctness and Correctness of Assurance Criteria

INFORMATION	E1	E2	E3	E4	E5	E6
SECURITY TARGET (theats, objectives, functions, mechanisms, evaluation level, S of M)	✔	✔	✔	✔	✔	✔
FORMAL MODEL OF SECURITY POLICY				✔	✔	✔
FUNCTIONS (informal)	✔	✔	✔	✔	✔	✔
FUNCTIONS (semi-formal)				✔	✔	
FUNCTIONS (formal)						✔
ARCHITECTURAL DESIGN (informal)	✔	✔	✔			
ARCHITECTURAL DESIGN (semi-formal)				✔	✔	
ARCHITECTURAL DESIGN (formal)						✔
DETAILED DESIGN (informal)			✔			
DETAILED DESIGN (semiformal)				✔	✔	✔
IMPLEMENTATION (hardware drawings amd source code)				✔	✔	✔
IMPLEMENTATION (object code)						✔
OPERATION (user/administrator documents, delivery and configuration, startup and operation)	✔	✔	✔	✔	✔	✔
	STATE		DESCRIBE		EXPLAIN	

LEVEL OF RIGOUR

Figure 1: Information obtained from a correctness assessment which is used to perform a vulnerability analysis

321

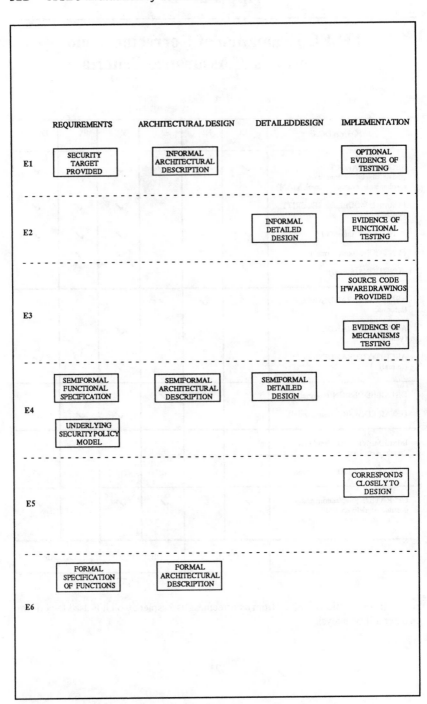

Figure 2: Correctness Criteria by Level - Development Process

Appendix E

Security Standards

STANDARDS PLAYERS

The main players in the area of security standarisation at the international and European level are within ISO, CCITT, ECMA, EWOS, and ETSI. The following lists provide a breakdown of these players into the various technical groups involved in the development of standards.

International

ISO/IEC JTC1

SWG ED1   (this group has now been disbanded)

SWG Security

SWFS   (Special Working Group on Functional Standards)

SC6   (OSI Lower Layers) - OSI protocol extensions at layers 1,3 and 4. Lower Layer Security Model.

SC17   (Identification Cards - WG4 IC Cards with contacts: logical card security.

SC18   (Text and Office Systems) - secure message handling MOTIS, distributed office automation security, ODA security, security work on the printer server standard.

SC21   (OSI Architecture, Management and Upper Layers) - OSI Security Architecture, and open systems security frameworks (WG1), databases (WG3), management and directories (WG4), FTAM, JTM and TP security (WG5), Upper Layer Security Model and OSI protocol extensions (WG6), ODP security (WG7).

SC22   (Languages) - POSIX security, formal methods

SC27   (IT Security Techniques) - Cryptographic and non-cryptographic based techniques and mechanisms, and supporting security related functions: including authentication, integrity, non-repudiation, modes of operation, access control, registration of algorithms, etc.

Note: There are other SCs within JTC1 which have an interest in security, although no specific activities are being undertaken at present. One such committee is SC14 (Representation of Data Elements) who has an interest in EDI security.

ISO & IEC

ISO/TC68   SC2   Wholesale security: message authentication, key management, data security framework, etc.
           SC4   Securities messages
           SC5   EDI and telecommunications
           SC6   Retail message security: message authentication. PIN management, key management, IC cards

Note: There are other TCs within ISO which have an interest in security, although no specific activities are being undertaken at present. These include (i) TC46 "Information and Documentation" - SC4 has an interest in information security for library systems, (ii) IEC/TC65 "Safety Related Control Systems", (iii) TC154 - an interest in EDI security, and (iv) TC184 - an interest in security as related to industrial automation.

CCITT

SGVII   Q18 - X.400 MHS security and EDI over X.400 security

SGVII   Q19 - Distributed Applications Framework (DAF) security: OSI security architecture, open systems security frameworks and DSASM, security infrastructure, secure applications and security techniques.

SGVII   Q20 - Directory System security: authentication and access control.

SGVII   Q24 - OSI management: security aspects.

SGVII   Q27 - OSI layers 3 and 4 security.

Regional

European Standards - Formal Groups

ITSTC   (IT Steering Technical Committee) : the following
                    two Expert Groups act in an advisory capacity to
                    ITSTC

       •   ITAEGV   (Advisory Experts Group on
              Information Security Standards)
       •   ITAEGM   (Advisory Experts Group on
              advanced manufacturing technologies)

CEN   European Committee for Standardisation

                    TC224 Machine Readable Cards, Related Device
                    Interfaces and Operation; the following groups are
                    currently concerned with security

       •   WG9 Telecommunication Applications
       •   WG10 Payment Specifications
       •   WG12 Health Applications
       •   WG14 Airline Applications

                    TC251 Medical Informatics

       •   WG6 Health Care Security and Privacy, Quality
              and Safety

                    TC278 Transport Informatics

                    WE/EE M4.D EDIFACT Security

CENELEC   the European Committee for Electrotechnical
                    Standarisation

ETSI   European Telecommunications Standards Institute

• SAGE (Security Algorithms Group of Experts) - responsible for producing, for ETSI Technical Committees (TCs) and sub-Technical Committees (STCs) report and draft standards concerning cryptographic algorithms and access protocols - this includes work on DECT, UPT and Teleconferencing.

TC/TE
- TE3 X.400 MHS security (joint ETSI/EWOS project)
- TE4 Security aspects of audio-visual services and telephony terminals
- TE6 Security aspects of directory systems
- TE9 Security aspects of intelligent card and card terminals
- TE10 Security aspects of teleconferencing

• TC/SMG Security for the pan-European Cellular Digital Radio system and (SMG5) for UMTS (work items not yet identified - former TC/GSM now renamed).

• TC/NA
- NA 7 Security aspects of Universal Personal Telecommunications (UPT)

• TC/RES Security for digital radio systems not elsewhere specified (includes, e.g., land mobile radio, DECT, CT2)

Note: ETSI are in the process of establishing a new security called STAG (Security Techniques Advisory Group). If approved by the ETSI/TA this group will commence work in September 1992.

The following group comes within the CEN/CENELEC framework, with participation of users' and manufacturers' organisations, provides a 'workshop function' which corresponds to the growing interest in the standarisation work and which aims at promoting international convergence.

EWOS European Workshop for Open Systems - European organisation for the development of functional standards. The following groups are concerned with several aspects of security within EWOS:

- EGSEC (Expert Group on Security)
- EG MHS (Expert Group on Message Handling Systems)
- EG DIR (Expert Group on Directory Systems)
- EG ODA (Expert Group on Office Document Architecture)
- EG LL (Expert Group on OSI lower layer profiles)

European Standards - Senior Officials Groups

In formulating Community policy, the European Commission is assisted by committees concerned in various ways with the whole standardisation process, from considering the need to start work on standards right through to putting standards to practical use. Three such committees are:

SOG-IS   Senior Officials Group for Information Systems Security
SOG-ITS   Senior Officials Group for IT Standardisation
SOG-T   Senior Officials Group Telecommunications

European Standards - Groups Promoting Standardisation

A major development in recent years has been the growth of 'pre-standardisation' bodies at the national and regional levels. These have various forms and objectives, but common to them all is the aim of ensuring action in the development and exploitation of IT standards in ways complementary to those of the formal standards machinery. These include ECMA (one of the oldest), EWOS (See 4.2.1.1.), SPAG, OSITOP, X/Open (see 4.4.4), etc.

ECMA   (European Computer Manufacturers Association)

- TC29 (ODA security)
- TC32
    - TG6 (OSI lower layer security, ISDN security)
    - TG9 (Security in Open Systems: Security Framework (TR46), Security Protocols, Data Elements and Services, authentication and security attributes, secure association management.

- TC36 (Security Evaluation Criteria)

OSITOP   European version of the TOP activity

-        WG5 Security

SPAG   Standards Promotion and Application Group - a
                  consortium of European suppliers developing
                  functional standards.

North American Standards

ANSI   EDI, banking, techniques/mechanisms and OSI
                  security.

IEEE   802.10 LAN security (SILS)
                  P1003.6 POSIX Security
                  P1157 MEDIX (Medical Data-Interchange)

OIW   OSI Implementors Workshop - OSI Implementors
                  Agreements based on international standards, e.g.
                  X.400 security, Directory security, security for OSI
                  management, lower layer security, security
                  architecture.

NIST   Workshop Integrity guidelines
                  FIPS: DES, message authentication, password usage,
                  Digital Signatures.

Other Standards Players

Government Procurement Specifications

GOSIP   Government OSI Profile - government defined
                  functional standards to help government departments
                  specify and purchase open systems equipment; the
                  GOSIP programme exists in several countries in
                  Europe, North America and the Pacific basin (UK,
                  US and Canada - OSI security profiles)

EPHOS   European Procurement Handbook for Open Systems
                  - France, Germany and the UK are currently working
                  on the specification of a European GOSIP for which
                  the CEC is funding the creation of EPHOS.

IPSIT   International Public Sector IT Group - informal association of public sector organisations - from Australia, Canada, the US, Japan, Sweden, UK, France, Germany and CEC - responsible for the development of open systems procurement profiles.

Evaluation Criteria

Various national criteria from the US, UK, Germany, France, the Netherlands, Canada, etc., including:

US/DoD   Trusted Computer System Evaluation Criteria (TCSEC) (Ref 12)

US/NIST   Federal Criteria (Refs 36 & 37)

UK,   Information Technology Security Evaluation Criteria
France   (ITSEC), Version 1.2, June 1991 (Ref 13)
Germany &   Information Technology Security Evaluation Manual
the Netherlands   ITSEM), Version 0.2, September 1992 (Ref 35)
Canada   Trusted Computer Product Evaluation Criteria, Version 3.0, January 1992 (Ref 38)

Others

IFIP   International Federation of Information Processing - Technical Committee TC-11 on Computer Security - 1.3 Secure Database Management Systems.

NATO   NATO OSI Security Architecture (NOSA)

SDNS   Secure Data Network Systems - OSI security programme funded by the US DoD - secure messaging, layer 2/3/4 security, access control and key management.

OtherGroups

General

IBAG   INFOSEC Business Advisory Group

User Groups

ITEF	Internet Task Force (has four working groups concerned with: privacy enhanced mail, GSS API, common authentication techniques and network management security)
MAP	Manufacturing Automation Protocol - set of functional standards developed under the auspices of General Motors in the US.
NIUF	North American ISDN Users Forum - This contains an ISDN WG on Security - user requirements, architecture design and applications
TOP	Technical and Office Protocols - a set of functional standards designed for the office environment, initiated by Boeing in the US. there is a joint MAP/ TOP user group looking at security requirements

Collaborative Research & Studies - CEC Research

There are several European collaborative research projects administered by CEC/DGXIII, which involve some work on standards attached to programmes such as:

RACE	Research & Development in Advanced Communications (Ref 25)
ESPRIT	European Strategic Programme for R&D in IT (Ref 26)
INFOSEC	Security Investigations Programme (Ref 32)
TEDIS	Trading EDI System (Ref 27)
AIM	Advanced informatics in Medicine
ENS	European Nervous System
ANSA/ISA	Advanced Network Systems Architecture

Collaborative Research & Studies - Other Research

EURESCOM   European Institute for Research and Strategic Studies in Telecommunications.

Vendor Associations

EUROBIT   European Business in IT

COS   The US based corporation for Open Systems

POSI   Promoting Conference for OSI

OSI NMF   OSI Network Management Forum

X/OPEN   Dedicated to the creation of an internationally supported, vendor-independent, Common Applications Environment based on industry standards.

Unix International

OSF   Open Software Foundation (e.g. trusted platforms TMAC, Distributed Communications Environment - Kerberos, DSF, etc.)

Conformance Testing & Interoperability Testing

ECITC   European Committee for IT Testing & Certification

EMCIT   European Testing of Electromagnetic Compatibility of IT Products

EOTC   European Organisation for Testing & Certification

ETCOM   European Testing & Certification for Office & Manufacturing Protocols

EurOSInet   Marketing association of IT systems and service suppliers whose collective mission is to promote the wider adoption of OSI in Europe.

OSIone   Open Systems Interconnection Organisation for
                       Network Establishment - a consortium of
                       demonstration networks including OSInet and
                       EurOSInet

OSTC   Open Systems Testing Consortium

Index

334 *Index*